COOLING THE FLAMES OF CREWE

MPIRE
BOOKS

Published in the United Kingdom by MPire Books of Crewe, 2022

email: markpotts7764@gmail.com

COOLING THE FLAMES OF CREWE

Gareth Roberts

CONTENTS

ACKNOWLEDGEMENTS

Thank you to everyone who has been involved in supplying information and contributing in any way to this book. This includes: Janssen Bostock, Rod Broome, Ralph Buckley, Elizabeth Cotton, Howard Curran, Ken Gardner, Geoff Goodwin, Andy Fox-Hewitt, Chris Hannan, Linda Hassall, Dave Holman, Peter Jacks, Terry Kelly, Barrie Lunt, Dave McCabe, Ethel Moss, Richard Moulton, Peter Neary, Mark Potts and Tony Marks (MPire Books), John Roberts, Steven Roberts, Peter Shields, Malcolm Smith, Ray Stafford, Caroline Sutton, Ian Swan, Chris Thorley, Dave Williams and Robert Wootton.

A special mention to local artist Jean Crocker who created the book cover and to Jerry Park who, as well as proof reading, edited sections of the book to include local information from the past that was relevant to the fire brigade.

Contributors to this book have kindly shared their memories. Their views should not be taken out of context, nor should they be taken to represent any of the policies or views of the organisations mentioned in this book.

The book is dedicated to the Crewe Firemen who lost their lives in the line of duty during the Second World War with proceeds from the book sales donated to the Firefighters Charity.

INTRODUCTION

This project about the fire service in Crewe began in 2020 as the UK entered lockdown due to Covid-19. It was over 10 years since my retirement from Cheshire Fire and Rescue Service (CFRS) and with the 'stay at home' advice in place; I felt it was an opportunity to recall my days as a firefighter in Crewe. My project grew to include the early years of firefighting in Crewe as I sourced information from copies of old newspapers (online), Cheshire Fire and Rescue newsletters, Fire Brigades Union journals and my collections of scrapbooks and fire service photographs.

Contributions to the project have been made by former fire officers who served at Crewe, some of whom remained fighting fires throughout their careers, while others took on specialist roles, such as Control Operators, Training Instructors and Fire Prevention Officers. Family members of past firemen also assisted, as did former fire officers and their families from Crewe Railway Works, Rolls-Royce Motors, Royal Ordinance Factory (Radway Green) and Crewe Hall.

Hundreds of firemen have served the town and the major industries in Crewe, as volunteers or in a part-time or full-time capacity, and additional firemen were recruited to protect the town during the Second World War.

In days gone by, it was common practise for firemen to take part in fire brigade competitions involving equipment such as ladders, hose and pumps. There was also a keen rivalry among firemen when it came to competitive sports, whether it was football, fishing, volleyball or running. Snooker tables were an integral part of fire stations and it was traditional for firemen to participate in this sport.

The fire brigade has always had a presence in the community at large, and present-day firefighters with the support of civilian staff, spend much of their time carrying out home fire safety checks in people's houses and working with other agencies to improve community safety. The challenges of Covid-19 have seen members of CFRS reaching further out in the community by supporting the NHS and the care sector by delivering food and medicine, visiting vulnerable residents and assisting at the vaccination centres.

With plans in place to build a new fire station at Crewe, it is fitting that we remember how firefighting in this railway town has emerged from the past to the present day. The new fire station will be a state of the art construction and built on the same site as the current fire station.

Gareth Roberts

WILMOT EARDLEY

FIRE
DG53 JNX

MY THREE DECADES ON THE PUMPS

As a young man passing through Crewe by rail from my native north Wales, I never imagined I'd spend 30 years fighting fires in this part of Cheshire - the land of luxury cars and rather less luxurious trains!

Even when I caught sight of the prominent 60 foot drill tower as I headed to the fire station for my first shift in June 1979, I was only planning a short stay, before heading back to fight fires in Wales. I never thought that Crewe Fire Station would become my 'second home' for the next 30 years.

Walking into the fire station, clutching my spotlessly clean fire kit, I was both excited and nervous. I teamed up with eight other rookie firemen who, like me, wanted to 'fit-in' and make an impression on their first day. The place looked spick and span with five shiny fire appliances lined up in a row. A fireman's pole caught my eye and I pictured myself sliding down and running towards the fire engine on a call-out. Before that could happen, however, a lengthy training session had to take place on the drill yard to assess what calibre of firemen had arrived from training school.

After performing several routine drills, that seemed quite painless after the military-style training on our recruits' course, the duty personnel began to warm towards us. We were introduced to the Divisional Fire Officers (John Blenkinsop and Dave Jones) at Cheshire Fire Brigade's C Division HQ, which was based on the first floor. C Division covered south and east Cheshire with other fire stations at Audlem, Bollington, Congleton, Holmes Chapel, Macclesfield, Middlewich, Nantwich, Poynton, Sandbach and Wilmslow.

We spent the rest of our first day familiarising ourselves with the fire appliances and other equipment, learning about the industrial risks in Crewe and practising tying knots with lines. By the end of the shift there had been no real excitement, except for a chimney fire at a domestic property and plenty of leg-pulling by the old hands.

Settling in at the fire station didn't take long after the demands of Lancashire Fire Brigade's Training School at Washington Hall in Chorley. The recruits' course was now a distant memory when more than 100 recruits from Cheshire, Cumbria, Clwyd, Tyne and Wear and Lancashire had come together during a cold February in 1979. Beforehand, I'd envisaged squirting water and climbing ladders for the full 12 weeks of the course, so I was surprised to find a syllabus that covered a wide range of topics including pumps and primers, foam making equipment, metrication, physics, chemistry, elements of combustion, ladders, first aid, building construction, hydraulics, fire hydrants, salvaging at fires, hose and hose fittings, electricity, radiation, ropes and lines, vehicle rescues, special services incidents, fire alarms, fire extinguishers, sprinklers and drenchers and water relays. Towards the end of the course we had been given a taste of real firefighting when all sorts of refuse was set on fire inside some derelict buildings.

Teamwork was encouraged and practical training mainly focused on pumping, ladder work and running out hose. To instil pride and efficiency, we were taught to march, and our appearance and uniform were inspected daily - as well as the cleanliness and tidiness of our billets. As some ex-servicemen on the course pointed out, it was organised like basic training in the armed forces. Earlier generations of firemen had often served in the Royal Navy - a disciplined background that made it easy for them to fit in. A flavour of the navy lingered on: a fire station shift was called a 'watch', the eating and recreation was the 'mess', and the working hours were very long.

A dozen or so recruits dropped out of the course at Chorley, unable to handle the discipline or cope with the physical or mental demands made on them. By the end of course, those of us remaining felt energised and at ease with the fire service way of life. After the showcase 'passing out' parade to show off our new skills, we exchanged our farewells and headed our separate ways. Welcome to the reality of firefighting as a probationary firemen in Crewe.

Our shift pattern covered 48 hours over eight days with two nine-hour day shifts from 9am, and two fifteen-hour night shifts from 6pm. At the start of each shift, we formally paraded in our fire kit.

Simon Snape was Commanding Officer at Crewe Fire Station, assisted by Roy Howarth. They presided over four watches:

Red Watch - Ray Mills (Sub Officer), Ken Gardner (Leading Fireman), Paul Bickerton, Philip Edwards, Peter Ennion, Geoff Humphreys, Terry Kelly, Chris Mannix, Jim Morrey, John Noden (Jnr.) and John Roberts (Firemen).

Blue Watch - Dave Greatorex (Sub Officer), Maurice Higginson (Leading Fireman), Frank Bratley, Mick Clays, Dave Hanley, Steve Herbert, Barrie Lunt, Gerry McCabe, Alan Ollier, Keith Roberts and Colin Tomkinson (Firemen).

White Watch - Dave McCabe (Sub Officer), Lindsay Johns (Leading Fireman), Kevin Birtles, Gordon Goodwin, Elfyn Hughes, Graham Lowe, Chris Norman, John Roberts, Ian Scrimgeour and Dave Williams (Firemen).

Green Watch - Richard Green (Sub Officer), Cliff Simpson (Leading Fireman), Adrian Breeze, Steve Doyle, Bob Hughes, Dave Langer, Gareth Roberts (myself), Keith Stubbs, Alec Thomasson, Peter Turner and Paul Whitby (Firemen).

To progress beyond the two year probationary period we had to attend courses in breathing apparatus and fire prevention and undergo firefighting assessments. It usually took four years to become qualified. This involved learning hose repair and breathing apparatus maintenance, acquiring in-depth knowledge of major local risks, and taking additional practical firefighting tests. By then, many had acquired a heavy goods vehicle driving licence (class three) and completed the 'blue-lights' training, allowing them to drive to emergencies. As well as keeping the public and the crew safe, drivers were expected to enhance the Brigade's reputation on the road and to remain calm and tolerant in all situations.

We were encouraged to sit our promotion exams early on in our careers. Passing the Leading Fireman's exam, gave exemption from taking the qualified fireman's tests. A pay rise was also an incentive to become qualified, with a further cash increase on completion of 15 years' service. In 1979 a qualified fireman with 15 years' service earned £111.05 a week.

In the main, we were content with life on the fire engine and dealing with everyday emergencies. Nonetheless, climbing the promotion ladder appealed to some

Recruit Training Course, February - May 1979
Lancashire Fire Brigade Training Centre, Washington Hall, Chorley

Back L to R: Hoosan, Grundy, Golder, Hilton, Barnes, Ormerod, Whitby, Herbert, Port, Braby, myself and Mountain. Middle L to R: Jones, Bratley, Smith, Spence, Marriott, Stuart, Bushell, Simpson, McVey, Newman, Tynan and Monk. Front L to R: Meeham, Hannah, Sub O. Culleton, Sub O. Copley, A.D.O. Mawdsley, Stn O. Halliwell, Sub O. Mares, Harris and Holden.

*Fire recruits learning new skills on the drill ground. (**Bottom right**) L to R: Recruits G. Roberts (myself), M. Ormerod, R. Harris, R. Port and G. Monk (front).*

and every opportunity was given to attend management courses at the Fire Service College in Moreton-in-Marsh. The post of Leading Fireman was the first rung of the promotion ladder. This was followed by the Sub Officer rank (usually the watch commander). Next in line was the position of Station Officer, who worked in the fire prevention or training departments or took charge of day staffing (covered by full-time firemen in the day and part-time at night) fire stations. Assistant Divisional Officers were in command of Cheshire's main fire stations and sometimes they took on specialised roles at the Brigade's HQ, which was based at Walmoor House in Chester. Divisional Officers were heads of divisions or HQ departments, while the three principal officers of Chief Fire Officer and his Deputy and Assistant took overall responsibility for the everyday running of their Brigade.

The Brigade's three Divisional Controls at Chester (A), Warrington (B) and Crewe (C) were linked to the Main Control at HQ. Divisional Controls had their own control operators (con-ops) who had been in post since the mid-1970s. Before then, firemen had taken on these roles.

Main Control, which was the public's point of contact during emergencies, issued emergency calls to fire stations by teleprinter. They obtained vital information from often distressed callers, and their local knowledge could be crucial. Like their firemen colleagues, they had to be aware of all the risks in the area. In a crisis, when the Main Control was out of action, any one of the Divisional Controls was expected to function in its place. Divisional con-ops dealt with emergencies when calls were made in person or if the automatic fire alarm panel activated. This panel was linked to alarms in high risk premises across the division. Another feature in the control room was a large whiteboard, charting the movement of fire appliances and fire officers across the division. The Royal Ordinance Factory at Radway Green in Alsager - one of the biggest risks in South Cheshire - had a direct private wire phone line to the control room in Crewe to ensure an immediate response. This line was tested twice a day with the Royal Ordinance's security staff.

The number of fire appliances turning out to emergencies was determined by the national standards of fire cover. Throughout the country, areas were categorised into level of risk:

A - Areas of substantial size and should contain a predominating concentration of properties presenting a high risk of life loss or damage to property in the event of fire.
B - Continuously built-up areas of substantial size with a predominating concentration of property presenting a substantial risk of life loss or damage to property in the event of fire.
C - Built-up areas of substantial size, where the risk of life or damage to property in the event of fire is usually low, although in certain areas the risk of death or injury may be relatively high.
D - Areas other than those classed as Remote Rural, not falling within categories A to C.
Remote Rural - Areas isolated from any centres of population and contain few buildings.
Special - Areas which need a first attendance over and above that appropriate to the risk which predominates in the surrounding area.

Each risk category had a time limit within which a set number of fire appliances had to attend an incident. Crewe was a B risk throughout the 1970s and most of the '80s, but was downgraded after review to C risk in the '90s.

Divisional Controls were discontinued in 1982 and their con-ops moved to HQ to join the Main Control team. The last of the Crewe con-ops included Rod Broome, Joe Dudley, Mike Fox, Reg Gilby, Les Hodgetts and Bert White. Their new workplace at Walmoor House overlooking the River Dee in Chester was a prestigious grade II-listed building and once the home to the Victorian Architect John Douglas. The building had been the Brigade's HQ since the late 1940s, and Main Control remained there until it was relocated in the mid-1980s to a new control centre at Vaughans Lane in Chester.

A typical morning at Crewe Fire Station was made of equipment checks on the fire appliances while drivers ensured their fire appliances were fuelled-up and roadworthy and their water tanks filled to the brim. This was followed by a keep-fit session, which usually included a game of volleyball, before the hour long slog on the drill yard. After the traditional 'tea and toast' break we knuckled down to routine testing and maintenance of equipment. As well as repairing our own equipment, we also repaired breathing apparatus for nearby fire stations and patched up their damaged hoses with a vulcanising machine. In the afternoons we reviewed database or visited high risk local premises. These were known as 11d visits, derived from Section 11d of the Fire Services Act, 1947:

> *'Provision of fire services - efficient arrangements for obtaining, by inspection or otherwise, information required for fire-fighting purposes with respect to the character of the buildings and other property in the area of the fire authority, the available water supplies and the means of access thereto, and other material local circumstances.'*

Fire inspections were also carried out at offices, shops and factories to ensure they had (among other things) adequate firefighting equipment and means of escape. Cheshire County Council buildings where life was at risk in the event of fire were also inspected.

It was reassuring to have the fire prevention department on hand to offer assistance and advise when these inspections threw up problems. Fire Prevention Officers Dave Holman and Dave Wilbraham were particularly helpful in my early days. Firemen were also expected to be familiar with the geography of their local area and with access points to water supplies. For this reason, fire hydrants were checked and tested for adequate water pressure.

The weeks before bonfire night were a busy period. In the lead up, we checked that outlets selling fireworks had safe storage. On some evenings, the number of calls to bonfires reached double figures as rival gangs lit each other's prematurely. To combat these problems, local council officials and fire prevention officers introduced safety campaigns and we highlighted the hazards of fire in talks to schoolchildren. In addition, Scouts, Guides and other youngsters regularly attended the fire station to earn their fire safety badges, and learn about the process of combustion and the dangers of fire.

One of the weekend jobs was scrubbing the floor of the four-bay appliance room (fire engine house). We soaked it until it became a lake of soapy water, and then attacked the grime and oil dribbles with an industrial scrubber. A team of squeegee operators pushed the water into the drains, before mop operators gave the floor tiles a final wipe that left them gleaming. Among other weekend tasks, we had to check the supplies of engine oil, petrol and diesel (stored in underground tanks on the drill yard) and update the route-cards that gave directions to every location in the Crewe area. Weekends were also a time when we attended community events by public request.

The fire appliances that full-time firemen staffed in 1979 included a pump hydraulic platform and an emergency tender. Either full-time or (depending on their availability) part-time firemen staffed a water ladder, water tender and a Land Rover. The water ladder housed a 13.5 metres ladder and the water tender's was 10.5 metres. Both had the same pumping capacity. The pump hydraulic platform had a three year stay at Crewe before it was replaced with a water ladder. Prior to the mid-1970s, pump escapes had been in use, before they were phased out.

Because of a shortage of part-time firemen, the water tender at Crewe was rarely used and in the early 1980s was taken out of service along with the Land Rover, which had been mainly used at agricultural incidents. The emergency tender was multi purpose: it attended all types of special service incidents, road traffic collisions and chemical incidents. It also operated as a control unit at large incidents and it functioned as a breathing apparatus main control when large numbers of breathing apparatus were in use.

A flat-back vehicle used to transport fuel to incidents was also kept at Crewe. It housed two metal containers filled with two dozen cans of petrol (2 gallons) and six cans of diesel (5 gallons), which were taken to protracted incidents to replenish fire appliances and portable pumps with fuel. Although this was its prime function, this vehicle could also be used to move equipment from large incidents. It was replaced in the late 1990s with a Bedford van.

At the rear of the fire station, a two-bay garage originally built for the Auxiliary Fire Service to store their fire appliance and equipment was used to keep non-mobile equipment. This gear, which included low level pumps, stack drags and pickles for deployment at agricultural incidents, and thermometers and probes for measuring the temperature at deep seated fires, was very rarely used in practise. The garage also housed a spare fire appliance and a mobile workshop, used by Vehicle Mechanic Dave Colclough, who served the Brigade for over 40 years. Dave and his assistant Fred Booton, serviced and carried out mechanical work on fire appliances throughout C Division, often using the inspection pit in the appliance room at Crewe Fire Station.

Drums of engine oil were stored in a small brick structure alongside the garage. The breathing apparatus chamber beside it was used for training - a dark, windowless, single storey building (20 metres x 5 metres) reeking permanently of smoke. The long side of the building was fitted with a cage from floor to ceiling. The cage had three levels which could be modified to create different routes and confined spaces. When filled with smoke, the room gave a real sense of working in darkness at a fire incident. A frequent drill involved crawling along the cage in darkness through smoke released from canisters to retrieve a 12-stone training dummy hidden inside. Training was also held at local industrial sites or other venues with specific risks to give a greater sense of realism. These venues included Crewe Arms Hotel (basement), Welcome Foundation at Crewe Hall, Rolls-Royce Motors, Air Products, Leighton Hospital, ROF Radway Green, Railway Station, Railway Works and the Railway Carriage Sidings.

The brick-built drill tower (five floors) was a landmark at this end of Crewe but it was more functional than decorative. A siren was fixed to the floor of the summit, and used to alert part-time firemen of a fire in days gone by. The tower was used in training hundreds of firemen to pitch and climb ladders and squirt water supplied from the underground water pit or from the hydrant in the drill yard.

To keep everyone focused, training had to be inventive, whether by simulating rescues, setting up water relays or applying foam in enclosed spaces. The toilet and shower room were occasionally filled with foam as part of a drill. This highlighted the difficulties for sight and hearing for anyone wearing breathing apparatus in expanded foam. But perhaps the drill was a shrewd tactic by the Station Commander: although it took a few hours to clear the foam, the walls and floor were left spotlessly clean! Other drills involved cutting scrap vehicles, sometimes at Barlow Bros Car Breakers, to provide the required skills at road traffic collisions. During the winter months, night-time drills were performed under powerful floodlights that illuminated all corners of the drill yard.

Heavy duty salvage sheets and canvas hose were dried in the enclosed section of the tower if they'd got wet or soiled at incidents. They were scrubbed, tested and then hoisted up the tower and hung out to dry, although most of the canvas hose had been replaced with rubber lined hose made with synthetic materials that didn't require drying out. The salvage sheets served several functions, from protecting floors and furniture at fires, to covering buildings after storm or fire damage.

A stand-out feature in the recreation room, indeed taking up most of its floor, was the full-size snooker table. Although snooker was a popular pastime with some firemen, the clacking sound of balls was only heard during break times or stand-down periods in the long night shift. Despite having this limited use of the snooker table, the public sometimes believed that firemen spent all their time playing snooker between attending incidents!

A telephone, housed in a wooden box, was also located outside the front entrance. This allowed the public to make emergency calls, if by chance they could get no reply from the fire station. A flag pole stood in front of the fire station and on occasions like the Queen's birthday, the Union Flag took to the air.

The other pole at the fire station was of course the Fireman's Pole. In emergencies, this provided a quick turnout from the first-floor dormitory to the appliance room. A tight grip when grabbing the pole was necessary before sliding down and landing on a foam cushion. Despite the benefits of poles on fire stations, they were removed in the mid-1980s for safety reasons.

Each watch was allocated a rack in the appliance room to store fire-kit. The racks resembled a formation of invisible firemen: yellow helmets proudly lined up on the top shelf above silver-buttoned black fire tunics neatly hung above shiny black fire boots, whose uppers were concealed inside the legs of the curled-up yellow leggings. A storage area next door housed a wall-mounted hose reel that passed through a hole in the wall to clean fire appliances in the wash-bay at the back of the appliance room.

Buckets of soapy water, brushes and sponges were also brought into action for this end-of-shift chore. It only lapsed in icy weather or when hosepipe 'bans' were imposed during hot weather. Over 30 lengths of spare hose and a dozen 25 litre drums of foam concentrate were also kept in this store. A small quantity of unravelled hose undergoing repair was also stored in an equipment room at the front of the fire station, together with spare fire-extinguisher equipment that was used until the mid-1980s to re-charge extinguishers for use at Cheshire County Council premises. The equipment room also included a facility for drying equipment and fire-kit and a small area for maintaining breathing apparatus and a compressor for charging their cylinders.

After a couple of days on the fire station, and by now having attended a handful of callouts, a 'shout' (as firemen call them) came in for a house fire at Woore in Shropshire. A thatched roof cottage was in flames when we arrived after a 15 minute journey. Under the leadership of Ken Gardner we immediately set up a couple of water jets and I joined a Staffordshire fireman on a ladder. We both adopted the 'leg-lock' position on the ladder, which freed our hands to hit the flames with copious sprays of water from the hose. The dry thatch absorbed gallons of water and despite our progress; we were continually greeted with fresh glows of fire through the thatch. As well as dealing with the fire, a race began inside the house to salvage some valuable furnishings at risk from water seeping through the thatch. Heavy duty salvage sheets blanketed larger items while smaller pieces were dragged from the burning building. It was also one of the few occasions in my career that the fireman's axe was put to good use as the thatch was stripped from the roof. This was my first proper blazing inferno. I was drenched in sweat, absorbed in smoke and had the blackened face of a coal miner. This was being a fireman in every sense. Bring on the next 30 years!

We regularly attended road traffic collisions throughout South Cheshire, and sometimes over the Staffordshire border. An incident I attended on the 23 February 1980 involved an overturned tanker loaded with 284 liquid hydrogen cylinders on a slip road under the M6 motorway at the Barthomley interchange (Junction 16). The tanker was on fire and the driver was trapped in his cab. If the tanker exploded, it would take out the motorway bridge and everybody in the vicinity. The Police moved swiftly to close the motorway and evacuate nearby properties. Desperate attempts were made to free the driver. There was no hiding place as the loud hiss of escaping gas was a constant reminder of the cylinders' potential to explode. Cooling jets of water were sprayed over them, and the flames were allowed to burn out of the expansion tube at the back of the tanker. It took 60 firemen from Cheshire and Staffordshire over three hours to make the scene safe, and free the driver from his cab; miraculously he sustained only cuts, bruises and an ankle injury.

On 18 May in the same year, a fire across several acres of deep peat at a farm in Oakhanger near Alsager took almost a week to extinguish. In the early stages we made desperate efforts to control the blaze using hand beaters. At one stage, we were surrounded by flames as gusts of swirling wind allowed the fire to gather pace. Fortunately, an escape route was sought.

Later in the year on 7 November, two railway workers were killed and another seriously injured when one goods train ploughed into the back of another near Gresty Lane in Crewe. Members of blue watch worked heroically to release the workers from the wreckage and were later praised for their efforts, with Maurice Higginson, Barrie Lunt and Colin Tomkinson commended by the Chief Fire Officer for their courage and dedication.

A steady increase in the number of callouts was noticeable throughout the 1980s especially for fires involving vehicles, buildings and refuse. Other incidents included vehicle collisions, users trapped in lifts, rings stuck on fingers, animal rescues, chemical and railway incidents and fires involving chimneys, grass and agriculture. At times, there were two or three house fires a week. Many of these fires occurred at council owned estates such as, Brookhouse Drive, Moathouse Drive, Leighton Park and Derby Docks, off West Street - all except the last now demolished.

On 23 July 1983, there was a major fire at the (now demolished) British Rail General Offices in Eaton Street. When the shout came shortly after 8.00pm, I made my debut as driver of a fire engine. Plumes of smoke were hovering over the entire town centre. The roar of the racing fire engine, the blaring two-tone horns and the continuous relay of radio messages gave me an adrenalin rush as I drove past a handful of cars along Macon Way. We dashed through Earle Street, as pedestrians in Saturday night clobber looked on, before entering the town centre and heading along Market Street towards Chester Bridge. The fire was ripping its way through the building as we arrived at Eaton Street, alongside the Royal Naval Club. My task as driver was to operate the pump and deliver water to the fire from the fire engine's 400 gallon water tank. It was a scramble to find a hydrant as the water was soon swallowed up by the flames that were raging through the dry timbers. To my relief, Keith Stubbs and John Spicer arrived on the emergency tender and raced into action to source a water supply. In the meantime, Alec Thomasson and Bob Hughes were at the 'sharp end' attacking the blaze as Richard Green, who was officer in charge, assessed the overall extent of the fire and how best to tackle it. The second fire appliance, staffed by part-time firemen from Crewe, was directed to fight the fire alongside the former railway cottages off Chester Street. Further reinforcements arrived as the blaze rapidly developed, but firemen attacking the fire from inside the building were forced to withdraw for their own safety. An aerial appliance, which was fed with water from Valley Brook near the Duke of Bridgewater pub, was later set up to douse the flames in the 160 metre-long building. The fire burnt through the night, leaving only the outer walls intact in one of Crewe's historic buildings constructed in 1876. Fortunately, no one was injured in what proved to be one of Crewe's largest blazes, but it had taken 15 fire appliances, one emergency tender and two aerial appliances to put it out.

Fire can bring injury, or even death, to firemen, so it was always reassuring to know that the Fire Services National Benevolent Fund was on hand to offer support. The charity was set up during World War II to support the bereaved families of firemen who had died during the Blitz. As the Fund relied on fundraising, it had been traditional to hold annual flag days in Crewe town centre to raise money. These were replaced in the early 1980s by yellow helmet days. Two or three fire station dances were also held annually and fire engine 'pulls' were organised to boost both the Fund and other good causes, such as Children in Need, Springfield Special School, South-East Cheshire Special Gymnastics and the Wingate Special Gymnastics in Wrenbury.

Joining us on the fundraising events was 'Welephant,' the fire service mascot launched by the Greater Manchester Brigade in 1984. He went national the following year and played a big part teaching young children about the dangers of playing with fire. Another successful initiative in the late 1980s was the Smokebusters programme which showed children how to escape from a smoke-filled room. Like 'Welephant,' this became a long-lasting aid to teaching the dangers of fire to children.

There were many advances in equipment during the 1980s. Thermal imaging cameras helped to detect heat in obscure places. Hurst cutting equipment improved efficiency at traffic accidents: its cutters, spreaders and rams were connected to hydraulic hoses and powered by a generator. This replaced the outdated 'Blackhawk' hand-pumped hydraulic equipment and air-powered cengar saw and zip gun, and enabled firemen to release people trapped in vehicles or machinery more quickly.

Station Commander Simon Snape moved on to further his career in the early 1980s. There was never a dull moment at the fire station while Simon was on duty, whether during drill or in our day-to-day activities. He made way for Scotsman Bert Gillies. Green watch welcomed some new faces during the '80s. Andy Bell, Peter Coan, Brian Sherratt, John Spicer and Peter Whittaker transferred from other fire stations in Cheshire, while Phil Edwards, Lindsay Johns, Graham Lowe and Derek Mellor came across from other watches. Bob Sweeney, who had featured as a recruit at the fire station's opening ceremony in July 1966, took charge of the watch and a trio of probationary firemen, Alan Corbin, Chris McHugh and Peter Shields joined the watch. It was traditional to play pranks on a newbie. A favourite trick was to tell him to phone 'Mr. Lyon from Payroll' about an enquiry concerning his wages - then give him the Chester Zoo phone number. Another prank on a cold, wet night was to ask the con-op to send a message that an aeroplane in distress had been last seen flying over Crewe. The probationer was then tasked to go 'on lookout' from the top of the drill tower, armed with a railway warning horn, red flag and torch.

Industrial Fire Brigades at Crewe Railway Works, Rolls-Royce Motors, Calmac Ltd at Crewe Hall and ROF Radway Green continued to operate throughout the 1980s. Their firemen often combined their duties with on-site security work. Some, such as Ralph Buckley, who served at Rolls-Royce for 31 years (28 years in the Fire and Security Department), were also part-time firemen at Crewe Fire Station. Part-time firemen were also known as 'retained' and received a retaining fee for their commitment. Their initial training consisted of four weekend courses. As well as attending incidents, they were expected to train for three hours a week. They received payment for a callout and for attending incidents and were then paid an hourly rate for their services. In September 1974, part-time firemen received £1.95 for a turnout, £1.06 for attending a fire and 87 pence per hour at an incident. It could be difficult to recruit part-timers, as most had family commitments and full-time jobs, but many were very loyal and proud to serve their community. Recruiting part-time firemen at Nantwich had been a challenge during the 1970s and 1980s, especially for daytime cover. As a result, Nantwich developed a 'nucleus' manning system with full-time firemen working during the day and part-timers covering alongside them at night. Nantwich Firemen covered a large area in South Cheshire and regularly worked alongside Crewe Firemen at incidents, often in rural areas. One such incident was a road accident on the Whitchurch Road at Newhall on 23 November 1983. After a collision with a wagon and a tanker, a van driver was on a life support machine for three weeks. Fortunately, after months of hospital treatment, he was allowed home. He showed his gratitude to the firemen who had rescued him from the wreckage, by inviting them to his home in Northern Ireland, and their friendship continued for many years.

Having time off during the week was one reason why some full-time firemen took on secondary jobs, although permission had to be granted by the Chief Fire Officer who stipulated that part-time employment should not exceeded 10 hours a week. Some worked as drivers, gardeners or window cleaners, and a few became match-day fire stewards at Crewe Alexandra FC, as new regulations on safety at football stadia were introduced. These resulted from the tragic fire in 1985 at Valley Parade, home of Bradford

City FC, when 56 people lost their lives as fire engulfed the stadium, and from the Hillsborough Disaster in 1989, when 97 people eventually lost their lives. Such serious incidents gave the fire service greater public exposure. So did the popular TV drama *London's Burning*, with its insights into the work of firemen and the lighter moments of station life. In being presented positively in this way, the fire service became a more attractive career prospect. Nonetheless, a truer reflection of the job lies in fire prevention and dealing with fires of an anti-social nature involving rubbish or cars. 'Headline' incidents were - and are - few and far between.

Firefighting had traditionally been carried out by males, but a drive to recruit females and people from ethnic backgrounds in the mid-1980s, made firemen tread more carefully in playing pranks with colleagues. Although a 'wind-up' on someone had been seen as character building, or a way of testing one's emotional strength, it could also be seen as bullying. Times change.

At one time, each watch had a mess manager, whose role was to provide food provisions for the tour of duty. He would also stock up a locker with sweets, soft drinks and tins of beer. The watch culture was quite relaxed during the night shift and it was quite acceptable to have a beer. A couple of the fire stations in Cheshire had their own bars, and part-time firemen sometimes responded to fire calls from the pub.

The work of a fireman can be strenuous, and when I joined the fire service I had to demonstrate my physical fitness by giving a fireman's lift to a 12-stone person and carry him around Chester Fire Station's drill yard. Keep-fit was encouraged in fire stations and volleyball was played to boost morale and help keep firemen's reactions in shape. Despite the benefits, this activity became less frequent towards the end of the 1980s, as health studies were carried out to improve overall fitness. Exercise machines were installed and fitness management programmes put in place to promote a healthier workforce. This also prepared firemen for their medical checks, a requirement for all operational staff when they reached their 40th birthday.

Sport was very much part of fire service culture and there was keen rivalry among firemen in Cheshire who competed against each other in snooker, fishing, volleyball and football. Marathon runs were also organised, with Brendan Grant and Geoff Shepherd flying the flag for Crewe. For the intellectual, there were quizzes to test one's 'fire brigade' knowledge. Crewe Firemen were crowned the Cheshire quiz champions in 1982 and 1984. For those who enjoyed a good argument, a debating society got off the ground for a short period. There were also inter-Brigade competitions, with opportunities to compete at regional and national level. Other sports that brought Brigades together included golf, rugby, sailing and clay pigeon shooting. Fishing was very popular, and I was fortunate to take part in many sea-fishing contests in North Wales, Lancashire, Cumbria, Yorkshire and the Isle of Wight. I was also privileged to represent Cheshire's football team alongside Green Watch colleagues Alec Thomasson and Bob Hughes and Blue Watch fireman Gerry McCabe. These matches took us to venues in Lancashire, Cumbria, Shropshire, Yorkshire, Greater Manchester, Merseyside, Staffordshire, Tyne and Wear, Glasgow and Belfast.

In the 1980s, these sporting feats were featured in the Brigade's aptly-named seasonal magazine 'The Vigil' (later called 'In Attendance'), which also featured news and humorous stories from fire stations. There was also a report from the pensioners association to keep retired members informed of the latest developments and maintain their connection with the Brigade. Putting pen to paper on behalf of Crewe was Phil Edwards, a former submariner, whose 'Crewe News' column made entertaining reading.

The Brigade's three divisions were reduced to two during the late 1980s with Crewe becoming part of A Division. Each division had a staff officer (Leading Fireman), who was at the beck and call of senior fire officers in their division. They also supported and assisted fire stations in their division, validated fire reports, organised fire officers' rotas and tested and maintained equipment that included radio blocks, pagers and alerters used by part-time firemen. Faulty communication equipment was taken to the Home Office Radio Workshops at the Police Training Centre in Nantwich Road, Crewe. Eric Taylor filled the role of staff officer at Crewe for many years until his successor, Lyndon Loweth was appointed in the mid-1980s. He was followed by Ian Swan, who was also tasked with making a smooth transition to A Division, as the days of C Division came to an end.

Ian Swan and Chris Spencer co-ordinated a fire engine pull in 1988, to raise funds towards the purchase of eight year-old Sarah Thopliss' electric wheelchair. This was one of many fund-raising events during the 1980s.

Crewe Firemen encouraged youngsters in the community to get involved in sport during the summer of 1989 when a Children's Sports Day was organised for the first time. It proved so popular that sports days became annual events for the next 20 years as running races, long and high jumps and tug of war competitions were battled out at various locations including the Cumberland Sports Centre, Victoria Sports Centre, Legends Sport Centre and Playing Fields at Macon Meadows near the fire station. Ray Stafford, who served as a part-time fireman from the late 1960s, until the early 80s, hosted these events and (for over 30 years) he was the mainstay of the fire station Children's Christmas Parties.

It came as no surprise when, in 1989, Crewe's two fire appliances became staffed by full-time firemen. Crewe had relied previously on their part-time colleagues for back-up, but these were disbanded as their numbers dwindled. Ralph Buckley, Iain Dowell, Neil Ridgway, Tony Wallace, Ronnie Whitehead, and Brothers Gordon and Roy Wood were the last remaining part-timers at Crewe before the reorganisation. The upgrade at Crewe created additional full-time jobs, some of which were filled by the small number of full-time firemen from Nantwich (Paul Bickerton, Kevin Bowen, Alan Corbin, Jay Haag and Ian Scrimgeour). Nantwich was now staffed solely by part-time firemen.

Fire crews from Crewe and Nantwich worked together at many incidents during the 1980s. A fire in the early hours at a Crewe nightclub known as 'G's' needed six fire appliances to deal with the blaze. The fire in the four-storey building in High Street was contained to one floor after starting in the DJ's console. High Street was also the scene of another major fire in the mid-'80s when 12 vehicles were destroyed by fire in the garage showrooms of John Street Ltd. The hazards included exploding petrol tanks and hydro-gas suspension units, flying fragments from the asbestos roof, and the threat of a propane cylinder explosion.

A 15-year-old boy had a lucky escape in February 1987 after he was trapped in quicksand for more than three hours at Tilcon Sand Quarry in Marton near Congleton. The emergency tender from Crewe assisted firemen from Congleton to free the boy by laying out ladders across the soft sand, pumping water from around the boy, and liquidising the sand by forcing compressed air through an 'air lance.'

Green Watch were involved in the rescue of a 10 year-old boy who was overcome by methane gas fumes in June 1987, after he explored a 7.5 metres-deep shaft at the Maw Green landfill waste site at Coppenhall. After arriving at the site, a 250 metres dash through mounds of rubble, lugging essential equipment, was made to the shaft. It became a 'race against time' as a ladder was hastily lowered into the shaft and Sub Officer Dave Langer quickly descended to make a desperate snatch rescue. A line was quickly tied around the boy who was then hauled to the surface. Fortunately the youngster survived the ordeal after paramedics treated him at the scene before rushing him to hospital. The actions of Dave Langer, whose bravery had clearly given the boy a chance of survival, was commended by everyone at the scene.

Another serious incident on 17 March 1988 involved a blaze at Gainsborough Junior School, as fire ripped through the single storey building. A few weeks later Pegasus Toys, a factory on the Weston Road Industrial Estate that produced rocking horses for luxury store Harrods, was destroyed by fire during the night. On 9 March 1989, a multiple pile-up between junctions 16 and 17 on the M6 following a diesel spillage sadly resulted in four deaths. On 4 July in the same year, fire tore through the plant processing room at MTM Chemicals in Elworth, scene of several fires during the 1970s and '80s. Nearby residents reported a huge explosion and 20 feet high flames leaping out of the factory. Up to 100 firemen turned out to tackle the blaze with many having to don chemical splash suits.

Chemical incidents were very rare and the likelihood of an incident involving radioactive materials was very unlikely. Despite this, a plan had to be in place for any eventuality. During the mid-1980s Crewe Firemen were put to the test at a training exercise at Basford Hall Railway Sidings. The staged accident involved a collision between a petrol tank wagon and a railway-carried flask wagon. It resulted in a fierce fire, which also involved a collapsed workman and overhead electric cables and those taking part were faced with the leakage of radioactivity. A decontamination and casualty zone was set-up and the damaged flask was sealed after the fire had been covered with foam. As well as the fire brigade, the exercise involved the ambulance service, British Rail workers and officials from Cheshire's Emergency Planning Committee and the Central Electricity Board.

I transferred to White Watch in 1989 to work alongside the fire station's most dedicated snooker players. Firemen Kevin Birtles, Chris Norman and John Roberts took every opportunity to hone their skills. Their perseverance paid off in 1991, when they were crowned the Brigade's overall snooker champions, with Alec Thomasson of Green Watch making up the four man team. Other members of White Watch included Terry Lewis, Cliff Simpson, Peter Townsend, Rob Benson, Paul Buckley, Paul Dunn, Gordon Goodwin and Bob Sweeney.

Shortly after joining White Watch, I submitted through the staff suggestion scheme that smoke detectors should be fitted in fire stations and fire brigade houses occupied by day-staffing firemen. It was astonishing that they weren't already fitted, especially as we were telling everyone else to fit them. For this suggestion, I was awarded £10 and labelled a 'Bright Spark' in one local newspaper! As well as advising people to install smoke alarms, we sometimes asked them not to park their vehicles over fire hydrants - a problem we often encountered during hydrant tests. Hydrants can be found on roads, grass verges or footpaths, so marker plates specifying the location and size of the hydrant's water main were fitted on nearby posts, walls or lamp posts. We also had problems on hydrant checks in negotiating fire appliances through narrow streets, especially if vehicles were parked on both sides. This was sometimes also the case when responding to incidents. Despite the benefits of hydrant testing by fire crews, this practise became a thing of the past in the 1990s with hydrant mechanics used for the task.

The 1990s was a decade of many changes. White Watch welcomed newcomers Richard Gorst, Nick Gough and John Griffiths from Chester, and Mark Coleman and Brian Tuohy arrived from Widnes and Runcorn Fire Stations. Alistair Mackie and Lee Cliffe also became part of the team after transferring from other watches. There was also a huge investment in special appliances at Crewe:

A eurocraft inflatable safety boat became part of the fleet in 1990. Its role was to provide safety at water incidents. It remained at Crewe until 1993.

A £40,000 American-built General Motor Company rapid intervention vehicle with a V8 engine replaced the emergency tender in 1990. It was lighter and smaller to manoeuvre and its four-wheel drive enabled it to cross rough terrain. It was kitted out with hydraulic rescue and cutting gear and its prime role was at road traffic collisions. It had the capability of towing the safety boat and was known as the rescue tender until 1994. It then became the operational support unit, designed to deal with incidents involving collapsed buildings and confined spaces. In 1998 it functioned as a hazard management unit, for use at chemical incidents, until it was taken out of service in 2004.

A Dennis fire appliance was converted into a foam tender in 1994. It was used at incidents requiring large quantities of foam and remained operational at Crewe until 1997.

A Leyland DAF for use at chemical incidents was based alongside the other special appliances in 1994; it was known as the special incident unit until 1998, when it then became the damage control unit, until 2010, designed to deal with incidents that had an effect on the environment.

Having special appliances at Crewe required an in-depth knowledge of decontamination procedures at chemical incidents. This involved decontaminating personnel and de-robing their gas tight or chemical splash suits. Specialists were on hand at chemical plants to support and advise firemen, while road and rail tankers transporting chemicals had to be fitted with Hazchem warning plates. These displayed an emergency code, detailing the actions to be taken in the event of a fire or spillage.

Attendance at incidents with the safety boat, the foam tender, operational support unit and damage control unit were rare, so hands-on training with these appliances was essential to maintain our proficiencies in their use. Training with the safety boat involved a journey to the River Dee in Chester or to the boating lake at Winsford Flashes.

A memorable shout on 19 August 1991 stands out for the wrong reasons, when I was among eight firemen that ended up in hospital. Ten minutes before the shift ended at 9.00am, two fire appliances (*E459 XLG* and *HFM 711*) were called out to an automatic fire alarm at Dennis Round Court Residential Housing in Alsager. On approaching the roundabout that links Weston Road to Old Park Road, near Weston, the two appliances collided with each other. I was sitting in the rear of the cab on the first appliance whose back end was shunted by the second appliance. After a forward-surge the first appliance overturned and came to rest on its side. The sound of scraping metal and cries of disbelief from my colleagues were heard from all corners as we were thrown out of our seats to end up in a heap amongst the fallen equipment. We could hear water gushing out of the tank as we struggled to stand up. In the commotion, I found myself clutching my painful right shoulder, as my colleague Phil Edwards scrambled his way out of the cab through the upward facing window. Shortly afterwards I headed for the same exit, and with Phil's help I clambered out before lowering myself from the overturned fire appliance. I took refuge on the roundabout as the distant sirens of the approaching Police cars and ambulances grew louder. Visibly distraught colleagues were comforting each another as ambulances arrived to treat the injured and transport us to Leighton Hospital. Robert Benson, Kevin Birtles, Steve Burrows, Phil Edwards, Alistair Mackie and Chris Norman all suffered minor injuries, while Terry Lewis fractured his elbow and had lacerations to his hand, and I ended up with a dislocated and fractured shoulder. In the meantime, other fire engines were mobilised to the incident in Alsager, which added insult to literal injury by turning out to be a false alarm. This prompted a headline in a local newspaper: 'FIREMEN HURT IN FALSE ALARM.'

A three months' lay off from work followed this crash. I came to appreciate how much the Fire Brigade Union had looked after my interests during this traumatic period. Their support motivated me to become a union representative. I also appreciated the work of the Fire Services National Benevolent Fund after the accident, especially after staying at one of their convalescent homes in Littlehampton. This was my second serious injury in the line of duty: a few years earlier, I had received hospital treatment for burns to my wrist following a house fire at Leighton Park in Crewe. Nor was this the first time that Crewe Firemen had been involved in fire engine crashes. Collisions had occurred over the years, with the most tragic of all in 1939, when two firemen lost their lives after their vehicle overturned. Another crash in December 1965 hospitalised three firemen when their fire appliance *(NTU 930)* tipped-over, and in the spring of 1979, Fireman Gerry McCabe sustained a fractured leg, while his colleagues, Maurice Higginson, Alan Ollier and Keith Roberts received minor injuries when the emergency tender *(DTU 912F)* overturned near Winterley Pool during an emergency call. After the Winterley accident, the Bedford emergency tender was written off and replaced with a Dennis tender.

Local MP Gwyneth Dunwoody always kept up with developments at the Brigade and occasionally visited the fire station. Visits were also made by Home Office Inspectors to check that high standards were maintained. The Inspector was usually a retired Chief Fire Officer who expected to find a pristine fire station and a smart turnout by everyone. He would then observe rescue drills, which had been rehearsed to perfection, and scrutinise the administration work, before drafting his report. By the early 1990s however these inspections had been discontinued and a few years' later formal inspections by senior fire officers also ended. They did however turn up at training exercises. On 23 October 1991, they accompanied Lord Ferrers - the Home Office minister responsible for fire services - to Air Products in Weston Road in Crewe to observe an exercise of firemen dealing with a gas leak. Lord Ferrers also received briefings on emergency planning at Brigade HQ. Crewe Firemen were involved in several major off-site training exercises during the 1990s. One such exercise was held at Manchester Airport. This demonstrated the difficulty of evacuating passengers from the confined space of a crashed plane fuselage. Another exercise at Crewe Alexandra FC's Gresty Road Stadium highlighted problems with communications and evacuation procedures.

Personal safety continued to improve as a new working rig was introduced - nato jumpers and flame retardant proban shirts and trousers. The new Nomex fire-kit with high-viz bands gave better protection from heat and fire, as did the new French Gallet helmet, which was introduced in 1994. Its detachable hood safeguarded the neck against heat, and its reflective heat shield visor protected the face. This new fire-kit was a sharp contrast to my first issue - Nomex fire tunic, yellow rubber leggings and a cork helmet that had been in use since the end of World War II. Despite these improvements, there was a tinge of sadness in our farewells to our prized cork helmets, some strewn with indentations from falling debris to remind us of battles at fire incidents.

Local journalist Daniel O'Driscoll, who worked for the *Crewe Guardian*, often called into the fire station on his way to work. Over a brew, he was given first-hand details about the shouts we attended. Reporters from the *Staffordshire Sentinel* and the *Crewe Chronicle* were also regularly in touch, especially the *Chronicle*'s Jan Roberts and Belinda Ryan, and their photographer Tim Jervis, whose images enhanced many of the fire-related stories.

After a change of watch in 1994, I teamed up with Leigh Bowen, Frank Bratley, Mitchell Clarke, Mick Clays, Phil Edwards, Rikki Harden, Chris Hughes, Steve Herbert, Ray Mills, Alan Ollier, Barry Rose, Craig Welsh and Ian West on Blue Watch. The tempo of this watch was noticeably less hurried than the others, although the professionalism was as high. The ageing Blue Watch was sometimes referred to as 'dad's army' until Philip Hales transferred to us from Ellesmere Port and Garry Moore from Chester. At the same time, the youthful Richard Gorst breathed fresh life into the watch as the new Sub Officer. He soon fitted in with his common sense approach, and it was no surprise to see him climb the promotion ladder after he was replaced by the calm-headed Lindsay Johns in the late 1990s.

By now, our job title had changed from 'Fireman' to 'Firefighter.' Local recruitment of women to a traditionally male-dominated occupation remained sluggish throughout the 1990s, although some of the larger fire brigades had employed women to fight fires from the early 1980s. At the same time, the Brigade encouraged recruitment from ethnic communities.

My generation of firefighters found themselves attending the over-40s medical tests during the mid-1990s. Firefighters hoping to return to work after a long period of sickness were also checked over. I attended one of the medicals with Red Watch's Ken Gardner, who was on light duties after a period of sickness. Part of the tests was to step up and down onto a 12-inch box for 5 minutes. Our heart recovery rate was then measured, and the medic granted us both a clean bill of health. On our way back to Crewe, Ken started to complain of an aching leg, which tightened up as we got closer to Crewe. "How did you both get on?" Station Commander, Roy Howarth, asked when we arrived back at the fire station. With a smile on my face I gave him the thumbs up, but Ken limped towards the boss and said: "The good news is I passed the medical. The bad news is I pulled a leg muscle doing those flaming step-ups, so I'm booking sick!" Yes, Ken was serious!

Crewe Firefighters were involved with numerous fundraising activities during the 1990s. Over £12,000 was raised for a Romanian Orphanage in 1994 when hundreds of tea chests filled with a variety of tea bags were sourced from the local Co-op Tea Factory. Donations poured in from family and friends of firefighters across Cheshire.

Towards the end of the 1990s, a sponsored walk (while carrying a fire ladder), and two Fire Engine Pulls, raised over £2,500 for the Fire Services National Benevolent Fund, the South-East Cheshire Special Olympics Fund and the Mayor's Charity Appeal. Joining us to entertain the young children at these events was 'Welephant' and 'Blaze Bear,' the Benevolent Fund's mascot.

'Trauma Ted' was a new bear on the block in 1996. Distressed children at fires or road traffic collisions were handed teddy bears for comfort. Post-traumatic stress had become more recognisable, and fire crews who were exposed to trauma at incidents were now offered counselling

A new corporate dress code was introduced, displaying the Brigade's logo on the open-neck shirts, jumpers and fleece jackets. This was a sharp contrast with the working-rig uniform of my early days, which comprised a cotton overall jacket and trousers. For more formal duties, we had a blue nylon shirt, black tie, black blazer jacket and trousers, a black gabardine coat and a flat peak cap. The storage of fire-kit on racks in the appliance room was identified as a hazard as exhaust fumes from fire appliances contaminated it with harmful particles. As a result, fire-kit was moved next door into the hose room storage area.

Towards the end of the decade all Brigade departments moved to one site at the new HQ in Winsford, which was officially opened in 1997. Local government reorganisation on 1 April 1998 saw the creation of a new Fire Authority as Cheshire County Council and Halton and Warrington Unitary Council became responsible for the fire service. It was 50 years since the formation of Cheshire County Fire Brigade. The two Divisions (A and B) were disbanded and basic recruit training (non-residential) was delivered in-house.

The focus of our work was now gradually moving towards making our communities safer by fitting smoke alarms and carrying out safety checks at private homes.

The 1990s was notable as one of Crewe Fire Station's busiest decades. Incidents of interest included a fire that severely damaged the clock tower at Webb House in Victoria Avenue on 16 June 1992. Five days later a carpet warehouse at 96 West Street was engulfed in a blaze that needed four fire appliances. In November 1992, a fugitive cow from the cattle market in Barker Street charged past the Fire Station, and was only captured in Sydney Road after a long chase by a fire crew. The derelict Kindlers Clothing Factory in Queen Street was set on fire on 29 September 1993. Eight fire appliances and one aerial appliance prevented the blaze spreading to nearby properties. A fire on 13 November 1994 at the BOC Transhield warehouse, where food was distributed for Marks and Spencer, required six fire appliances. The former Foden Works in Elworth was the scene of a major fire on 23 September 1995 when over 70 firefighters attended, and 140 residents had to evacuate their homes. In Wistaston on 5 November 1995, a wheelie bin fire spread to the adjoining Mormon Church and destroyed its roof.

Assistant Divisional Officer Peter Wilding was in command at Crewe Fire Station as we approached the Millennium. Each watch had 14 members of staff:

Red Watch: Jay Haag (Sub Officer), Philip Kilgour, Nigel Pordes and Dave Williams (Leading Firefighters), Steve Burrows, Alan Corbin, John Dunne, Adrian Dunning, Christopher Holmes, Anthony Kitchen, Martin Poole, Mark Sopp, Daniel Wade and Gary Williams (Firefighters).

Blue Watch: Lindsay Johns (Sub Officer), Philip Edwards, Rikki Harden and Terry Lewis (Leading Firefighters), Kevin Birtles, Leigh Bowen, Frank Bratley, Mitchell Clarke, Mick Clays, Paul Gresty, Steve Herbert, Alan Ollier, myself and Craig Welch (Firefighters).

White Watch: Paul Rowlands (Sub Officer), Christopher Elson, Peter Townsend and Jim Yarwood (Leading Firefighters), Steve Benbow, Robert Benson, Philip Boone, John Caulfield, Lee Cliffe, Gordon Goodwin, Brendan Grant, Andy Mills, Philip Moorcroft and Ian Selby (Firefighters).

Green Watch: Dave Hanley (Sub Officer), Paul Hanby, Colin Tomkinson and Andy Wainwright (Leading Firefighters), Janssen Bostock, Max Higginson, Bob Hughes, Steve Hughes, Paul Leigh, Ian Seel, Peter Shields, Philip Smith, John Speed and Alec Thomasson (Firefighters).

Civilian Staff: Dianne Farrington, Caroline Roper, Jenny Steele, Hazel Jones and Jackie Hancock.

The Millennium was celebrated in style at the fire station with a sell-out dance in the appliance room for 200 people. These functions had raised thousands of pounds for the Fire Services National Benevolent Fund, but towards the end of the decade, the plug was pulled on holding such events in fire stations, which was considered an inappropriate location.

Later in 2000, on 18 July the fire station opened its doors to the public in a different way with its first Open Day for over 30 years. Hundreds attended and donations of over £1,500 were made to the Fire Services National Benevolent Fund and other charities. The following year, over £2,000 was raised for good causes with a Fire Station Car Wash and a challenging Ladder Climb in Crewe town centre. On 11 September 2001, the world was stunned by the 9/11 attacks on the World Trade Centre in New York when 353 firefighters were among the dead. The tragedy touched many hearts, and Crewe Firefighters raised £1,500 for the appeal fund through a ground collection at Crewe Alexandra FC's home match against Wimbledon FC. Other fundraising events for the appeal included a football match (Crewe Firefighters v Macclesfield Firefighters at Moss Rose, home of Macclesfield Town FC) and several bucket collections in Crewe pubs.

Earlier in 2001, Crewe Firefighters had been put on alert as the foot and mouth epidemic threatened farms in Cheshire. The damage control unit at Crewe was kitted out with specialist equipment and disinfectant for any decontamination that was needed at incidents. Fortunately, only two outbreaks were detected at farms in South Cheshire. Incidents of interest in 2002 included a fire that burnt out two rail carriages in the sidings off Weston Road, and a few weeks later, the side of a house in Crossway in Crewe was blown out by a lightning strike. Numerous derelict houses on the Leighton Park estate were deliberately set on fire over several months during the same year, as they waited to be bulldozed. In the same area, a serious fire destroyed most of Underwood West Nursery and Infant School on the evening of 21 November 2002.

In the summer of 2002, firefighters in the UK argued that they were underpaid for the work they did. This resulted in several periods of strike action as the culture of the fire service came under attack from the Government. It was the first major dispute since the nine-week strike in 1977/78, although there had been periods of working-to-rule as protests against worsening conditions of service and increased pension contributions. From being portrayed as heroes after the 9/11 tragedy, firefighters became overnight villains, as public opinion was influenced by the headlines on some national newspapers. The first strike began on 13 November, and further strikes followed over the next eight months. A breakthrough in the dispute was eventually reached in June 2003, after an independent review was commissioned. This recommended radical changes in the organisation and management of the fire service. Fire services became known as Fire and Rescue Services to better reflect their developing roles. One of the requirements of the Fire and Rescue Services Act introduced in 2004 was to focus on preventing fires by educating the public. As a result, Cheshire Fire and Rescue Service set out its mission to create safer communities, rescue people and protect local interests.

To achieve these objectives, safety initiatives were introduced, and youth engagement programmes and partnership work with other agencies were developed. Crewe's former Auxiliary Fire Service garage was flattened and a new community safety office was built. This became a hub for meetings with other organisations. Space was allocated for a fire cadet unit to provide young people from 12 to 17 years an insight into the fire service and opportunities to develop their personal and social skills. A new statutory instrument - the Regulatory Reform (Fire Safety) Order 2005 - came into force in 2006, replacing other regulations that dealt with fire precautions. This shifted the responsibility to individuals within an organisation to carry out risk assessments to identify, manage and reduce the risk of fire. National standards of fire cover were replaced by Integrated Risk Management Plans. These plans are based on risks to life and injury in the community to make the fire and rescue service more responsive to local needs and locating resources appropriately to best protect the community.

Time spent training on the drill yard appeared to fall as more computer-based activities were introduced. The breathing apparatus chamber became redundant as a training facility, and personal development handbooks were issued. A new continual professional development payment scheme replaced the long-service pay increase. A role-based structure replaced the fire service rank system and promotion examinations were scrapped. Leading Firefighters became Crew Managers and Sub Officers became Watch Managers. Other new roles included: Station Manager, Group Manager, Area Manager and Brigade Manager. The new leadership culture allowed civilians with no fire service background to be appointed into senior management positions.

Brigade traditions came under fire. The interiors of Cheshire fire stations were revamped. Out went snooker tables and dart boards. Reclining chairs replaced the beds used by firefighters on the night shift. Space was made available for community use. The jobs of fire station cooks who prepared meals for firefighters on the day shift were lost. New firefighters looked in disbelief when we told them that fire stations once had bars and beer lockers!

Cooks and administration staff had been part of the team at Crewe Fire Station, supporting many of the Firefighters' activities. Hazel Jones, who replaced Janet Darlington-Lea as cook in the mid-1990s, played a big part organising the Ladder Climb for the Ruskin Sports College Appeal in 2001. Jenny Steel, who served as fire station clerk for over 24 years, immersed herself in fund-raising for the Romanian Orphanage Appeal in 1994. Other civilian members of staff, including Sue Bebington, Cath Dodman, Bev Dyer, Diane Farrington, Jackie Hancock, Caroline Roper and Tracey Williams also supported many events.

Following the success of the Millennium event, Open Days were held bi-annually. They attracted bumper crowds to the fire station as did the annual charity car washes. By 2009 over £15,000 had been raised for the Fire Services National Benevolent Fund (now known as the Firefighters Charity) and other causes since 2000. One memorable fundraiser was a football match between Crewe Firefighters and their colleagues from all over Cheshire at Nantwich Town FC's Jackson Avenue ground in 2006. The event was held to support the South Asian Disaster appeal following a catastrophic earthquake in 2005. Crewe Firefighter Majid Ullah, who took part in the football match, flew out to Kashmir to assist with humanitarian aid. International support had also been provided by Crewe Firefighters (Mark Coleman, Keith Roughley, Chris Spencer, Andy Wainwright, Ian West and Gary Williams), who were part of the Cheshire Fire and Rescue Service Search and Rescue Team, responding to international tragedies caused by earthquakes or flooding in: Armenia (1988), Iraq (1991), Montserrat (1996/1997), Rwanda (1997), Macedonia (1999), Turkey (August and October 1999), Mozambique (2000), India (2001) and Indonesia (2009).

The 2006 Open Day commemorated 40 years since the opening of the fire station. Norman Turner, who had been Station Commander at Crewe in 1966, was the guest of honour. Guests at previous Open Days included Bruce Jones, aka Les Battersby from 'Coronation Street' (2000), Paul Spencer, local musician with Dario G (2002), and Gwyneth Dunwoody MP (2004). Councillor Margaret Simon, who served on the Fire Authority, was guest at the 2008 Open Day, which highlighted the growing number of vehicle fires in the Crewe area by displaying a burnt out car. The emphasis on this type of anti-social behaviour was prompted by the 45 vehicles that had been torched around Crewe during the first half of 2008, compared with 28 for the whole of 2007.

Later in the year, Mersey Regional Ambulance Service NHS Trust delivered First Responder training, as preparations were made for Crewe Firefighters to attend medical incidents. The aim was to provide a joint response with the Ambulance Service to pre-determined life-threatening illnesses, and to provide a flexible, efficient and resilient response to medical emergencies. Despite all the planning, the initiative failed to get off the ground as it was judged to be outside the scope of firefighters. Meanwhile a recycling initiative had a successful outcome as Firefighters Leigh Bowen and Alan Ollier influenced the local authority to supply industrial wheelie bins to recycle glass and paper at the fire station.

Although many of the local industry fire brigades had been disbanded, we continued to make 72d (previously known as 11d) visits to high-risk premises. This requirement to *make arrangements for obtaining information needed for extinguishing fires* derived from Section 7, subsection 2 (d) of the Fire and Rescue Services Act 2004. Training exercises continued to be held at the sites to test the procedures in the event of an emergency. On 10 March 2005, an exercise at ROF Radway Green involved eight fire appliances when the COMAH (Control of Major Accident Hazards) plan was put to the test. The scenario was a magazine fire/explosion involving 13 tonnes of propellant caused by spread of fire/explosion of 750 kilos of propellant being carried by a fork lift truck. The initial fire was caused by an electrical fault on the fork lift truck. Firemen at ROF Radway Green had been well equipped in earlier years and were trained to high standards at the Defence Fire Training and Development Centre at Manston. They were disbanded, however, and by the late 1980s their expertise and local knowledge was no longer available.

Towards the end of my career, huge efforts were made to reduce the number of emergency calls. Over 60,000 home safety assessments were completed in Cheshire over a single year, through the combined efforts of firefighters and civilian staff. The new Cheshire Fire and Rescue Service newsletter, (re-named 'Alert') boasted about safety initiatives and the fire service's community involvement. It contrasted sharply with the focus of 1980s newsletters on the activities of the Brigade's sports and welfare association, fire station humour, incidents of interest and new developments within the fire service.

The introduction of new equipment continued. High-pressure hose reels on the pumps, and positive pressure fans to rapidly ventilate buildings, improved efficiency at fires and made life easier on the fire-ground. Despite these advances and the huge investment in community safety initiatives, the number of incidents in Crewe had not yet fallen significantly. In June 2007, Blue Watch were first on the scene at Aztec Chemicals on the Crewe Gates Industrial Estate, at one of the biggest blazes in Crewe for several years. The fire involved a cocktail of chemicals, propane cylinders, drums of solvent and a mass storage of liquid petroleum gas. Fortunately no one was injured, largely because the premises were swiftly evacuated.

Blue Watch had seen many comings and goings since the start of the Millennium. Some members had short stays, while others remained on the watch for the long haul. The arrivals included Matt Barlow, Steve Barnes, Janssen Bostock John Caulfield, Iain Dunne, Andy Hewitt, Max Higginson, Anthony Jones, Mark Latham, Leon Parkes, Ian Seel, Nigel Swan, Graham Thomas, Kirsty Townsend, Adam Wagstaff, Alan Williams and Ryan Younger. Station commanders had also come and gone. Norman Turner, who was the first in 1966, remained at the helm for four years and was followed by: Norman Nicholson (1970-1975), Dennis Davis (1975-1977), Simon Snape (1977-1981), Bert Gillies (1981-1984), Ian McDonald (1984-1989), Roy Howarth (1989-1993), John Lloyd (1993-1998), Peter Wilding (1998-2001), Mark Abram (2001-2002), Clive Pickering (2002-2006), Carl Hanson (2006-2008) and Derek Dickson (2008-2009). The post had sometimes been filled temporarily, but it was Roy Howarth who had played the biggest part in keeping a steady ship at the fire station. Before taking charge in 1989, he had served as the Station Commander's Deputy since 1976.

Crewe and Nantwich are twinned with Bischofsheim in Germany, Macon in France and Dzierzoniow in Poland. Roy Howarth's successor, John Lloyd, was awarded the German Fire Service Silver Medal for International Co-operation in 2005 for his commitment to forging links between firefighters in Crewe and Nantwich and Bischofsheim. John's award was made during centenary celebrations at Bischofsheim, which were also attended by former Crewe Firefighters Lindsay Johns and Dave Langer.

To further a career, firefighters were usually expected to serve at other fire stations, or in other departments such as fire safety or training. However, many were content to remain at the same fire station throughout their firefighting days. The eight recruits who began their careers with me in 1979 took different career paths. Steve Doyle and Philip Edwards found their niches in the fire safety departments, while Dave Williams became a full-time FBU official. After a couple of years, Paul Whitby embarked on a different career, while Jim Morrey headed to Canada and ultimately retired as Captain of the Toronto Fire Department. Chris Mannix became a fireman in his home town of Winsford, before taking charge of the part-time firefighters at Nantwich. Like me, Frank Bratley and Steve Herbert were content with fighting fires in Crewe throughout our careers. Frank and Steve were among a handful of firefighters who remained on blue watch for most of their careers, as did Mick Clays and Alan Ollier. John Dunne, Anthony Kitchen and Martin Poole stayed loyal to Red Watch, as was Gordon Goodwin and Philip Moorcroft to White Watch, and Bob Hughes to Green Watch. I served on all the watches, apart from Red Watch and it wasn't uncommon to be detached to any of the full-time fire stations in Cheshire (Chester, Ellesmere Port, Macclesfield, Wilmslow, Birchwood, Warrington, Runcorn and Widnes) for a shift during a tour of duty. Similarly, firefighters from these fire stations came to Crewe for their shifts. It was while on detached duties at Warrington that I attended my last serious building fire in May 2009.

Firefighters have their own tales to tell about incidents they've attended during their careers. Large scale fires, fatal incidents, rescues involving people or animals, and (in recent times) attacks from groups of youths are embedded in one's memory. Comforting casualties trapped in their vehicles could be harrowing, as we fought alongside paramedics to keep them alive. Sometimes our voices were the last they heard.

But there were many humorous moments as well. The rescue of a cow from the frozen water of a canal near Nantwich caused both mirth and sadness. An animal sling, which was used to rescue animals trapped in water or mud, was wrapped around the cow in readiness to haul it out of the water. The vet in attendance reckoned that the cow would have suffered brain damage after being in the frost for so long and should be put down. On hearing this, everyone looked dejected, but a quick response from Nantwich Fireman Kevin Bowen brought hope to everyone's faces, when he asked the vet if brain damage would matter to the cow as she wouldn't be taking part in any pub quizzes! After some laughter, however, it became clear that the vet's word was final and the cow was eventually put down.

Another attempted rescue involved a Canada goose, which appeared to be tangled in fishing line while perched on a roof behind a supermarket in Crewe town centre. It had been reported that the bird had been stranded and unable to move for several hours. We pitched a ladder against the building and I climbed to within touching distance of the bird, armed with a pair of pliers. Sure enough, the bird was tangled in fishing line and appeared to be trapped in the guttering. As I reached out, pliers in hand, towards the bird, it suddenly flicked its neck, flapped its wings, and took off into the sky. I looked down at the cheering onlookers as a handful of feathers drifted towards them. Everyone thought I had the magic touch as I slowly descended the ladder feeling ten feet tall after my so-called act of valour. In truth, I had probably been more terrified than the bird and just relieved it hadn't taken a swipe at me as I clung to a ladder 20 metres off the ground. It certainly brought on the goose bumps!

Early on in my career, I attended a fatal road traffic collision involving a man who was trapped in a vehicle. The aim of our team was to release the casualty from

Green Watch 1985. L to R: Ken Gardner, Dave Langer, Chris McHugh, Peter Shields, Keith Stubbs, Peter Turner, myself and Graham Lowe.

*(**Above**) Blue Watch Firemen - myself and Phil Hales training on the aerial appliance in 1995. (**Above right**) Blue Watch 1999. L to R: Craig Welch, Gary Moore, Steve Herbert, myself and Terry Lewis at an incident.*

Blue Watch 2004. Back L to R: Jon Caulfield, Leigh Bowen, Majid Ullah, Alan Ollier, Frank Bratley and Steve Barnes. Front L to R: Andy Anderson, myself, Kevin Birtles and Paul Gresty.

Blue Watch 2009. Back L to R: Alan Ollier, Graham Thomas, Leigh Bowen, Andy Hewitt, Matt Barlow, Ryan Younger, Nigel Swan and Andy Anderson. Front L to R: Janssen Bostock, Paul Edwards, Iain Dunne, myself, Adam Wagstaffe, Mark Latham and Paul Gresty.

the wreckage and lift him onto the stretcher. After freeing him, the order was given for everyone to lift at the same time. I was holding tight to one of his legs waiting for the order. As the order was given, I suddenly realised the casualties leg had become detached from him. I was horrified that I'd made things worse, before I realised that the casualty had an artificial leg. Predictably, I had my own leg pulled after that shout!

A fire in a terraced house in Stalbridge Road, Crewe, brought the fear of God to me one evening, as I searched the first floor of the smoke-filled house for someone reported to be trapped inside. With my breathing apparatus partner, I shuffled into a bedroom searching for a casualty in the darkness of the dense smoke. Within a few moments of entering the room, the back of my hand struck an obstacle directly in front of me. It brought me to a sudden halt, and within seconds, I was met face-on with a gentle thud. I instinctively backed off, wiped the outer lens of my facemask and stepped forward to catch sight of an image of a face swaying backwards and forwards in the haze of the smoke. I concluded that a lifeless person was dangling from the ceiling. I nervously closed-in again, and to my relief, I discovered I was face to face with a punch bag. It was marked with its eyes, nose and mouth and suspending from the ceiling. There was only one thing to do - land it a whopping right hander!

Chimney fires were attended quite frequently in my early days. These could be problematic, as the exact location of the fire was often uncertain. They could be fought from the grate using rods attached to a hose fixed with a nozzle, or from the roof top by pouring water down the chimney. The preferred option was from the grate. Not only was it safer, but there was always the possibility of pouring water down the wrong chimney from the roof top. This happened on occasions, but fortunately not while I was on duty.

I lost count of the number of incidents I drove to and prided myself on not causing any accidents when sitting behind the steering wheel. There were a couple of near misses though. On one occasion, I was reversing in a tight space when my colleague, who was checking the rear of the fire appliance, shouted "Go!" I carried on reversing and he came running to my window and shouted: "I said Whoa! Not Go!" Luckily no damage was done.

I was also pleased with my disciplinary record, although it was blemished towards the end of my career, when I was among seven members of Blue Watch who were disciplined for a breach of IT protocol after a watch member emailed several Cheshire MP's suggesting how proposed changes, as laid out by the Cheshire Fire Authority, might be detrimental to the fire service. Each watch was allocated an email address, and on this occasion, the email was sent from Blue Watch's email. We were informed that one of the MP's made a complaint about the email, so an investigation took place. As no watch member owned up to sending the email, the seven firefighters who happened to be on duty were disciplined. Despite pleading our innocence, a 'note for file' for misconduct was served to all seven firefighters as punishment.

The last shift of my 30-year career arrived at the end of June 2009. The years had passed in the blink of an eye and I left with mixed feelings. Like my first shift, my last had offered no real excitement, apart from a few small refuse fires and a couple of false alarms. It was also a time to reflect on those tragic incidents when people lost their lives in front of our eyes, often from road traffic collisions. Memories of drilling on the yard, which had been a big part of my working life, flooded back - climbing ladders, running out hose, mauling equipment, spraying gallons of water and crawling through smoke donned in breathing apparatus while dripping in sweat. The prospect of training wasn't always welcome, but there was usually a sense of satisfaction at the end of a session.

Before I finally 'stood down' from the fire service there was one ritual to be completed - the presentation to me of a firefighter's axe. The chrome plated axe was mounted on a wooden plinth with my fire service cap badge, medal ribbon bars and a brass breathing apparatus tally, inscribed with the dates I joined and left the fire service. The tallies are designed to show the time you went under air when wearing breathing apparatus to tackle a fire and the time you were due to come out of the fire, so this was a fitting gift for someone who rode the pumps for three decades. The axe now takes pride of place alongside my fire service long service and good conduct medal and my 25 year FBU badge.

A pleasant surprise was waiting at my presentation evening at the Flying Lady Pub, when a young man called Gavin McLean turned up with his father Edward to pass on their best wishes. In 1987, Firefighter Peter Shields and I had been involved in the rescue of Gavin, then nine months old, from a house fire in Oxford Street, Crewe. Gavin was fortunate to survive the fire, and our paths hadn't crossed since that day. After the fire, Chief Fire Officer Dennis Davis had commended our actions for 'acting within the highest traditions of the service and effectively rescuing baby Gavin McLean'. My career had been full of unpredictable moments, but meeting Gavin, who was now in his early twenties, and tracked down by my colleague Nigel Swan had to be my 'number one' surprise!

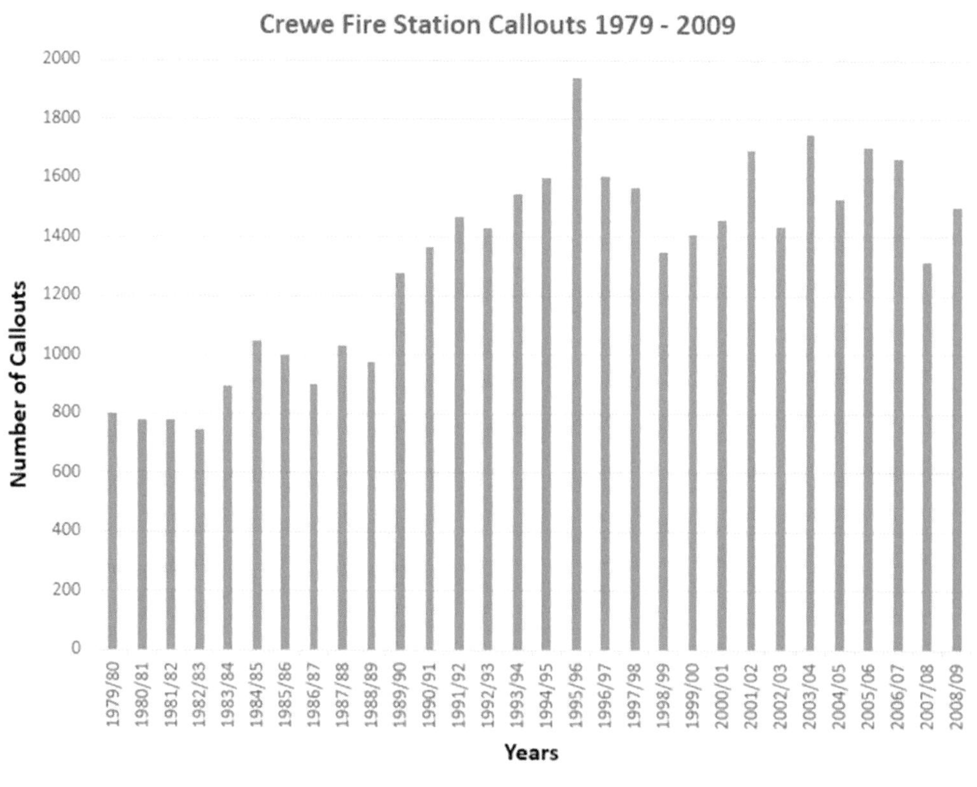

FIREFIGHTING IN CREWE

THE BEGINNING

Fire can be devastating for both country and town, but its potential causes and its potential destruction of people and property has always been greater in heavily-populated areas. It is no surprise that the crowded cities of Edinburgh and London were the first to develop defensive building regulations and fire brigades.

Less than 200 hundred years ago, the township of Crewe was rural - essentially a country district dominated by Crewe Hall, its local Big House. Its fire risks reflected this, with newspaper reports of rick blazes or infernos at properties built in the local vernacular style with timber frames. Like many country houses, Crewe Hall ran its own limited fire service, manned by volunteers, with the priority of protecting the mansion and the 50 farms and 200 cottages that made up the estate.

But the nature of South Cheshire was about to change with astonishing speed. First, the Grand Junction Railway, linking Warrington with Birmingham, bisected Madeley Parish. Then the Crewe-Chester-Birkenhead link was established in 1840. When Nantwich and Newcastle-under-Lyme each turned down its chance of becoming a railway junction, Monks Coppenhall was chosen instead and rechristened Crewe. By 1842, the Liverpool line converged at the same station.

The Grand Junction Railway Company wanted to move its small works at Edge Hill in Liverpool to a green-field site. After making surveys at Winsford, the Company decided to build its new workshop alongside the Chester railway line at Crewe. Engine-repairs began there in March 1843 with just 161 staff. From February 1845, however, the Company began to build new locomotive engines at the Crewe Works. The Grand Junction Railway had already absorbed the Liverpool and Manchester Railway. In 1846, it amalgamated with the London and Birmingham Railways to create the London and North-Western Railway, with the headquarters of its Northern Division in Crewe. By this time, the extent of the Works had increased to 30 acres, and the number of staff to 600 (and to 1,100 by 1847, and 1,600 by 1848). By 1851, Crewe's population was 5,000 and rising. To cope with this growth, the Railway Company had built houses for its workers. The first 32 cottages in what became the centre of the town were occupied by the end of 1842. By 1848 there were 520, and by 1858 well over 700.

Throughout the 19th Century, local newspapers (see *Shouts* chapter) continued to report the incidence of cottage and farmstead fires across rural South Cheshire. These included some of the most destructive blazes - such as the near-destruction of Crewe Hall in January 1866 - but it is clear that the railway itself, and the industries supporting it, and the new chemicals and substances they introduced, were now a major cause of fire. These stories often make two implicit points. First, that fires were for many people an irresistible public spectacle. Even alarms raised in the middle of the night attracted large numbers of spectators. Second, that fire could bring ruination to householders or businesses: newspaper accounts often estimated the cost of the fire damage and reported whether the victims carried insurance. A more explicit and tragic aspect was that children were sometimes the victims of fire - a distressing outcome for firefighters, then as now. Animals, too, regularly perished in farm fires.

Some causes of these fires have a modern ring. Several were believed to derive from smoking or the careless use of matches. It is difficult to tell whether fires blamed on 'Bonfire Night' or 'incendiarists' were speculation in default of anything more definite. The Law recognised at least some of the fire risks. Under the Town Police Clause Act 1847 it was an offence to wilfully set fire to a chimney or even to allow a chimney to accidentally catch fire. Unswept chimneys and poorly constructed hearths and vents were one of the main causes of blazes in the 19th Century. In July 1874 three Crewe residents - James Durrant, William Goldsmith and Susannah Swan - were each fined 2s.6d (12.5p) for allowing their chimneys to catch fire.

One or two of the newspaper stories do not shed a uniformly positive light on the fire services available. The fire had occasionally gone out by the time the firefighters arrived on the scene - perhaps not so surprising given the Brigade's voluntary character although the numbers turning out were usually impressive. Water supplies were not always readily accessible, and equipment listed suggests an uneasy mix of the primitive 'wicker baskets' with state-of-the-art technology.

By the middle of the 19th Century, Crewe effectively had three fire services: a volunteer brigade serving the town and its residents, a service based on the Crewe Hall estate, and a service based on the LNWR Works. The first of these was part of a growing pattern of community-based facilities - with an incentive of avoiding discriminatory premia imposed by insurance companies - and made use of other services such as a water supply that local government was starting to provide. Although each of the three providers had its own sphere of influence, there is ample evidence from newspaper reports that the services often, though not always, supported each other when necessary and could even rely at times on help from a brigade based at Nantwich. Yet as late as 1887, the Crewe Hall engine remained the first port of call when the alarm sounded on the estate.

AN INDEPENDENT VOLUNTARY FIRE SERVICE

Around 1860, a volunteer fire service of sorts existed in Crewe, with a London Fire Brigade model fire engine for local use under the direction of Mr. W. Watson. This was housed in the yard behind the Royal Hotel, while Mr. Henry Irving of the Star Inn provided the horses to pull it. As Crewe's population approached 20,000, the Local Board decided in June 1870 that the town should have its own organised volunteer fire brigade. A group of men offered their services, but their equipment was limited to a fire cart containing hoses, nozzles and standpipes. This led to a successful public appeal for funds to commission a proper fire engine. Members of the Brigade at this time included: Inspector Morris, Captain Edward Floyd, Lieutenant and Honorary Secretary George Watson, Sergeant Plant, Sergeant Samuel Wood, Second Sergeant John Porter and Firemen George Chatfield, J. Coonan, John Farr, John Heath, T.H. Heath, E. Herd, George Hollin, Henry Hough, John Jones, John Mason, W. Mason, Israel Moor, H. Proudlove, G. Turton and W. Wood.

In November 1872, the volunteer firemen asked the Local Board to provide an engine-house and to convert the bell of the town clock into an alarm that would alert the firemen to fire emergencies. They also asked for use of the Corn Exchange for drill purposes and pointed out that the water main was sometimes turned off when they were training. As a result, the Local Board gave approval for the fire brigade to store its tender in the former Methodist chapel, built in 1847 alongside the Market Hall in Earle Street, with the keys kept at the Market Tavern next door! At the same time, arrangements were made to maintain effective pressure in the water main.

A report in the *Guardian* in January 1873 described delivery of the new engine funded by the public appeal. It was common practice at the time to mark such an arrival with a procession or naming ceremony.

'The engine was purchased from Mr. T. Rose, the well-known fire engine manufacturer of Manchester. Members of the Brigade celebrated its arrival with a procession and a dinner. Mr. Charles Welch of the Royal Hotel, with his usual good nature, kindly lent a pair of horses to draw it. At three o'clock the men mustered in the engine-house, and under the command of their Captain (Mr. Floyd), they marched to the Royal Hotel for the engine. The horses were yoked and the procession, headed by the Captain and the Lieutenant Mr. George Watson (the Brigade's Honorary Secretary and subsequently its Captain), started for the town. Unfortunately, they did not follow the example of other processions - circus processions invariably start at one o'clock, when the men are turning out - so the admiring crowd at the heels of the Brigade were the school children, the representatives of their fathers. As they marched into Crewe with the engine everybody turned out, not only to look but to do honour to the brave firemen, who are courageous enough to enrol themselves as volunteers to face danger of the fiercest kind, for the benefit of their fellow townsmen. After walking till they were tired they mounted the engine and rode full speed down Victoria Street and along Market Street, to the engine-house. As they galloped along, the burly form of the Captain, the smart, soldierly appearance of the Lieutenant, were particularly noticeable, and the glitter of the helmets and formidable hatchets of the men revealed that they were ready to rush into danger. It had been intended to get Mr. Moon to photograph the engine and Brigade, but the day was too advanced and the portrait is deferred till a more favourable opportunity occurs.

The engine was purchased at a cost of £100 and is both powerful and handsome. It is known as a 'Seven Inch Brigade Engine' and contains every improvement that science has discovered. It will draw from pond or cistern and can be supplied into itself by the mains or buckets; will deliver one or two jets at once, the water going in behind the engine and delivered from either one or both sides. It possesses two seven-inch gun metal cylinders, gun metal valves and seatings, large copper air vessel and suction receiver. It is supplied with pole and swingletrees for two horses, a pair of shafts for one horse, also drag handle for the men. It has two large oil lamps, is beautifully painted and lettered, and is a credit to the maker.

On reaching the market the men dismounted, uncoiled their horses, and set to work in earnest to pump the engine. Mr. Wright, the manufacturer's manager, gave them a good drilling, and a jet of water was thrown several feet beyond the clock tower. Two jets were then tried, and both were thrown higher than any building in Crewe. The engine was supplied from the mains, and afterwards a large tub was procured, and the water drawn from it. It was then found to project the water as far as when it was supplied direct from the mains. The mains were busily engaged in supplying water to the engine, but they barely kept it going. There is no doubt about the engine's capabilities, and when the men get thoroughly instructed and initiated into the art of working it, Crewe need not fear fires for want of a good engine. The Brigade are able-bodied men and not afraid of hard work.'

Mr. Watson went on to say:

'The Crewe Local Board acted very wisely when they laid down the water mains throughout the town, in fixing, at stated distances, hydrants of the most approved kind. These hydrants they could have access to without turning off the water from the mains, by fixing their standpipes, and the apparatus was so simple they could have the water turned off at a minute's notice. In many towns and in the metropolis itself, a standpipe could not be fixed without previously shutting off the valves to turn off the pressure of the water. When the old fire plugs were used, as was the case with the fire at the Crewe Town Hall, the Company's (Railways) Fire Brigade were about 20 minutes after reaching the fire before they could begin to operate. They had to go to the top of Chester Street to turn off the pressure before they could begin and then they had to turn it off after having connected it. Since then the Company had adopted the Local Board's system of hydrants. At that fire one of the Company's foremen asked him for the loan of their standpipe which enabled them to have the water playing on the fire in less than two minutes.

Immediately after he (the speaker) had received orders from the Local Board to wash the market out, and thinking as the Company had used their standpipe etc, they would have no objection to lend them their hose, so he made application to Mr. Stubbs for it. That gentleman replied, "No; the Local Board must find hose for themselves." He did not blame Mr. Stubbs, although it was scarcely courteous, but afterwards he thanked him for it. He thought, "Why should not the Local Board have hose of their own." Although they had hydrants they had no means of quenching the fire, and on laying the matter before the Board he was instructed to order some. He communicated with Mr. Rose, of Manchester, and he recommended the apparatus now in the fire cart, which contained about 150 yards of hose, standpipes, and other necessaries.

He then recommended to the Board to adopt some means of forming a Fire Brigade, and some members suggested that it should be formed of their own men. One of them lived at Gresty, another at Coppenhall, and the only man living near to was old Abraham Bailey. He did not like the idea of old Abraham being the leading hand, so he put a notice in the market inviting persons to join a Fire Brigade on the voluntary principle. He was glad to say that the appeal was responded to very cordially, and from that grew the

Crewe Volunteer Fire Brigade, They soon found out that they required men to distinguish them from the public at a fire, and he was deputed to ask the Local Board to provide clothing for them, To this appeal the Board cheerfully responded by giving them a good uniform at a cost of about £60. Inspector Wood drilled them, and the next thing they wanted was a good fire engine, and to the Local Board they applied. They said they would include it in next year's estimates, but when the next year came they discovered that they could not possibly afford to buy a fire engine.

The Brigade then sent out 100 circulars to 100 gentlemen, and to those 100 circulars only one reply was received, which was from the Marquis of Westminster, enclosing a cheque for £3. People did not generally respond to circulars, so they tried again, and by means of several letters sent to numerous individuals they received a great deal of help. The first was from the Manchester and Liverpool District Bank for ten guineas. Then three guineas and two guineas began to flow in rapidly until they got far more than they anticipated. Circulars were sent out stating that unless £100 was promised the money would not be collected, but he was happy to announce that they had now £149 and £15 promised not yet collected. They would be surprised and gratified to hear that Mr. Martin, Lord Crewe's agent, had sent them a cheque for £5, being his lordship's subscription. It had resulted in the purchase of a useful fire engine. The Local Board had promised to provide extra hose if required, but the Brigade was in a position to buy hose for itself. The engine had been tried, and they had given general satisfaction. That afternoon they had thrown a three quarter inch jet over the weathercock on the tower, and with two jets they could reach the clock face.

The next consideration was who were to be the custodians of the engine. Was it to be invested in the hands of the Local Board or in the hands of the public? Besides, the engine would need maintaining. After an elaborate speech by Mr. Floyd, it was agreed that the fire engine be absolutely invested in the hands of the Local Board.'

Striking while the iron was hot, on 28 January 1873, Watson wrote to the Local Board members:

'Gentlemen. In the name of the Crewe Volunteer Fire Brigade, and in accordance with the wishes of the subscribers towards the fund for the purchase of the fire engine, I beg to present to the town of Crewe, to be vested in the Chairman of the Local Board for the time being, the new engine recently purchased by subscription, together with new standpipes, suction and delivery pipes, ladders etc. also other fire apparatus ordered, but not yet to hand, amounting in value to upwards of £150. The only condition being that the Crewe Volunteer Fire Brigade may have full control over the working of the engine and apparatus in the same way that the Board granted them the use of the other fire apparatus purchased by the Board so long as the Brigade continues to act. Also, that the Board will provide an engine-house and little necessary repairs from time to time.'

Later in 1873, Lieutenant Watson was appointed Captain and Mr. E. Herd replaced him as Honorary Secretary Herd pointed out in the annual report issued in January 1874 that the previous year had been eventful for the Brigade, who had regularly demonstrated the benefits of their new engine. As the *Chronicle* commented a few months later:

> *'The rising town of Crewe is generally very free from fires, and when a fire does break out it is crushed out on the shortest notice by our energetic firemen.'*

Its first important outing was to a fire at Eardswick Hall in July, when farm buildings were largely destroyed. Although the alarm was given in the middle of the night, very few minutes elapsed before the Brigade was mustered, and speedily arrived at the scene of the fire. In the following month, a haystack fire in Hightown, belonging to Mr. William Heath, confirmed earlier fears that there would be little or no water supply for any blaze in the higher parts of the town. In theory, the presence of an engine was unnecessary because the fire was within easy distance of some of the street hydrants. In practice, the water pressure in the main was so low that the standpipe, hose and jet were useless when connected. A great deal of time was lost in sending for the engine and shutting off the water from various parts of the town before beginning operations.

As well as volunteering their time to develop their firefighting skills, Crewe Firemen regularly visited places of interest in South Cheshire and North Staffordshire. In April 1874, the *Chronicle* reported that the Brigade harnessed three superb animals to their engine and headed to Crewe Hall. His Lordship (the third Baron Crewe) was away at the time, but the Brigade were shown around the magnificent gardens and other features of interest. The party then went on to Betley, where they stopped at a comfortable hostelry, put the engine into working order, and went through their usual exercise. After that, they proceeded to Madeley and from there to Woore in time for 'a regular feed.' On the last lap, they headed back to Crewe via Doddington Park and Wybunbury.

A couple of months later, members of the Brigade drove over to Winsford. As the engine sped along onlookers asked, *"weere the foire wur"* (where the fire was). After refreshments at the Red Lion, the Brigade headed to the large salt-works on the banks of the Weaver, where they were shown the processes of pumping, evaporating and drying brine. They then set up their pump on the riverbank and sent a stream of water over the top of the Town Hall weathercock. After proceeding to Middlewich for an enthusiastic welcome, refreshments and a tour of the church, they made their way home, reaching Crewe at 10.30pm.

In 1877, extra space was allocated next to the fire engine-house for a new fire escape that the Royal Society for the Protection of Life from Fire had presented at an estimated cost of £100. The following March, thanks to Mr. Bibley, of Messrs. Rylands and Co. Ltd, the Great Britain Insurance Company of Manchester donated three guineas in recognition that the Brigade did not charge for attending fires. By now, the Brigade could take satisfaction that since their foundation they had obtained a more powerful engine than they had hoped for, four lengths of hose, and mounted harness for two horses. In addition, the firemen themselves had purchased Glengarry caps to wear when helmets were too heavy or inconvenient for ordinary practice and drill.

In April the following year, the *Guardian* reported a Brigade visit to Trentham Hall:

> *'That beautiful mansion is the seat of the Duke of Sutherland. Thither the 20 men of the Brigade, with their friends, went in the beautiful morning on the engine, drawn by three horses, followed by several private conveyances. The route was really beautiful, being through Betley, Wrinehill, Keele, Butterton Park and Trentham. After the ride of three hours and a half, the party arrived at the gates of the court yard of Trentham Hall; and the men of the Crewe Brigade were courteously met by Mr. Robertson, and the men of the Duke's brigade, which seemed to augur for them the kindest and most generous treatment for the rest of the day. Business began by a large mass of wood heaped together and steeped in some inflammable oil, being ignited, and when the flames had grown fierce and strong the Duke's Brigade immediately extinguished the flames by means of one of the Duke's chemical fire extinguishers. Eight of the Crewe men were then put through drill by Captain Watson. The Duke's Brigade, led by Captain Roose, with their manual engine, next threw a jet of water over the clock tower about 90 feet high, and with Shand Mason steam fire engine, costing £1,200 they threw jets an immense distance with an inch and quarter nozzle. It was the admiration of all beholders, and, no doubt, the next subscription started in Crewe will be for a Shand Mason engine. Mr. Robertson then took the visitors through the fine old church; after which they sat down to dinner in the servants' hall.'*

But the firemen's life was not all beer and skittles. Quite apart from the constant possibility of being called to a fire, members of the Brigade carried out drills every fortnight and met on the first Monday of each month for street practice with their apparatus. And even their country house itinerary generally included equipment drills.

Crewe Fire Brigade continued to play an active part throughout the district. In 1883 the Brigade was under the leadership of Captain George Watson, Lieutenant John Porter and Sergeants George Turton and John Farr.

In August 1886, the Brigade's brass band under the command of Lieutenant Herbert Green competed against other local bands at Crewe Horticultural Society's annual show at the Borough recreation grounds. In the following July, the Crewe Brigade and the Works Fire Brigade displayed their fire engines and joined in the celebrations to mark the golden jubilee of the LNWR Company's foundation on 4 July 1837.

The bell on the Market Clock Tower summoned the firemen to the engine-house in the event of fire. In June 1891, however, the *Chronicle* reported that the alarm had sometimes failed to sound and was 'a positive disgrace.' The paper subsequently claimed that when a messenger attempted to ring the fire bell, it was found not to work, and as a result there was a long delay before the firemen had assembled at the engine, let alone reached the blaze itself at a bakehouse in Victoria Street.

At this time, the Brigade was involved in controversy when the Broughton Arms invoiced Crewe Corporation for 31 gallons of beer that had been consumed when the engine was called to a fire in Haslington. The blaze was fought by 15 Firemen over several hours. At a Council meeting, Councillor Hodgson claimed that townsfolk were very dissatisfied with the present operation of the Brigade, alleging that even though the Brigade had reached the fire, they had seemed more interested in consuming a wonderful amount of beer. Following this meeting, the Mayor of Crewe received a letter of complaint from members of the Brigade, which appeared in the *Chronicle* on 4 July 1891:

'We, the members of the Crewe Volunteer Fire Brigade respectfully offer our protest against the unfounded and cruel charges brought against us at the last Council meeting by Councillors McNeill and Hodgson. We are all, with one exception, in the employ of the London and Northern Weston Railway Company, and the charges of intemperance's and neglect of duty made in the presence of the manager of the railway company (Councillor Earle) is calculated to us a serious injury. We therefore ask that the charge be proved or withdrawn. If the Council deem it advisable to have an enquiry, we are quite willing to be called before them to refute the undignified accusations made against us. We have every confidence in Superintendent Lumb, whose great aim is to make himself efficient as well as ornamental, and who always answers to the call of duty. For many years the Crewe Volunteer Fire Brigade has held a high place in the estimation, not only of the people of Crewe, but also of the surrounding districts, and whenever brought in competition with other brigades, has always upheld the motto of our borough. We may say in conclusion that we are severely handicapped in not having an electric communication, similar to that of Crewe Works Brigade. Anxiously waiting your reply, we remain, Mr. Mayor and gentlemen, your humble and faithful servants, Sergeant Farr, Sergeant Turton, Corporal Proudlove, Firemen Chatfield, Ollier, Harding, Weaver, Roberts, Dunn, Walker, Brookes, Wycherley, Evanson, McNichol, Belfield (hon sec).'

Councillor McNeill denied that he had made any charge against the Brigade and he could not understand why there had been so many complaints made within the last year or two about the fire alarm. The Brigade's Superintendent, Councillor Wallace Lumb, defended the firemen and encouraged the Council to hold an enquiry. In a letter to the *Chronicle,* Mr. Bellfield (Honorary Secretary) appealed to the public:

'The Crewe Volunteer Fire Brigade has been made the target by certain individuals and we ask that the public will not come to any conclusions till the members of the Fire Brigade have been heard at the inquiry which they have demanded, when they will be able to refute the dastardly charges against them.'

The *Chronicle* also published a letter of support for the Brigade from Ann Webster of the Broughton Arms:

'I feel it my duty to defend a body of workingmen against the cruel and untruthful charges made by Councillor Hodgson, and which are calculated

to do them a serious injury. In the first place, it will be remembered that the fire at Mr. Martin's broke out early on Sunday morning, and sometimes before the Crewe Fire Brigade arrived, Mrs. Martin came herself and ordered me to send a barrel of beer for the large number of people who were assisting to put out the fire, but not having assistance at hand to deliver the beer in bulk, it was taken away by the helpers (and not by the Crewe Volunteer Fire Brigade) in large milk cane and jugs. What beer and refreshments I supplied to the Crewe Volunteer Fire Brigade I mentioned in separate items in my account to Mr. Martin, and which amounted to the sum of 3s. 7d. For the satisfaction of the public and in justice to the men who have pints of beer, I give an exact copy of my account rendered to Mr. Martin. I must also mention that people spoke in the highest terms of the working and conduct of the Crewe Volunteer Fire Brigade. In conclusion I beg to hope that the charges will be withdrawn, and the stain removed from the characters of a number of workingmen who were anxious to make themselves useful to their fellow-men. If an inquiry is held I am willing to give evidence.'

Some weeks later, the Council referred the matter to its General Purposes Committee which declined to appoint an arbitrator, and as a result the decision was made not to proceed with charges against the firemen.

A CORPORATION FIRE BRIGADE

Despite these occasional spats, the Brigade continued to function in its existing form - for example, in December 1891 they held a concert at the Town Hall to help fund their new uniforms.

But change was in the air. In October 1892, the Crewe Volunteer Fire Brigade was abolished and the service taken over by Crewe Corporation after paying an honorarium of £50 for the helmets, clothing and fire appliances. A total of 33 applicants were eager to join the new brigade, and at a special meeting of Council's Cemetery, Market, Lighting and Water Committee on 15 December 1892 chaired by Councillor Charles Welch, the following were enrolled into the Brigade: Mr. Eaton-Shore (Superintendent), Hedley W Grieves (Lieutenant), George Harding (Captain), Benjamin Howarth and William Roberts (Sergeants); Firemen Allman, Brockley, Brookes, Collier, Druce, Dunn, Jervis, Naylor, Ruham, Salmon, Walker, and Waver; and Reserve Firemen, Booth, Coope, Heath, Meakin, Whitehouse and Young. Although the firemen were now paid for their services, the Brigade kept the title of Crewe Volunteer Fire Brigade because the firemen were still part-time. They were generally employees of the Railway or the Corporation. Crewe Works Fire Brigade continued to work alongside the Crewe Volunteer Fire Brigade at fires and both brigades came together at social functions for their members and guests.

Mr. Arthur Irvin of the Angel Hotel in Victoria Street provided horses to pull the fire engine. When he retired, Ward Bros. of Ye Olde Hostelry in Hightown took over the arrangements. Crewe historian Howard Curran described the role of the horses when fire broke out:

"On hearing the sound of the fire alarm bell at the Market Hall Tower in Earle Street, the horses started to gallop as they headed to the fire station without any encouragement to do their duty. It is said that if the horses were being used by the omnibus at the time of hearing the fire bell, the passengers would be left abandoned, as priority was given to the Fire Brigade. For almost ten years the Hostelry was unoccupied, then in 1882 three brothers, William, Thomas & John Ward started to use it for their local horse drawn bus service. This provided a service from the George Hotel, West Street via Mill Street to the Royal Hotel at Nantwich Road. For the next few years the horses were stabled at Ward Brothers Hostelry. These arrangements remained in place until the Brigade made their own provision for horses after they relocated to their new fire station, which was complete with stabling, in 1906 in Beech Street East."

When the fire engine-house, the Market Tavern and a barber's shop were to be pulled down in 1903 to make way for the construction of the new Municipal Buildings, the Crewe Fire Brigade used a wooden hut in the Town Yard (previously used as a boxing booth) as their temporary quarters until its new premises were completed in Beech Street.

Beech Street was Crewe's first purpose-built fire station and once again, new premises led to acquisition of a new engine. The 'Greenwich Gem' steam fire engine was so heavy that it needed three horses to pull it through Crewe for delivery to the fire station in June 1903. Steam fire engines were operated by heating the boiler with wood soaked in paraffin. This was lit in the grate, coal was added, and a hand-operated blower was on hand. As the fire engine headed towards the fire, sparks could be seen coming out of the chimney as the boiler pressure built up. On reaching the fire, hoses were laid out and the suction tube was put into the water supply. The steam cocks were then opened and the pump started to work.

The new fire engine was supplied by Messrs. Merryweather and Sons Ltd of London, and had a patent double cylinder engine similar to those adopted by the Metropolitan Fire Brigade and those of many other British towns and cities. The engine was capable of delivering water at the rate of 450 gallons per minute and was equipped with all the latest equipment. Many years later, the *Chronicle* described how Alderman Abraham Jervis had:

'brought before the committee the question of an up-to-date engine, and a sub-committee was formed to go into the matter. After discussing it for about two years, the Corporation decided to purchase one, and a deputation including himself visited Messrs. Merryweather's works at Greenwich to purchase a new engine, either motor fire engine or steam. They recommended the purchase of the 'Merryweather Gem'. There was no christening ceremony, but as a compliment to Councillor Charles Welch, who was the first chairman of the Fire Brigade Committee, it was decided to name it after him, in recognition of the splendid work he had done years before on behalf of the Brigade. That engine had done good work for the town'.

Proprietor of both the Robin Hood Public House and the Royal Hotel, Charles Welch (1840-1895) was a well-regarded and influential Crewe figure. The former Deputy Mayor (1893) had a long association with the Crewe Volunteer Brigade and was largely instrumental in its transfer to Crewe Corporation in 1892. Almost a century after its commissioning, the original name plate and coach lamps of the 'Charles Welch' fire engine were formally returned to Cheshire Fire & Rescue Service.

Before Council members could attend a formal demonstration of the new engine, the steamer was put to the test for real when in August 1903, it was summoned to a serious fire at the Corporation Council's Stack Yard in the West End.

As well as the steam fire engine, the Corporation Fire Brigade had its own manual pump, wheeled escape cart, ancillary firefighting equipment - and shortly its new fire station, which the Mayor (Councillor T. Smith) formally opened as the *Chronicle* reported in March 1906:

> *'Crewe is now in possession of a fire engine and station worthy of any municipality. For many years the want of an up-to-date depot has been felt, and when it became necessary to do away with the 'old shed' in Earle Street for the purpose of utilising the site for the present Municipal Offices, the council were determined to erect premises which would meet the requirements of the town for many years to come. The new station is situated at the east end of Beech Street, and behind the Co-operative Stores, and although there has been much diversion of opinion as to the suitability of the site, it is one of the most central parts of the borough. The building is a really useful and magnificent structure, and has been designed by Mr. W.J. Ball, assistant borough surveyor, who by carrying out the work has saved the ratepayers a great deal of expense. The engine house is 64ft. by 33ft., and contains ample room for the engines. At one side is erected a firemen's mess-room, which is 24ft. long by 15ft. 6in. wide. This can be used by the firemen as a kind of club room, where they can assemble at night and indulge in various kinds of sport and amusement.*
>
> *There are up-to-date lavatories fitted up, and all sanitary conveniences adjoining, and at the rear there is a large tower 60ft. high and 10ft. square. This will be used for hose drying. The walls of the engine-house, hose tower, lavatories, and conveniences are faced internally with glazed materials, and the floors are granolithic. The walls of the men's room are finished in plaster, and the floor is of wood blocks. The roof of the engine house is carried by steel trusses and lined internally with pitch pine boarding. The main entrance doors of the engine house open outwards, without automatic appliances. The engine house contains ample space for any future development in equipment, and there is provided at the back accommodation for four horses, with a gangway leading there from directly into the engine house. There is a heating chamber below the hose tower, and the buildings are all heated on the low pressure system. The whole structure externally is faced with Accrington facings, terra cotta dressings, and green slates, with the exception of the hose tower and gangway roofs, which are built of steel concrete. The work has been carried*

out by Mr. J.T. Gresty, builder, Willaston, and the total cost, exclusive of stables and town's depot buildings, is about £2,000.

The firemen, under the command of Superintendent Eaton-Shore, Lieutenant Roberts and Captain Harding were present, and looked exceedingly smart in their shining helmets and well-groomed uniforms. Representatives of other brigades also attended, as well as several Councillors and Superintendent Pearson of the Cheshire Constabulary.

After the opening of the building by the Mayor, who was glad that the Council had thought fit to provide the town with a fire station, he complimented the firemen and the designer of the building. After an inspection of the building, the company proceeded to the Angel Hotel, where they were entertained by the Mayor to dinner. A smoking concert followed, interspersed with a number of toasts.

The Mayor spoke of the progress of the town since his connection with the Council. He admitted that the new fire station was not replete with everything which went to make a fire brigade perfect, but as time went on and the town grew they might have what they all desired. However the fire station and the engines were a credit to the town, and could not be improved upon. Everything connected with the building was first-class and up-to-date. He thought the drying room and the mess-room for the firemen were two splendid inventions, and he was sure that they be fully appreciated by the men. He was looking forward to the time when the Corporation would have their own fire engine horses. They required four useful steeds, and two always ready for action.

Concluding, Councillor Booth said he noted with pleasure that the Council were contemplating having their own fire buzzer. He trusted that in the very near future the odd ding dong fire-bell, which had disgusted so many of them, would be a thing of the past.

Superintendent Eaton-Shore marked a striking epoch in the history of Crewe Fire Brigade by stating that in past years the Crewe men did capital work. They led the country as regards efficiency. Of late years, however, owing to the rapid advancement of the equipment which went to make a perfect brigade, they had fallen off somewhat. They had not been able to take advantage of the advance owing to unfortunate circumstances over which they had no control, but now they were nearing the boundary line if they had not already passed it. He had worked with the men for about twenty years and he had great confidence in them. They would now, he was proud to say, take up their old position, and with the excellent facilities which the council had given them they would in a brief space of time be able once more to hold their own with any brigade in that part of the country.

Mr. Eaton-Shore commended the work of Captain Harding and the members of the brigade, and the Mayor made presentations to Captain Harding and Fireman Collier for their services to the brigade, and long service awards were made to Lieutenant Roberts, Sergeant Done and Firemen Holman and Weaver.'

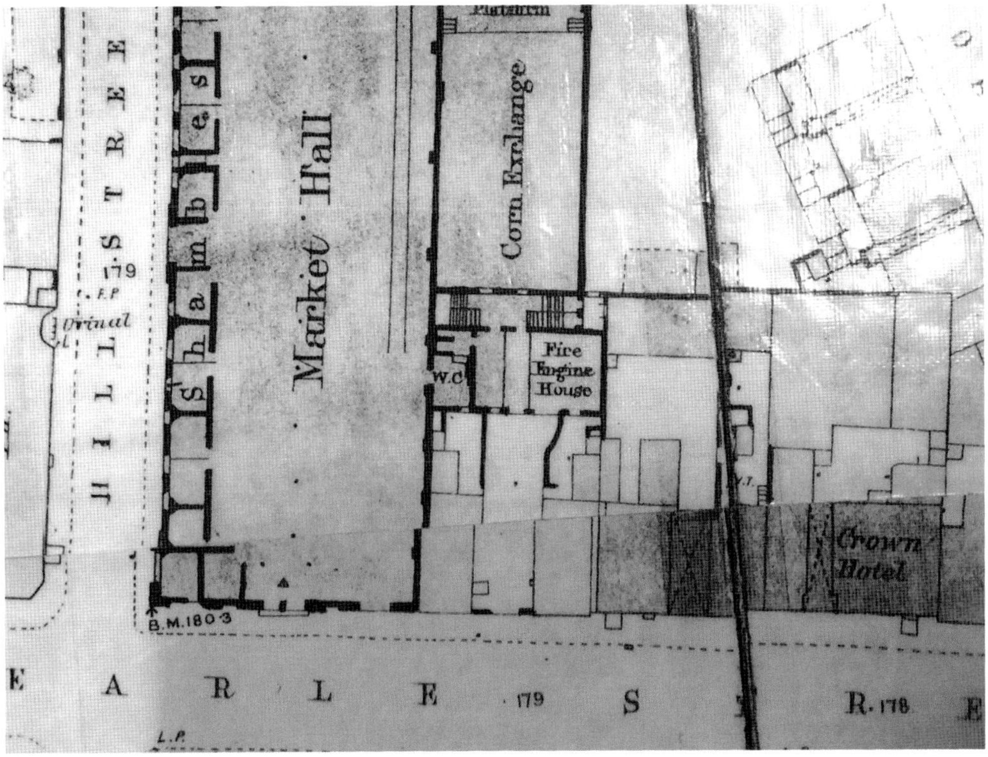

*(**Above**) A plan showing the Fire Engine House alongside the Market Hall in Earle Street where the Municipal Building is now located. (**Below**) Crewe Corporation and Crewe Works Fire Brigades as listed in Eardley's Crewe Almanack, 1896.*

Fire Brigade (Crewe Corporation).

Superintendent, Mr. George Eaton-Shore, 180, Edleston road. Captain, Mr. G. Harding, Delamere street. Lieutenant, Mr. W. H. Grieves, 179, Edleston road. Sergeants, Messrs. W. Roberts and I. Jervis. There are 12 Regular Firemen and 6 Reserve Firemen in addition to the above.

Fire Station—Entrance to the Corn Exchange, Earle street, where the Engine, Fire Escape (presented to the town by the Royal Society for the Protection of Life from Fire), and other Apparatus are kept.

The Bell on the Market Clock Tower is rung as an alarm in case of fire. Keys kept at the Market Inn.

Fire Brigade (Crewe Works).

Superintendent, Mr. Kerr. Captain, Mr. J. Kenyon. Lieutenant, Mr. G. R. Gibson. Sergeants, Messrs. G. Thomas and J. Turner. Engineman, Mr. W. Ankers; and 16 Firemen.

Notice of fire to be given to the Works Watchman, at the Central Fire Station, Deviation Entrance; or to Mr. Kenyon, 6, Hill street.

*(**Above**) Crewe Fire Brigade at the Cottage Hospital procession, 1906. (**Below**) The Charles Welch Fire Engine name plate and lamps.*

Crewe Corporation Firemen were inspected in November 1907, as reported in the *Chronicle*. The men fell-in looking exceedingly smart in their full-dress uniform with brass helmets. After Captain Harding had completed the inspection, Lieutenant Roberts put the firemen through a series of foot drills. The Mayor (Alderman H. Hoptroff) was an interested spectator, and afterwards congratulated the men. He was delighted that they now had a modern fire station and hoped the Brigade would soon possess their own horses properly trained and ready for emergencies.

Despite the Brigade's efficiency, the lack of pressure in the water mains sometimes hampered their performance at fires. Blazes in May 1907 at the Co-operative Stores, the Baptist School and 'Hilldene' (the Nantwich Road home of Miss Hill) highlighted this problem. To make matters worse, firemen had arrived late at 'Hilldene' due to the non-arrival of the horses at the fire station.

The *Chronicle* described how members of the Brigade were given the opportunity to prove their competency at Queens Park in April 1908, as they entertained the public during their annual inspection. A series of competitive drills and demonstration tests with their steam fire engine followed the inspection - much to the delight of the onlookers.

The Crewe Memorial Hospital Fete was always supported by both the Corporation and Works Fire Brigades. In spite of tensions that followed the declaration of War on 4 August 1914, the event went ahead during the same month. Two months later, the *Guardian* reported that Harry Jones (16), who was employed by the Crewe Bus Company, stumbled in Beech Street while riding one of the horses to the fire station. The animal threw him off his back and then rolled over him, leaving him seriously injured. In November the following year, the *Staffordshire Sentinel* reported that the Brigade's fire engine, on its way to a Coppenhall fire in dense fog, had ended up in a ditch - fortunately without serious injuries.

Crewe was made the centre of an area of about 160 miles during the Great War, under the control of the Superintendent Eaton-Shore, the Brigade's Chief Officer. Reserve firemen were drafted in to carry out firefighting duties as Brigade numbers fell below strength with firemen enrolling for the armed forces.

Despite the demands of the War, the day-to-day work of fire brigades continued. Crewe's steam boiler was given its periodical examination in 1915 by engineers from Merryweathers. The following report was read out at a Council meeting:

> *'The boiler was opened out and thoroughly cleaned. The pitting did not seem in any way serious at present. The tubes are badly pitted, especially in the bottom row of J's and straight tubes. There was a water test put on the boiler of 200 lbs. and passed by the Ocean Assurance Inspector. All new steam joints were made, and steamed and tested and left in good working order. All the engine piston and pump rods required dressing up, which was done by Mr. Button. All the cross-heads had to be re-faced and centre brasses let together. Crank re-scrapped in. New valves fitted in pump and bucket leathers. All valves and cocks ground in and glands re-packed. New leather joints on by-pass cover. Steam valve ground in. The engine was steamed and passed by Mr. Eaton-Shore to his satisfaction.'*

In 1916, the Council appointed Councillor Abraham Jervis as Honorary Superintendent with Councillor Pemberton as his assistant, following the death of Mr. Eaton-Shore.

It was reported in the *Chronicle* in February 1917 that Councillor Jervis presided as councillors gathered at the fire station to welcome a number of recruits who were enrolling into the Brigade. The Mayor, Alderman J.H. Kettell, also praised the services of Lieutenant Roberts (31 years) and Fireman Downing (15 years) who were retiring. The Mayoress then presented five years' bars to several members of the Brigade. Captain Harding, on behalf of the Brigade, presented Lieutenant Roberts with a walking stick, pipe, tobacco and pouch, and Fireman Downing with a pipe and pouch.

Newcomers into the Brigade included J. Ashley, C. Hancock, J. Harthern, W. Harding, G. Simon, G. Shuker, A. Walley, J. Twenlow and T. Ault. The following were signed-up as reserves: H. Barnes, T. Gibson, J. Fisher, L. Harthern, S. Trickett and J. Taylor. J. Bevin was appointed as the fire engine driver and caretaker of the town's depot.

The Council procured its first motor-driven fire engine from Leyland Motors Ltd in 1922 at a cost of £1,460. The *Crewe Chronicle* gave an account of its 'christening' at Beech Street Fire Station on 21 September - an event attended by Council members and officers as well as several townspeople. George Wilkinson, who had been appointed Superintendent of the Brigade, officiated as chairman. He called upon the Mayoress to perform the 'christening' ceremony. This she did by breaking a bottle of champagne and pouring its contents over the bonnet of the fire engine as she said: *"I christen this Abraham Jervis."* She then uncovered the name which appeared on the front portion of the fire engine above the bonnet.

Abraham Jervis, after whom the new engine was named, was active in Crewe's civic and social life. Jervis was a volunteer fireman who rarely missed a fire, and for several years was captain of the Brigade. For 28 years, he was chairman of the Corporation's Market Committee, which - a tad bizarrely - was also responsible for the Fire Brigade. A builder by trade, he was elected to Crewe Council in 1889, became deputy mayor in 1907, and served as mayor in 1910/11 and 1911/12. Jervis was also a magistrate, ultimately 'father' of the Crewe Bench and chairman of the Licensing Justices. During the First World War, he worked on munitions as an assistant in the Fitting Shop in Crewe Works to assist in munitions production. Some months later, he became a wages clerk and timekeeper in the Deviation Time Office. He worked there for 11 years and was the only member of staff, who remained on duty throughout the General Strike of May, 1926. He was also a keen sportsman and for many years was involved with the Crewe Alexandra Athletic Club, winning prizes on the cycle track.

After the Mayoress had 'christened' the engine, Alderman Jervis said his first duty was to thank her for doing so. Following the speechmaking he hoped they would honour him still further by their presence in the adjoining room to drink success to the new engine, either in water, wine or beer. Of course water was the usual thing used by firemen and fire brigades in the carrying out of their duties at fires, but he was reminded of the lines written by the Scottish judge, Lord Neaves, who said cold water was the best, but qualified the statement, by the lines:

'Plain water is the best of things, the Grecian poet sings
But who am I that should want the very best of things?

Let Princes revel at the pump, and Peers enjoy their tea,
Whisky or beer, or even wine is good enough for me.'

It was not for him to say what they should drink, but he only hoped they would find something in the adjoining room to suit their palate.

He described (when he had been appointed to the Market Committee), how he at once began to enquire into the reasons why certain things relative to the better working and efficiency of the Brigade were not carried out.

'It was no use having officials and chairmen if they took no interest in the affairs which came under their control. The equipment of the Brigade consisted of the manual fire engine and a red cart, with very few other appliances. The new engine was fitted with a 40hp engine and could reach a speed of about 45miles per hour. 'She has a capacity of 300gallons and the pump is known as Rees Roturbo. By using a three quarter inch jet a pressure of 180 - 200lbs. can easily be obtained. There is also fitted a first-aid tank (capacity 30gallons) with hose and reel, which is capable of extinguishing small fires without coupling up the hydrants. A 35ft. light extension ladder is also included in the equipment. When tested on delivery, the engine had thrown a jet of water high over the top of the Power Station chimney in Electricity Street - well over 100 feet.'

Jervis went on to explain that:

'when Captain Wilkinson was appointed Borough Surveyor, he was informed that one of his duties would be control of the Fire Brigade, but he admitted having had no experience in that direction. However, he assured the Council that he would soon qualify, and without a doubt he had done good service for the Brigade. One of the first questions he consulted (Jervis) on was that of a new motor fire engine, and he made reports as to the necessity for one, seeing that the two they had were 52 and 20 years old respectively. He thought it was time the department was brought up to date. The result was the appointment of another sub-committee, and the result of their efforts was seen that evening. He took it as a great honour that the Council (had) named the new motor fire engine 'Abraham Jervis' and he hoped he would not in any way betray it. It was the name his father bore, and perhaps after he had ceased his membership of the Council his son, who also bore the same name, would follow in the footsteps of his father and grandfather.

In Superintendent Wilkinson they had an officer who was keen, alert and alive to the business, and was ably backed up by Lieutenant Miles, so that Crewe would live up to its motto: NEVER BEHIND. With regards to the other members of the Brigade, he had nothing but praise for them. He considered, for a Brigade that was not constantly engaged in fire work, there was nothing to touch them in the North-Western Division. This was proved by the fact that last year they won six prizes, and this year five prizes. He was hoping that next year the Crewe Brigade would carry off the blue riband of Fire Brigade competition in the North of England, with the Crosfield Challenge Shield. He called attention to the honour, secured by Fireman Whiston, who was selected with two others out of 270 on parade at Buxton, as being the smartest.

Councillor Pemberton added that:

'with such an up-to-date fire engine at their disposal they would never be held up to ridicule. With horses, valuable time was lost, but now they had a motor fire engine.'

In April 1923 the *Manchester Evening News* reported an alarming incident when the steering malfunctioned and the powerful new fire engine, bound for a fire scene, mounted the footpath and crashed into the doorway of a Co-operative store, missing its large windows by inches. All the firemen jumped, but the engine was badly damaged.

It was customary for Brigades to hold dinners to celebrate their achievements and for the dignitaries to pay tribute to their work and success at Brigade competitions. In September 1923, Sergeant Yates of the Corporation Fire Brigade won a special prize for the most smartly-dressed fireman at a competition in Helsby. A few months later, in January 1924, the Brigade held their annual dinner at the Municipal Buildings, when Alderman Jervis complimented the firemen and also suggested that the alarm should be replaced by an electric siren on the tower at the fire station. It would be heard across Crewe and be distinguished from the Works Fire Brigade buzzer.

The Brigade continued to attend ceremonial events. When George Harding retired in 1926 after an association of 40 years with the Brigade, he was presented with an inscribed gold watch. Alderman Jervis recalled how Mr. Harding had also accompanied each Mayor to his respective place of worship on Mayoral Sunday for 39 years, missing only one occasion due to illness. Another task that often fell to a fireman was that of mace bearer. On 12 September 1927, Brigade members were present when the freedom of the Borough was conferred on Alderman A.H. Badger JP (Mayor) and Sir William Hodgson JP (Chairman of Cheshire County Council) as Crewe celebrated the 50th anniversary of its incorporation as a municipal borough.

In January 1927, a new Dennis fire engine TU 4187 was delivered to Crewe. The *Chronicle* reported that the Mayoress (Mrs. A.H. Badger), accompanied by her daughters (Mrs. Blackbourne and Mrs. Bullough), 'christened' the new fire engine in which the Council had invested £800. Council members were again out in force, together with the Brigade in full-dress uniform:

'The chairman of the Market and Water Committee (Alderman A. Jervis), before calling upon the Mayoress, gave a brief but interesting outline of the Fire Brigade during the past half-century, and alluded to the period when a small ralli-car (horse drawn cart) and pump was sufficient to meet the needs of the Borough. Now they had two of the latest motor engines, and he was proud that one of them bore his name. Since the war they had had only one engine and the Corporation felt that this was entirely

inadequate in view of the rapid growth of the town and the extension of businesses premises. He expressed the view that the Corporation had acted wisely in securing a second engine which, he believed, would satisfy their requirement for the next twenty to thirty years.

Alderman Jervis mentioned that they now had a first-class brigade consisting of Corporation employees and they were all enthusiastic in their work. He hoped to have the pleasure of entertaining them in the near future to commemorate the 'christening'. Chief Officer Collier also spoke of the need of a second engine, and said that now they had secured it, a great deal of anxiety had been removed from his mind. They were now fully equipped and ready for all emergencies; in fact he believed that they had the finest equipment in Cheshire.

Chief Engineer Trimbell then assisted the Mayoress to mount the front of the engine and having cut the strings of the Union Jack, which was suspended to the bonnet of the car, broke a small bottle of champagne over the engine and formally 'christened' the machine 'Jubilee' which, she said, synchronised with jubilee of the town. She also expressed the hope that the new engine would do all that was required of it.'

Members of the Brigade petitioned the Corporation in 1928 for a billiard table for the fire station. The following year, ladders of the latest design were purchased, enabling firemen to reach the highest buildings in the town. In April the same year, a representative of Messrs. Allen-Liversidge of London, who were building a factory in Crewe, gave a demonstration of acetylene flare lights at the fire station. The Chief Officer, Mr. Frank Collier, strongly advocated the provision of flares, due to the difficulties encountered when dealing with fires in darkness, especially in the countryside. For the same reason, the Brigade also proposed the purchase of two searchlights.

'A magnificent performance' was how Colonel Watts of Haslington Hall described the Brigade's prompt response to a fire at his home in April 1929. In a letter to the Chief Officer of the Brigade, he wrote that he felt more secure now he knew what the Brigade could do. The letter was read out to members of the Brigade when Alderman Jervis presented 20 years' long service medals to three firemen - Second Officer Yates, Sergeant Butler and Fireman Foden.

Later in the year, Crewe Corporation offered for sale their old horse-drawn fire engine, which had served the town since 1903. It was a reminder of the days when horses dashed to fires at a moment's notice.

The *Staffordshire Sentinel* reported in October 1929 that a fire at a shop might have been less calamitous if the Brigade had been called out sooner. It was suggested that amateur firefighters had struggled with the blaze for an hour before the Brigade was notified. Chief Officer Collier told the *Sentinel*.

"We cannot put fires out if we are not called to them. There is a tendency on the part of some people to attempt to deal with fire themselves, by pouring water on it, either because they fear that they will be charged for the services of the Brigade or because they lose their heads. No householder living in the boroughs need fear that he will be charged for Brigade services. The Brigade

is paid out of the rates. It is no use blaming us for being late when we have not been called for."

Some fire brigades charged for their services, usually when attending fires outside their area. A fire in Alton Street during the late 1930s brought a pleasant surprise to a Crewe resident. Colin McLean recalls this incident at his father's house:

"A decorator was burning paint off the bay window when the timber inside the frame started smouldering so the fire brigade were called to check if it was safe. My father was expecting a bill from the Corporation after the callout, but none arrived."

The potential risks to firemen from blazes on premises with electric high tension insulations were brought to the Corporation's attention in 1934. The Borough Surveyor reported that he had arranged for the Brigade's Chief Officer to be informed of the locations of cut-off switches for several neon signs and related apparatus in the town.

The Brigade was seeking a new fire alarm in April 1935 as the steam buzzer at the Crewe Electricity Works would no longer be available due to the closure of the Electricity Works.

In February of the following year, the Brigade joined all sections of the community in a civic procession. They also formed a guard of honour for the Mayor (Councillor H. Jones) and two firemen carried the mace and sword.

Mr. W. Nuttall was appointed Chief Officer when Mr. Collier retired on 31 December 1936. An article in the *Chronicle* explained how Mr. Collier joined the Brigade. The veteran officer said that after watching a fire drill 45 years ago, the Brigade Secretary persuaded him to draw on a pair of fire boots and tunic, which incidentally were three sizes too large for him. Having donned the tunic and dragged on the boots, the secretary said: *"Now you're a fireman."* He had been one ever since and was appointed the first Chief Officer of the Brigade in 1926. Before then, the most senior title was captain or superintendent. Mr. Collier served at Earle Street and Beech Street Fire Stations. He went on to say that a man must be physically fit to undertake firefighting because he could be called out day and night, and in all kinds of weather. He recalled the old days when the Brigade had a manual engine and a fire escape forty or fifty feet long and the horses were kept at the Angel Hotel in Victoria Street. They now had a well-equipped fire station, a club for the men, and two engines; and the Brigade was equal to any in the north of England.

In the year after his appointment, Mr. Nuttall lost his bicycle when attending a fire at Leighton. On receiving the alarm, he had mounted his bike and was cycling along West Street when the fire engine stopped to pick him up. He dismounted, hurriedly asked a passing couple to look after his bicycle, and climbed aboard the fire engine. He retired in August 1941 - without ever seeing his bicycle again!

It was not the last of Mr. Collier however as he was recalled to duty in September 1939 and attended several fires.

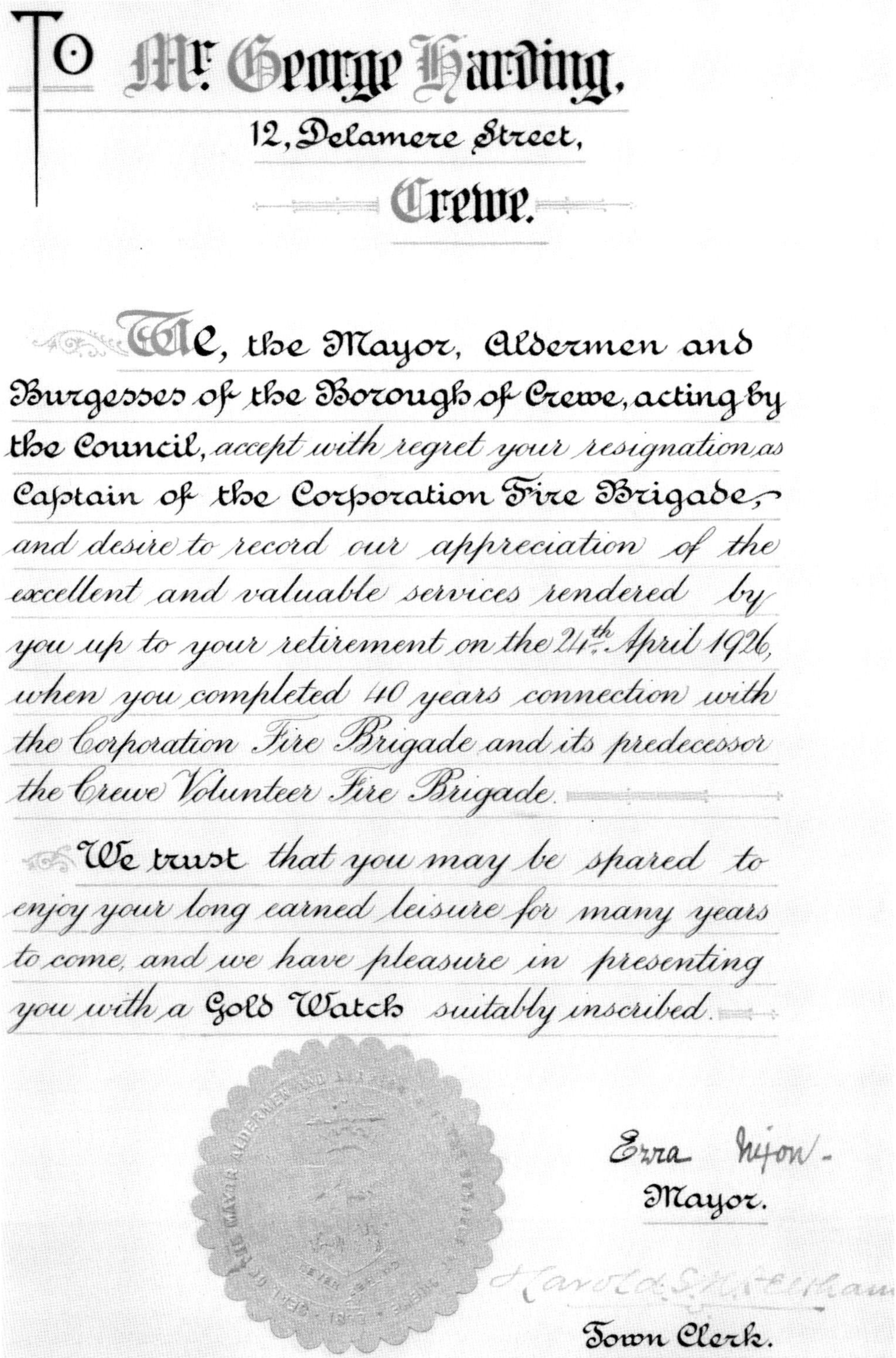

To Mr. George Harding,
12, Delamere Street,
Crewe.

We, the Mayor, Aldermen and Burgesses of the Borough of Crewe, acting by the Council, accept with regret your resignation as Captain of the Corporation Fire Brigade, and desire to record our appreciation of the excellent and valuable services rendered by you up to your retirement on the 24th April 1926, when you completed 40 years connection with the Corporation Fire Brigade and its predecessor the Crewe Volunteer Fire Brigade.

We trust that you may be spared to enjoy your long earned leisure for many years to come, and we have pleasure in presenting you with a Gold Watch suitably inscribed.

Ezra Nixon
Mayor.

Town Clerk.

Certificate of service for Captain George Harding.

*(**Above**) Superintendents of the Crewe Fire Brigade - Wallace Lumb (left) of the Volunteer Fire Brigade, George Eaton-Shore (middle) and Abraham Jervis (right), who both served with the Corporation Fire Brigade. (**Below**) Crewe Corporation Fire Brigade, 1936 - Winners of the Arden Challenge Cup (Warrington) for Motor Wet Drill. Back L to R: A. Yoxall, H. Houghton and H. Welch. Middle L to R: J. Sutton, A. Hood, Jack Alcock, Jim Alcock, B. Johnson, A. Dodd, J. Bevin (Driver), F. Hancock and H. L. Jacks. Front L to R: W. Wooldridge, Sergeant J. Foden, Chief Officer W.W. Nuttall and Second Officer S. Yates. Sitting L to R: Alderman Frank Bott (Chairman), Councillor H. Jones (Mayor) and Admin Officer L. Reeves.*

A WAR TIME FIRE SERVICE

In the 1930s, the threat of another major European war was linked in the public imagination to the likelihood of blanket aerial bombing: *'The bomber will always get through',* Prime Minister Stanley Baldwin gloomily pronounced in 1932. In the event of war, therefore, effective firefighting would be essential. As it turned out, the extent of bombing, and even the numbers of casualties and fatalities, though devastating enough, was wildly over-estimated. Nonetheless, Crewe's railway network and its large industries made it a likely target of enemy bombing.

A national Auxiliary Fire Service (AFS) was established in 1938. Mr. Nuttall and Leonard Reeves (who as Borough Engineer and Surveyor was also the Brigade's administrative officer) were responsible for the recruitment, training and equipment of the local AFS. By 1939, 164 citizens had signed up in Crewe.

Given the limited space available at Beech Street fire station, schools at Edleston Road and West Street were requisitioned as AFS training centres. When even more space was needed, they were replaced by larger schools in Bedford Street and Ludford Street. Sir Donald Somervel, the Attorney-General and MP for Crewe, toured the Borough's civil defence services in January 1940, and was impressed by the town's preparedness against air raids. His visit included an inspection of the fire station, sub-fire stations, first aid centres, air raid control room, air raid wardens' posts and decontamination and rescue centres.

Air Raid Precautions (ARP, but re-designated as Civil Defence Service in 1941) exercises were organised as part of War preparations. The 'despatch carrier service' was tested in the south and central wards of the Borough one evening in February 1939. Fire messengers, who played a key role during the War, were recruited from the Boy Scout and Boys Brigade movements. These lads, aged 16 and 17, were tasked with delivering communication messages if bombing destroyed alternative means of communication. Information was received at the sectional wardens' posts in both wards and then passed to the report centre at Edleston Road Police Station. The receiving and passing of information from the report centre to the required services was then observed under strict supervision. The messages were sent at intervals of five minute and decontamination squads and the AFS took action in response to the information received.

Contingency plans were laid to counter air raids. One such plan was to obtain water for firefighting from the Valley Brook using a temporary water main, as it was feared that the only supply of water into Crewe, via the Railway company pipeline from Whitmore, might be cut off. Another concern was that the escape ladder, owned by the Crewe Corporation for about 40 years, could only reach 43 feet when the tallest building in Crewe was 60 feet high!

On 17 May 1939, another ARP exercise ended in two tragic deaths. A Home Office vehicle with a trailer pump attached was conveying 12 firemen to the exercise at Cliffe Road in Crewe when it was involved in a road traffic accident in Underwood Lane. Two Firemen - John William Alcock (37) and Cyril Langley (29) - were trapped and later died from their injuries. John Alcock of Ludford Street was a popular figure with his colleagues. He served in the Crewe Corporation Fire Brigade and often represented them in inter-Brigade competitions. As well as serving as a fireman, he worked as a general labourer with the Corporation. Cyril Langley of Goulden Street served with the AFS in Crewe. He was a prominent member of the Order of Oddfellows and worked as a fitter in the brass finishing department at Crewe Works. His brother George also served in the AFS. A public funeral was held at Christ Church, Crewe, for both firemen whose coffins were mounted together on a Brigade fire engine. It was probably one of the largest funerals seen in Crewe in living memory, with 5,000 mourners and a cortege over a mile long. Other firemen who were injured in the accident included John Blakemere, William Henry Clutton, John William Dockery, Walter A. Fisher, Arthur Henshall, Albert Herring, William Hodkinson, Herbert Peake, H. Preston and Leonard Woodbridge.

A memorial for Alcock and Langley presented by their Brigade colleagues was unveiled at the fire station a year after the accident. It was made up of photographs of both firemen in an oak frame inscribed 'In Memoriam'. Relatives of the firemen and members and officers of the Council and the Brigade attended the ceremony. Alderman Frank Bott (Chairman of the Fire Brigade Committee) who performed the unveiling, spoke movingly of the work done after the accident by doctors and civilians. He added:

> *"These men served and died for their country just as much as any soldier on the field of battle."*

The Mayor, Alderman R. Dutton, said that he appreciated the thought that had led the firemen to establish a permanent memorial to their late colleagues. Councillor J.H. Kettell, (Father of the Council) also paid his tribute.

Fire Brigades were also established at Rolls-Royce and at the Royal Ordinance Factory (ROF) at Radway Green, which began to manufacture ammunition for the British armed forces in 1940. A fire at the factory could have been catastrophic, so a fire service was established with a purpose-built fire station. Contingency plans were prepared, and fire precautions included provision of a large reservoir easily accessed for pumping. In addition, a private wire telephone line linked the factory to the control room at Crewe Fire Station to give an early warning of fire.

Former Crewe Corporation Fireman Harold Welch was appointed Chief Fire Officer at the ROF, and some of his firemen had already served with the AFS. One of these was Thomas Hassall whose nine months with the AFS in 1939 stood him in good stead as an ROF fireman. His granddaughter Linda Hassall remembers him recalling his days at the plant:

> *"It's heart-warming to know that my grandfather played a part in defending the ammunition factory as a fireman throughout the War. He often spoke with pride about his time in the Brigade as fears grew that the factory was a target for enemy bombing. He continued to serve after the War and was awarded the long service and good conduct medal with two of his colleagues (Firemen W. George and L. Dale) in 1961."*

The potential dangers soon became real enough. Enemy bombing caused an explosion in Crewe on 29 July 1940 close to the Cheshire Cheese pub. Fortunately there were no casualties, but much damage was caused. On the same day the following month, another bomb caused substantial damage near Bedford Street School. Further bombing followed on 26 September, with the biggest blast at Ruskin Road. The Rolls-Royce factory was targeted on 29 December, when 18 people were killed.

More followed on 8 April 1941 when bombs falling at the junction of Earle Street and Hall O'Shaw Street injured 30 people and killed 14. One of the dead was Fire Watcher William Arthur Roberts (38). The fire watcher scheme had been introduced in January that year and played a vital part in the nation's defence against fire. They provided a round-the-clock look out for fires caused by bombing. Many fires were prevented and extinguished by fire watchers and fire guards, who were organised and co-ordinated by the local authority and worked in tandem with ARP wardens and the Brigade.

After attending a fire at Ettiley Heath in July 1940, the Brigade were criticised for not having called the AFS at Fodens to the scene. It was claimed that the Brigade didn't know the position of the hydrants, and when they were found, they could not be unfastened. There was also considerable delay in coupling up, and when the water was sourced it lacked volume, so another supply of water was sourced from the canal at a distance of 800 to 900 yards.

On 18 August 1941, the National Fire Service (NFS) was established. The bombing raids of the War were exposing the inadequacies nationally of a system that relied so much on voluntary effort and varied so greatly between districts. The Fire Services (Emergency Provisions) Act 1941 amalgamated all local authority fire services into a single National Fire Service divided into regional areas. Of the 12 regions of the new NFS, the North West (Region 10) had four Fire Force (FF) Areas in its region, combining 46 separate brigades. These Areas were numbered 26, 27, 28 and 29. Crewe was in Area 26 with its HQ at 'Holly Mount', Mill Lane, West Derby, Liverpool.

Fire Force Area 26, which was controlled by a former London Fire Brigade officer, included the local authorities of Alsager, Bebington, Birkenhead, Bootle, Chester, Congleton, Crewe, Crosby, Ellesmere Port, Formby, Haydock, Hoole, Hoylake, Huyton-with-Roby/Litherland, Liverpool, Middlewich, Nantwich, Neston, Newton-le-Willows, Northwich, Ormskirk, Prescot, Rainford, Runcorn, St Helens, Sandbach, Tarvin, Wallasey, Warrington, West Lancashire, Whiston, Widnes, Winsford and Wirral. In September 1942, the NFS (Alteration of Fire Areas) Regulations created three new Fire Force Areas in the region. One of these (Area 41) covered the districts of Crewe, St. Helens and Warrington with a HQ at 'Thelwell Heyes' at Grapenhall in Warrington.

The fire station at Beech Street was completely re-equipped with Home Office appliances, including an Austin K4 turntable ladder, and became the hub of a very large NFS District. The Crewe area had several divisions and the number of full-time firemen at Beech Street was increased from 18 to 80, with 200 part-timers.

Crewe Corporation also rented the Co-operative stables across the street from the fire station as a store for the increased supplies of firefighting equipment. Other items such as spare hose were kept in the coach house and stables of a Corporation property, 'Brooklands' off Broad Street, where a control centre was also set up. Fire sub-stations were located on Derby Street and behind the Brunswick public house on Nantwich Road.

Tragedy again hit on 29 November 1941 when Joseph Dack Entwisle (40), a Column Officer with the NFS was electrocuted at a fire that gutted the ground floor at 52, Stafford Street, Crewe. The *Evening Sentinel* reported Company Officer Johnson was helping a colleague to play a hose on the flames when Mr. Entwisle came up behind him and asked to pass him. Shortly afterwards a length of flex apparently touched

Mr. Entwisle's helmet, and he suddenly collapsed with a groan. Despite heroically attempting artificial respiration in turn, Company Officer Johnson and Police Constable Burton were unable to save Mr. Entwisle's life.

Following in the footsteps of his father and grandfather, Mr. Entwisle had served for 20 years in the fire service. In 1928, he had been awarded the King's Police Medal for conspicuous bravery in a hotel fire in Farnworth when three people had perished. He had come from Barnoldswick as Chief Officer of the Crewe Brigade, Administration Officer, and Commandant of the Crewe AFS. When the NFS was formed, he was appointed column officer in command of a wide area in Cheshire. Mr. Entwisle was given a fire brigade funeral in his home town of Farnworth, attended by dignitaries and firemen from across Cheshire and Lancashire.

The names of Joseph Entwisle, John Alcock and Cyril Langley are inscribed on the Firefighters Memorial, located opposite St. Paul's Cathedral in London, and together with Fire Watcher William Roberts, their names are also recorded in the Firefighters Memorial Trust's Book of Remembrance (online).

Crewe Corporation appointed a chief fire guard in November 1941. Each NFS station area was divided into fire guard sectors, and each sector was sub-divided into street party areas.

Two years later, almost 700 fire guards in the area had received instruction from wardens including the use of firefighting appliances for those fire guards with the necessary qualifications. Wardens were responsible for making sure that no lights were visible during the 'blackout' and for issuing gas masks, ensuring the availability of air raid shelters, searching for survivors after bombing raids and recording information about bombs and the damage they caused.

One of the wardens was the father of former Crewe Works Fire Officer Chris Thorley. He recollects the role that his father played during the war years:

> "*On hearing the air raid siren we once took cover in an Anderson Shelter at Badger Avenue. Incendiary bombs were heard dropping in the distance as we nervously waited in the shelter with a handful of other people. Suddenly a loud crashing noise was heard as a bomb hit a house a couple of doors away from the shelter. The aftermath of the bomb left us trapped as debris and rubble from the blast covered the shelter. Fortunately a young fellow named Fred Philips eventually dug us out. After all those years, I still talk about this incident to my family and friends. I also recall walking along Underwood Lane with my mother when the air raid siren sounded. We quickly made our way to the rear of the Pioneers Club where access to a large underground shelter about 20 feet in depth was down a steep iron ladder. The shelter was built with concrete to withstand the V2 rockets that were intended for bombing cities, such as Liverpool. Fortunately on this occasion we were given the all-clear to emerge out of the shelter and no damage was seen nearby. A similar shelter was located at the Samuel Street recreational ground. As a Warden my father checked properties to ensure they were in darkness during the night. I remember him recalling that he knocked on the door of a house in Naylor Street and told the resident that he needed to keep his middle door shut, as on the*

previous night, a light could be seen. To my father's amusement the occupier responded by saying that he'd cut the bugger (door) up, to keep the fire going!"

Crewe's surrounding villages, such as Haslington, Hough, Shavington, Warmingham and Willaston, were provided with basic firefighting equipment. This included buckets with sand and fire extinguishers. These villages had their own fire guards and firemen, and some were equipped with their own fire motor car. Among the Haslington Fire Guards were George Harrop, Lou Holdcroft, Samuel Jones, Frank Lowe and Lou Whiston.

Philip Roberts served as a fireman at Willaston and remembers how the fire team got started:

"I enrolled as a fireman on 18th July 1940. Willaston's fire car was a Ford V8, bought for £80 with donations from the village people. It towed a trailer pump and carried the ladder and firefighting equipment. As well as serving in Willaston and Nantwich, I also spent time firefighting at Liverpool, Slough and Windsor during the War years."

After his discharge from the NFS on 17 July 1946, Philip married Crewe Firewoman Miss Cissie Edge. Members of the Willaston Fire Brigade included: Captain A. Smith, G. Alcock, G. Eaton, A. Hallett, Len Hancock, F. Lunt, George Lunt, Philip Roberts, Frank Robinson, Herbert Taylor, Eddie Thomasson, Bert Wetton, Jack Wright and Tom Wright.

Willaston's fire car was kept in a garage opposite the Lamb Hotel. Bella Thomasson, who was married to Fireman Eddie Thomasson, remembers those days and one occasion in particular:

"The fire car was kept at our house and was always ready to deal with any kind of emergency. I'll never forget the day I was due to go into hospital for the birth of my first child in 1942. It was suggested that I went to hospital in the fire car, but the firemen had to get approval from the Brigade Control. After a long delay, with everyone getting anxious about my condition and the firemen saying that I should be given priority, permission was finally granted and I was driven to hospital. I felt so relieved and quite honoured. But after all, it was an emergency! I'm glad to say that my son John was born. I was also pleased that 27 years later, in 1969, my youngest son Alec enrolled into Lancashire Fire Brigade as a junior fireman. He transferred to Crewe in 1976, where he served as a fireman until 2001."

Many firemen and their families gave their support to the Fire Services Benevolent Fund. In March 1942, members of the Shavington NFS held a fundraising dance at the local school with NFS representatives of Crewe, Burland, Haslington, Hough and Willaston joining in. Members of the Crewe NFS Orchestra (Dickenson, Ford, Kurnoff and Pemberton) provided the entertainment with Leading Fireman M. Jobson as Master of Ceremonies.

Twelve months later, planning for post-war brought the closure of fire stations at Alpraham, Aston, Burland, Hough, Norbury, Winterley and Wrenbury as arrangements were made to attach Alpraham to Bunbury, Winterley to Haslington and Hough to Shavington.

In July 1944, several exercises tested the civil defence service and NFS. One took place in Sector 305 involving fire guards at an 'incident' laid at the railway company's premises at Thomas Street. Another was set in Sector 306 where a fire was 'staged' at some distance from the emergency water supply. The trailer pump crew were given some problems to solve and as a result learnt many lessons. An exercise was planned to test the revised method of summoning the NFS and use of the trailer and wheelbarrow pumps. It was at this time that 30 volunteers enrolled in a single week to form a new street fire party (fire guards) in Wheelman Road. Fire Guard Area Captain Mr. Taplay, put this down to the good work of G.F. Snape and T. Pennington.

Fireman William Edward Butler was tragically killed following a cycling accident in 1944. He'd served with the Crewe Corporation Fire Brigade for 25 years before enrolling into the AFS in 1939 and re-assigning into the NFS in 1941. His son Terry recalls his father's time as a fireman during the war years:

"My dad was a builder by trade and carried out his business from a builder's yard in Ludford Street, Crewe. The premises are still there but have long since been used for other purposes. When the War was declared I was only four years old and it was obvious that there wouldn't be a great deal of work for builders like my dad. Events proved that to be so.

During the First World War dad had been in the Royal Engineers and had served at Verdun the Somme and Ypres and perhaps, because of his military training, he soon found another 'string to his bow' with the AFS at Crewe, once it was obvious that the War was not going to be short term. From that day to this I cannot understand why my dad was a fireman rather than a member of the Home Guard. Perhaps he had no wish to be a soldier again.

As my dad lived in Albert Street it was natural that he should be based in the town's fire station in Beech Street, situated opposite the old Co-op bakery. Over the years this area was redeveloped and now forms part of Vernon Way, the fire station having moved to its present site in Macon Way. For the next four years, I remember I was the son of a fireman. My dad must have been important because I recall a bell was placed in the house and had a direct link with the fire station. He was a Section Leader, whatever that meant. Whenever he was needed the bell rang.

From that time forward all dads' spare time was spent as a fireman. He was presented with a motorcycle and sidecar, to enable him to visit other sites in the District. One of those was situated at the Brunswick Hotel on Nantwich Road, and I recall they had a small fire appliance. Surrounding villages also had their own fire brigade, one of those villages being Shavington, who fitted their ladders onto the roof of a car that served as a fire tender.

The Brunswick Hotel brings back many memories, because the fire brigade used to show films of Charlie Chaplin and George Formby. How lucky we were! How lucky I was to have a dad in the fire brigade. I particularly remembered his very 'posh' shiny helmet and his fireman's axe strapped to his waist.

As the War progressed, my dad's builder's yard was used as an out base for the fire station. I remember it being a 'fire station' within a builder's yard, with all mod cons, including two bunk beds. Many an hour I spent fire watching at the age of eight, only to burst into tears when dad sent me home to sleep instead of letting me stay the night.'

Throughout the War years, the town of Crewe was ringed with smoke machines (by the Pioneer Corps), which were lit at night to provide a smoke screen to hide the town from enemy aircraft. These did have their problems. There were occasions when they got out of control and the fire brigade were called out. Sometimes the smoke screen provided excellent cover, so much so, that when my dad's chimney caught fire, the firemen put the water down the next door neighbours' chimney. However they were very understanding!

To keep the Brigade in top physical condition they used to play War games with the Home Guard, stalking each other around the streets of Crewe. If a fireman caught a member of the Home Guard, as punishment they would take them captive to the fire station and turn the hoses on them. If a fireman was captured then I'm told they were given a good hiding. Many a time my mates and I would direct the Home Guard into the arms of a fireman.

Sadly before the War ended, my father who had survived the great battles of the First World War was involved in an accident on his bicycle in September 1944 and suffered fatal injuries. He was not forgotten; the funeral was for a Fireman, complete with guard of honour and a fire tender to carry the coffin. And to this day I shall never forget the help given to my mother by the Fire Services Benevolent Fund.

To finish on a happy note it is gratifying to know that my dad's grandson, Colin Tomkinson, carried on the tradition of being a full-time fireman and served at Crewe Fire Station from 1973 to 2001."

By the time the War was over in 1945, full-time firemen worked a shift system of 24 hours on duty followed by 24 hours off duty, with part-timers undergoing training for two hours each week and responding to fire emergencies as they occurred. The NFS remained in place for the time being, and in April 1946 a team of NFS firemen from Weston challenged those from Crewe to darts, snooker and table tennis at a games evening.

A couple of months later, former Crewe Corporation Superintendent Abraham Jervis died at the age of 81.

The following year, the country's firemen were set a target of raising £4,000 for the NFS Benevolent Fund. It was suggested that one shilling should be raised for every firewoman who had served during the War. About 150 firewomen had served in Crewe. The target set for the North West was £1,200 - yet more than £5,000 was raised. This was presented by Miss E.M. Leverson, (Regional Senior Woman Officer) at a ceremony in Didsbury attended by Crewe Leading Firewoman Pickthall.

A recruitment appeal for the Auxiliary Fire Service in 1938.

***(Above left)** Crewe Fireman John W. Alcock. **(Above right)** AFS Fireman Cyril Langley.*
***(Below)** Funeral of Firemen John Alcock and Cyril Langley.*

*(**Above**) Unveiling of a plaque in memory of Firemen John Alcock and Cyril Langley. (**Below**) Crewe AFS, (Central Squad). Back L to R: G. Dodd, J. Healey, R. Cohoon, W. Tanner and F. Page. Front L to R: S. Wilkinson, H. Jacks, W.W. Nuttall (Chief Officer), E.W. Wilding, C. Talbot and T. Roddan.*

(**Above**) *Crewe AFS with Crewe Fireman Harold Jacks, seated on the right.* (**Below**) *Crewe Fire Brigade at Queens Park, July 1941. Back L to R: A. Dodd (2nd Officer), W.W. Nuttall (Chief Officer), Councillor F. Roberts (Chairman), J.D. Entwisle (NFS Column Officer), B. Johnson (3rd Officer). Front L to R: T. Colclough, H. Cummins, C. Emerton, R.A. Roberts, C. Moss, J. Lowndes, J. Steventon and J. Rowlands.*

*(**Above**) Shavington's Wartime Fire Brigade. (**Below left**) Willaston's Wartime Fire Brigade. L to R: Frank Robinson, Len Hancock, Bert Whetton, Jack Smith, Eddie Thomasson, Herbert Taylor and Jack Wright. (**Below right**) Willaston Fireman Eddie Thomasson alongside the trailer pump.*

NATIONAL FIRE SERVICE

CERTIFICATE OF SERVICE

Name (in full) Phillip Llewellyn Roberts

National Fire Service No. 297868 *Date of discharge* 17th July, 1946

Rank on discharge Fireman

Cause of discharge At Own Request

	WITH LOCAL AUTHORITY FIRE BRIGADE	WITH NATIONAL FIRE SERVICE
WHOLE-TIME SERVICE	*from* ——	*from* 30.3.42
	to ——	*to* 17.7.46
PART-TIME SERVICE	*from* 18.7.40	*from* 18.8.41
	to 17.8.41	*to* 29.3.42

17th July, 1946 .... *Fire Force Commander.*

Phillip Roberts' NFS Certificate of Service.

NATIONAL FIRE SERVICE

CERTIFICATE OF SERVICE

Name (in full) Edge, Cissie

National Fire Service No. 935518 *Date of discharge* August 15th 1945

Rank on discharge Fireman

Cause of discharge Reduction of Establishment

	WITH LOCAL AUTHORITY FIRE BRIGADE	WITH NATIONAL FIRE SERVICE
WHOLE-TIME SERVICE	*from*	*from*
	to	*to*
PART-TIME SERVICE	*from*	*from* 12.12.42
	to	*to* 15.8.45

August 15 1945 .... *Fire Force Commander.*

Cissie Edge's NFS Certificate of Service.

*(**Above left**) Fire Watcher William A. Roberts. (**Above right**) NFS Column Officer Joseph Entwisle. (**Below left**) NFS Section Leader William Edward Butler. (**Below right**) ROF Radway Green Fireman Thomas Hassall.*

*(**Above left**) Firewoman Barbara Edgerton. (**Above right**) Firewoman Cissie Edge. (**Below**) Crewe NFS at Beech Street Fire Station, 1946. Among the firefighters are: Chris Saxon, Bill Hare, Harold Howard, Ken McKenzie, Mary Pickthall, Tom Fish and Horace Sumner.*

*(**Above**) AFS and NFS badges. (**Below**) Beech Street Fire Station.*

A COUNTY FIRE SERVICE

After the War ended, it was clear that the existing arrangements would end with it, if not necessarily at once. It was equally clear that there could be no going back to the muddled and ill-funded fire services of the 1930s.

Relevant legislation would have to take its Parliamentary turn, and meanwhile some War-time changes in the private sector were clearly here to stay. Crewe Railway Works, Rolls-Royce and ROF at Radway Green retained their industrial fire teams. ROF had a reputation for taking part in - and often winning - firefighters' competitions across the region. In 1946, the ROF's Chief Officer Harold Welch and two of his colleagues attended the Sixth International Congress on Fire Protection and Extinction in Paris, and were honoured with medals and certificates that conferred honorary membership of the National Federation of Firemen of France.

Another private fire brigade joined the other three in 1946 when Crewe Hall became the headquarters of Calmic Ltd, and subsequently of Wellcome Pharmaceuticals. The company went on to employ over 800 people at its height. A nearby stream and a large pond were conveniently located behind the mansion, and fixed water installations were positioned in the gardens to support the control of water supplies if fire broke out. Geoff Goodwin, who worked in the transport department from the mid-1950s, became a member of the fire team at Crewe Hall. He recalls his time as a fireman:

> *"I was one of six firemen on-call at the site. The firefighting equipment was kept in a red Ford Anglia van, until a Commer fire engine replaced it. The fire team regularly checked the water supplies, and often trained with the equipment, sometimes climbing onto the roof of the mansion during the training sessions."*

As the NFS was approaching the end of its reign its Crewe members entertained over 50 children at a Christmas party in December 1947. It was the last of its kind organised by the NFS. The children delighted in party games, a film show and carol singing accompanied by hand-bells played by the firemen at the fire station, before presents were handed out by Father Christmas.

Under the 1947 Fire Services Act, the NFS was to be disbanded from April 1948. Fire brigades were returned to the control of local government - but at county council or county borough (unitary authority) level. This led to the establishment of Cheshire County Fire Brigade, which was made up of five districts: North East Cheshire (controlled from Hyde), East Cheshire (controlled from Wilmslow), Mid Cheshire (controlled from Crewe), West Cheshire including Malpas, Runcorn and Tarporley (controlled from Brigade Headquarters in Chester) and the Wirral (controlled from Ellesmere Port). A training school was established at Heswall Fire Station, and a workshop and stores at John Street, Winsford. County Brigade expenditure in its first year was £200,000; twenty years later, it had risen to £1,120,000.

Paradoxically, as the Cold War got colder in the late 1940s, the Civil Defence (Fire Service) Regulations reconstituted the AFS with effect from 29 November 1949 as part of planning the emergency responses to a nuclear attack. The local AFS operated under the control of the Crewe Division of the County Brigade. A three months' recruitment drive for firemen began in June 1951 with the aim of re-establishing the AFS on its wartime footing. Up to 60 recruits were needed, of whom 10% were to be women. Although they now filled many posts in the fire service, women were as yet excluded from firefighting teams. In an early recruitment exercise, a *Chronicle* reporter was 'rescued' from the roof of the four-storey Crewe Odeon. A sea of upturned faces watched anxiously as Sub Officer J. Skeat attached the reporter with a life-line to a 60 foot turntable ladder before lowering him to the ground. Station Officer E. Ball and Odeon manager Roy Raistrick organised the event.

Fortunately the post-war AFS were never called upon to perform their grim tasks for real, though their training did result in some accidental loss of life. This was the era of the green fire engine aka the 'Green Goddess.' The AFS along with the civil defence corps were disbanded on 1 April 1968 and much of their equipment went into storage. Many of the Green Goddesses were stored at a disused hanger at Prees Heath in Shropshire.

Over time, the type and number of fire calls was changing. The summer of 1949 was exceptionally dry, which led to a 33% increase in the number of calls to the County Brigade. Cheshire's Chief Officer Boulton told the *Chronicle* that the number of farm fires, which could spread all too quickly and cause serious loss, had increased in recent years. Such losses were particularly serious at a time when the materials destroyed were critical to the nation's economic recovery. One disturbing factor was that many fires were caused by human carelessness - naked lights, poor disposal of smoking materials and sparks from mechanical appliances that were used too close to inflammable materials. Sadly, the number of malicious calls also rose - a worrying trend that continued until 1956/57 - with 53 of them attended.

The Fire Services Benevolent Fund was 'robbed' on an October Saturday in 1952 when Crewe Firemen had to abandon their 'flag day' in the town for the more urgent task of dealing with a fire. The outbreak, involving hay and unthreshed corn at Bank Farm in Haslington, occupied the firemen from 2.45pm on the Saturday until 10.45am on the Sunday. The Flag Day raised only £40 against the £100 the firemen had hoped to raise.

Beech Street Fire Station was also the base for Crewe's municipal ambulances before they moved to their purpose built ambulance depot at Badger Avenue in 1953. Just as new fire engines were welcomed with 'christening' ceremonies, new ambulances were also given a similar reception on their arrival at the fire station. The father (Ray Roberts) of former Crewe and Nantwich Borough Council Mayor, Steven Roberts (2004/05), served as an ambulanceman at Beech Street and was also a part-time fireman and a member of the Crewe AFS. Steven added:

> *"My Father often spoke about his days at Beech Street East Fire Station. In the old days it was home to the Crewe Fire Brigade and the Crewe Ambulance Service. Crewe Corporation workers, whose builder's yard and garage was located at the rear of the fire station, were also often on the scene. There was a great deal of camaraderie and co-operation between the three services, and friendships formed that lasted even when the three services went their separate ways."*

A fire engine on its way to a blaze in Catherine Street, Crewe, collided with a car containing four passengers in July 1953. The accident happened in Edleston Road, which had recently been re-surfaced. Together with rainfall, this was believed to be a contributory factor. The injured occupants of the car, who were all employed by Calmic Ltd at Crewe Hall, were all admitted to Crewe Memorial Hospital for treatment.

Over the years, Crewe Firemen have been recognised by their community and beyond. The *Chronicle* reported in May 1954 that Crewe Firewomen Sheila Broadbent, Barbara Cookson, Margaret Goode and Molly Jones were among 24 women from the County Brigade's Auxiliary Service who had been inspected by Staff Officer Miss V.M. Garner MBE of the Home Office Fire Service Department. Apart from their work in the watch room and on specialist duties, such as radio communications, catering and first aid, the women auxiliaries were trained in civil defence and fire brigade routine, both active and administrative. The women also inspected some of the latest fire appliances, including a water tender with a powerful pump and an auxiliary pump, which could be easily removed from its compartment and carried anywhere.

A County Brigade report in 1954 pointed out that the main causes of blazes in Cheshire remained those of previous years: chimney fires (540); fires caused by various sparks (296) or children playing with *e.g.* matches or fireworks (248); overheating fish fryers (17); and linen or clothing 'aired' too close to open fires (20). Other jobs that fell to firemen included the rescue of trapped animals (51) or administration of first aid after accidents (14). The County Brigade received a total of 2,838 calls in the 12 months to 31 March 1954.

In March 1956, the bell at Crewe Fire Station sounded even though no fire had broken out. It was the signal for 'the last call' to be taken by former Chief Officer Frank Collier, who had served with the Corporation Brigade for 45 years. With local officers in attendance, a fire tender bore his coffin to St. Michael's Church and later to Crewe Cemetery. A firemen's helmet was placed above the coffin. Mr. Collier, who lived in Middlewich Street, was 89 years of age. He had joined at the age of 25 in January 1891, in the days when firemen were unpaid volunteers and horses drew the fire engines. He rose to the rank of junior sergeant, then to senior sergeant, and then to lieutenant. When the Brigade was reorganised he was appointed Chief Officer and combined his job with that of Corporation road foreman in the surveyor's department. During his long career as a fireman, which ended with his retirement in 1936, Mr. Collier had had many exciting experiences and a few narrow escapes. On one occasion, attending a fire that had broken out in the cabinet shop of the Crewe Co-operative Society, the roof fell in. He was knocked unconscious by debris and large quantities of molten lead which came pouring down. His helmet alone saved his life. The fire that destroyed the old Lyceum Theatre on 11 March 1910 was the biggest he attended, though he fought another large blaze at the Municipal Buildings in 1929. The following year, he showed conspicuous bravery in rescuing an unconscious woman from a blazing shop. He also served on the north-west Committee of the National Fire Brigades Association. Bearers at Mr. Collier's funeral from Crewe Fire Station included: Sub Officers Beacall and Farrall, Leading Firemen Jacks, Sutton and Walker and Fireman Shepherd, with Station Officer H. Whalley in charge.

Firemen who completed 20 years service were recognised with long service and good conduct (LSGC) medals. Prior to 1954, some local authorities issued their own medals, while others relied on medals issued by the National Fire Brigades Union (later known as the National Fire Brigades Association) and the Association of Professional Fire Brigade Officers of the British Empire (later known as the Professional Fire Brigades Association). Both associations amalgamated in 1949 to form the British Fire Services Association. In 1954, the Fire Service LSGC medal was introduced by Royal Warrant for eligible uniformed members of the fire brigade.

In February 1960, Crewe Fireman N.L. Greenhalgh received a LSGC medal after completing 20 exemplary years service. He'd joined the AFS in 1938 and served with the NFS from 1941 to 1946, before becoming a part-time fireman. Firemen E. Bosson and I. Shufflebottom were also recipients of the LSGC medals after starting their careers with the AFS.

The Royal Society for the Prevention of Cruelty to Animals presented a framed certificate to Crewe Firemen in March 1960 for rescuing six trapped animals between April and October 1959. The animals were a dog trapped in cast iron railings of a school at Ludford Street, a cat stranded on the roof of 29 Goddard Street, a cow stranded in the mud of an empty pond in Manor Way, a cow stranded up to its shoulders in the mud of a pit at Vine Tree Farm, and a horse trapped in the mud of a dried-up pond in Ravenscroft Road, Wistaston. Miss M.A. Lewis-Dale, an honorary official of the local RSPCA auxiliary who had devoted most of her life to the welfare of animals, handed the certificate to Station Officer H. Whalley, who received it on behalf of the 25 full-time firemen and 20 part-time firemen at Crewe.

Perhaps predictably, a Fire Prevention Week in November 1961 had raised little local enthusiasm. Adult visitors to the fire station were few and far between, but schools in Crewe took full advantage to send parties of pupils on a tour of the premises to see firefighting equipment and vehicles. They were also given a clear grasp of all the many causes of fires in homes - from open fires to electrical, gas and oil appliances - and the means of preventing, fighting or otherwise controlling them. Each child carried out a practical telephone exercise in making a 999 fire call, and a few had the thrill of being hoisted high in the air in a rescue sling from an extending turn-table ladder.

The County Brigade had dealt with 7,450 callouts in the 12 months ending 31 March 1963, an increase of 2,231 on the previous year. Of the total number of calls, 730 were from neighbouring fire authorities; 3,740 were to actual fires; 915 to chimney fires; 1,301 to special services; and 24 to standby duties at industrial premises. There were 422 calls to false alarms with good intent; 275 malicious false alarms; and 31 calls to false alarms caused by defective equipment. The busiest month was March 1963, when 1,203 calls were made to the Brigade. Crewe had answered 284 calls for the year.

In May the following year, Sub Officer Harold Howard was presented with his LSGC medal by Mr. Archie Warren, the Brigade's Chief Officer. Mr. Warren recalled that Harold's father, Charles Howard had given him his initial training when he joined the fire brigade in 1936. Charles, who retired in 1955, had served with Brigades in Manchester and West Yorkshire and with the NFS during the War. Harold was based at Crewe for over 25 years after transferring from Manchester Fire Brigade in 1946. He also had a brief spell at Runcorn Fire Station.

Another Sub Officer who served at Crewe Fire Station for a similar period of time was Horace Sumner, who retired in December 1964. He was also dedicated to Crewe Alexandra Football Club, and filled roles of director, public relations officer and secretary of the Club's Supporters' Association.

By the 1960s, the Crewe Brigade had outgrown its Beech Street premises, and a new fire station was built by the roundabout at Crewe Gates. This was open to the public to have a look around in May 1966, although the official opening would not take place until 18 July. The opening itself was attended by Chief County Fire Officer A. Warren and representatives of the County's Fire Brigade Committee. The Mayor of Crewe, Councillor H.P. Vernon, welcomed the visitors and the Chairman of Cheshire County Council; Alderman Sir Wesley Emberton then invited the Rt. Hon. Alice Bacon CBE MP to declare the building open. The Chairman of the County Fire Brigade Committee, Alderman F.D. Gee, proposed a vote of thanks, and this was followed with a dedicatory prayer by the Vicar of St. Paul's, Crewe, the Rev R.E. Tostevin. Displays of drills were then performed by the County Fire Brigade recruits.

The fire station's opening commemorative brochure gives details about the new fire station and its staffing numbers, fire appliances and equipment:

'The Crewe Fire Station became Station C.1., and also the District Headquarters for 'C' District of the County Fire Brigade controlling nine Stations. The fire station is manned by 29 whole-time Officers and men supported by 24 part-time (retained) personnel drawn from various walks of life. There were also a number of Auxiliary Fire Service men and women and women attached to the fire station.

The appliances include a Pump Escape, which carries a 50ft. wheeled escape and extending ladders, and a water tender which carries 350 gallons of water. Both these appliances and most of the fire appliances in Cheshire are powered by Rolls Royce engines, which are manufactured in Crewe. The ancillary equipment of each appliance includes breathing apparatus, foam, salvage and lighting equipment, lamps and tools. The fire station is also equipped with a Land Rover, used mainly as a supplementary appliance capable of negotiating rough ground in rural areas, and a Petrol Carrier. Blackhawk jacking equipment and oxy-propane cutting apparatus is held for dealing with road accidents.

The fire station provides cover for the Municipal Borough of Crewe, Alsager Urban District and parts of Nantwich and Congleton Rural Districts, and they turned out to other neighbouring areas, as required.

The new fire station has a four-bay appliance room, drill tower and drill ground. It's provided with all the requirements of a modern fire station, including, control room with teleprinters, offices, dormitory, drying rooms, showers, with facilities for messing, recreation and study. There is a District Headquarters administrative section and oil-fired heating system. A smoke chamber for training of breathing apparatus operators, and a 2-bay garage for emergency fire service appliances are provided in the yard. The buildings were designed and the construction supervised by Mr. Edgar Taberner, A.R.I.B.A., the County Architect. The main contractors for the buildings were Messrs. Elsby Bros., of Burslam, Stoke-on-Trent. It came at a cost of £84,200.'

A new fire tender with an array of equipment arrived at Crewe Fire Station in May 1968. The Bedford Emergency Tender was designed to deal with all kinds of emergencies including road traffic accidents, animal rescues and fires. It operated throughout south and mid-Cheshire. It was also fitted with a large 4,500 watt electricity generator to work floodlights and power saws etc. Another new appliance was housed at Crewe shortly afterwards - the latest Dennis F38 water tender with a capacity of 400 gallons.

Crewe Firemen had to abandon the children's annual Christmas party at the fire station in December 1968, when they were summoned to an emergency at a house in Gainsborough Road. Father Christmas (Sam Caruth) later handed a present to each child and the party was followed with a social evening for the firemen, their wives and friends.

A Christmas fire safety message by Cheshire's Chief Fire Officer Warren appeared in the *Chronicle* in December 1969:

> *'Most people will be looking forward to a Happy Christmas enhanced by the glitter and splendour of seasonal decorations. Unfortunately, the use of flammable decorations etc, and the additional heating required to combat cold weather, frequently leads to an increase in the risk of fire with sometimes tragic consequences. I therefore urge special vigilance'.*

During the same year, about one third of calls to the Brigade involved chimney fires or fires caused by children playing with matches. Sparks from railway locomotives were also a problem, and in 1972, the Brigade dealt with 10,726 fires and other emergencies - the highest number in its history - compared with 9,557 the previous year. In February 1976 Fire Officer Dennis Davis, who was based at Crewe, explained to Willaston Women's Institute that most fire accidents were caused by human error, with the very young and very old being the most at risk.

The Home Office made a request that all black fire helmets be painted yellow during the late 1960s. This was intended to make firemen more visible when working in the dark or in smoky conditions. This move coincided with all personnel being issued with yellow waterproof over-trousers to replace the previous black leggings that had been worn since before the Second World War.

Further changes took place in 1974 as part of the national reorganisation of local government in England and Wales. The word 'County' was dropped from the title of Cheshire Fire Brigade and the 23 fire stations were divided among three Divisions: Chester (A), Warrington (B) or Crewe (C).

The Brigade campaigned to recruit more part-time firemen during April 1975, which actually led to a waiting list of candidates wanting to sign up. Successful applicants received a retaining fee of up to £117 per annum and a payment of not less than £1.95 for each fire attended.

A national fireman's strike began on 7 November 1977 and lasted for 12 weeks. It was followed throughout 1978 by a recruitment drive for full-time firemen as a new shift was created. The weekly rate of pay for firemen during the first six months was £70.60, rising for qualified staff to £88.30 during the fifth year of service.

FIRE ENGINES AT CREWE
1940s - PRESENT DAY

An Austin K4 Turntable Ladder *(GXN 223)* was based at Crewe in 1944 after the National Fire Service took control of the UK fire brigades. Dennis fire appliances were the preferred options in Cheshire following the reorganisation in 1948 when local authorities took charge of fire brigades. This continued for over 50 years.

Other fire appliances at Crewe were manufactured by Bedford, ERF, Land Rover, Leyland, General Motors Company, Mercedes and Scania. Special appliances have included: Petrol Carrier (PC), Emergency Tender (ET), Pump Hydraulic Platform (PHP), Rescue Tender (RT), Operational Support Unit (OSU), Foam Tender (FT), Hazard Management Unit (HMU), Special Incident Unit (SIU), Damage Control Unit (DCU), Breathing Apparatus Command Unit (BACU). Some of the appliances based at Crewe Fire Station are listed below:

DENNIS

F12 - *NTU 930* (1951 - 1973)
F8 - *TLG 887* (1954 - 1968)
F38 - *DLG 416F* (1968 - 1982)
F28 - *508 PLG* (1960s)
F45 - *JTU 775G* (1969 - 1987)
R61 - *EFM 560S* (1978 - 1990) - ET
RS133 - *HFM 708X* (1982 - 1991)
SS133 - *HFM 711X* (1988 - 1991)
RS133 - *SDM 556V* (1990 -1994) - FT
SS135 - *E459 XLG* (1990s)

LAND ROVER

YMA 815 (1956 - 1978)
DDM 336S (1978 - 1986)

BEDFORD

RLHZ Green Goddess 1960s - Auxiliary Fire Service
TK - *DTU 912F* (1968 - 1978) - ET
CF - *WMA 607M* (1973 -1985) - PC
CF - *A320 RFM* (1985 - 1990) - PC

ERF

FLG 649K (1972 - 1988)
TCA 861R (1975 - 1981)
NMA 397P (1976 - 1979) - PHP with a 50 foot Snorkel

GENERAL MOTORS COMPANY

F368KTU (1990 - 2004)
(1990 - 1994) - RT, (1994 - 1998) - OSU, (1998 - 2004) - HMU

LEYLAND DAF
J299 HCA (1994 - 2016)
(1994 - 1998) - SIU, (1998 -2016) - DCU
J781 HCA (2016 - Present) - BA Command Unit

MERCEDES (Introduced during the 1990s)
1124 *K631 KMB*
1124 *L973 TFM*
Atego *DG53 JNX*
Sprinter *DA52 YZF* (2004 - 2016) - HMU

DENNIS SABRE (Introduced after the Millennium)
R47 FMA
N707 GFM
N711 GFM
XL *V895 JMA*

SCANIA
P320 *PO11 FZR* (2011 - 2021)
MX67 JUE (2017 - Present)
MX21 EFW (2021 - Present)

CHESHIRE CHIEF FIRE OFFICERS 1948 - 2021

1948 - 1957	A.A.F. Boulton OBE MIFireE Chief Officer, Cheshire County Fire Brigade
1957 - 1973	A.H. Warren OBE FIFireE FIPET Chief Officer, Cheshire County Fire Brigade
1973 - 1978	A.R. Brannon OBE FIFireE Chief Officer, Cheshire County Fire Brigade (1973 - 1974) County Fire Officer, Cheshire Fire Brigade (1974 - 1978)
1978 - 1986	A.N. Lightbody OBE QFSM FIFireE County Fire Officer, Cheshire Fire Brigade
1986 - 1999	D.T. Davis OBE OStJ QFSM CEng FIFireE CIMgt MIntE Chief Fire Officer, Cheshire Fire Brigade
1999 - 2009	S. McGuirk CBE QFSM DL MIFireE Chief Fire Officer, Cheshire Fire & Rescue Service
2009 - 2018	P. Hancock OBE MBA DMS QFSM FIFireE Chief Fire Officer, Cheshire Fire & Rescue Service
2018 - Present	M. Cashin QFSM FIFireE Chief Fire Officer, Cheshire Fire & Rescue Service

Information for this chapter sourced from: Cheshire Fire and Rescue Service, The Chronicle, The Guardian, Evening Sentinel, Staffordshire Sentinel, Terry Butler, Howard Curran, Geoff Goodwin, Linda Hassall, Colin McLean, Jerry Park, Philip Roberts, Steven Roberts, Alec Thomasson, Chris Thorley and Colin Tomkinson.

RECOLLECTIONS FROM THE PAST

HAROLD JACKS

Fireman Harold Jacks' brass fire helmet has been a fixture at Crewe Fire Station since the mid-1990s after it was donated by his family in his memory. Harold spent most of his working life as a fireman, after becoming a member of the Crewe Corporation Fire Brigade, in 1933. His son Peter Jacks recalls his father telling him many tales about his firefighting days.

My dad often spoke about the various roles he carried out as a fireman for the Crewe Corporation. These roles included that of Mace Bearers and escort to the town's Mayor. Their smart appearance with polished helmets, shiny buttons and stylish tunics were a spectacle on special occasions. He also mentioned day to day life on the fire station and how they were regularly drilled to ensure they were fully efficient to deal with fires. They also took part in pumping and ladder competitions against other fire brigades.

The firemen also had their own cat at Beech Street Fire Station. Its job was to keep out the mice. On one occasion the cat chased a mouse that was running for his life all over the fire station before it found a safe haven inside a hosepipe, which had been rolled out on the floor after being cleaned and tested. The mouse's movement inside the hose was followed by the cat along the outside of the hose as the mouse tunnelled its way through the hose. As soon as the mouse appeared at the outlet, it was pounced upon by the cat. Fortunately the cat was playful and was content to tease the mouse rather than kill it. Scenes from Tom and Jerry came to mind!

After his temporary promotion during the war years, my dad was transferred to the Annexe Fire Station, behind the Brunswick Hotel on Nantwich Road. This location was chosen as it allowed for a quick response to the railway station in the event of enemy bombing.

It seemed that this fire station was also infested by mice as they were often heard rustling about under a workbench as the firemen rested in their quiet dormitory during the night. As soon as the light was switched on, it was quite amusing to see the mice scuttle all over the floor and stumble over each other, before crashing into the door. Desperate efforts to squeeze under the door came to no avail as they searched for cracks and gaps to escape from the room.

It was entertaining and boosted morale to have light hearted moments while being on constant alert for enemy attacks during the War. It was also true to say that the fire brigade also had their fair share of property fires to deal with in the Crewe area at this time. On one occasion we chuckled after my dad returned home from a house fire near the flashes in Elton. While discussing the extent of the fire damage with his boss on the ground floor, a thundering sound was suddenly heard from above. They both looked up to see a cloud of dust and a fireman's leg dangling through the ceiling amongst the rubble. In an instant, my dad knew who was involved in this calamity. He recognised the big sized fire boot. There was only one fireman with feet that big. It had to be his colleague Jack Sutton.

Jack was one of our neighbours at Gresty Terrace, as were part-time Firemen Arthur Dodd and Fred Ellis. In the Wartime years the full-time firemen had plaques fitted on the front of their houses. These signs allowed members of the public to contact them for advise or if they had any 'fire related' concerns.

The period of war brought many challenges to my dad and his colleagues. On many occasions he was detached to Liverpool to provide relief cover to the fire officers who suffered day and nightly bombing of the docks. I recall him telling me of returning to the fire station in Scotland Road after a bombing raid when the fire station was the only building left standing in the street.

After the War, it was back to the normal work routine for my dad and the other firemen as they returned to Beech Street Fire Station. It was business as usual during the week with some relaxation on Saturday evenings, as the firemen played snooker and their wives were invited to the fire station for a whist drive.

As the UK Fire Brigades were reorganised in 1948, my dad who'd served as a fireman for the Crewe Corporation and in the NFS, now found himself part of Cheshire County Fire Brigade. On reaching the age of 55 years, which was the retirement age for firemen, my dad was given dispensation by the Chief Fire Officer and continued working for a further three years. During this time his main duties were checking hydrants and inspecting premises, such as schools, until he retired in 1968.

ELLIS MOSS

Ellis Moss joined Cheshire County Fire Brigade in the late 1940s at a time when the number of firemen and firewomen in the County was under 250. In the early 1950s, Ellis was involved in training members of the Auxiliary Fire Service (AFS) and later, became a prominent part of the establishment at Crewe Fire Station, where he remained until his retirement in 1978. Ellis' wife Ethel recalls his time in the fire brigade.

Ellis, who was brought up in Biddulph, was keen to become a full-time fireman and crossed the border from Staffordshire to Cheshire to achieve his ambition. After his basic training, he was posted to Beech Street Fire Station. A few years later he was seconded to the Home Office Civil Defence Training Department where he was tasked with training the AFS to perform rescues from buildings and fight fires, as the UK planned its emergency response to the Cold War nuclear attack. Ellis was detached to the Ministry of Defence Training Centre at Washington Hall in Chorley, Lancashire in

1955, and as the threat of War intensified, he sometimes attended briefings at the Home Office in London.

By the 1960s Ellis was back to his operational firefighting duties. He was quite eager to get on the promotion ladder and briefly took up a post at Northwich Fire Station, but it was at Crewe where his heart lay and he was glad to eventually return to his old stomping ground.

As a rule Ellis rarely spoke about the incidents he attended, although he did talk about unusual and amusing moments or tragic accidents. The foot and mouth epidemic in 1967 and the hot summer of 1976 seemed to drag on for an eternity, so those incidents were often spoken about. A train crash at the railway crossing by Nantwich Railway Station, involving a passenger train and a car in July 1964, was also remembered. This accident left the car driver and his wife having to be freed after becoming trapped in their vehicle. As well as the many road traffic accidents he attended, Ellis also mentioned other harrowing incidents, in particular, the distress that was caused when attending drowning incidents.

Every now and then Ellis and his colleagues were called out to rescue animals, which often included cattle stuck in ditches. One particular cow was very challenging to restrain and a local newspaper compared the actions of the firemen to a 'rodeo' as they struggled to control the stubborn cow who was thrashing about as the firemen attempted to wrap ropes around it.

Ellis had a fearful experience at one of the house fires he attended. He was in the confined roof space when surrounded by flashes of crackling sparks. Everyone was baffled as they attempted to discover the cause while struggling in the smoke filled attic. It had the hallmark of November 5th, as it seemed that fireworks were being set off all around them. After a thorough check of the area while carefully treading on the roof joists, the mystery was eventually unfolded as they discovered the electrical wiring was faulty.

Lighting fireworks in the garden on bonfire night was always an exciting time for us as a family, but naturally we always waited for Ellis to arrive home from his shift before setting them off. He would always err on the side of caution, which was no surprise as he'd spent many years instructing firemen how to fight fires in a safe manner. His skills as an instructor were put to good use throughout his career, as he often visited nearby part-time fire stations, such as Holmes Chapel, Nantwich and Sandbach to deliver training on new equipment.

Firemen were encouraged to take part in all types of sport. Ellis was at his happiest when playing snooker or fishing and he regularly represented the Crewe Fire Station teams with his fishing rod or snooker cue. It was the fire station's Sports and Welfare Association that organised the sporting competitions, as they did with events such as the children's parties at Christmas. These occasions brought the firemen's families together to give lasting memories of meeting Father Christmas. My grown up children, Steve and Kam, still remember those parties when they climbed onto the fire engine and dressed up as firemen and played games before receiving their presents. The social evenings were also fun times as the fire station was transformed into a dance hall. It was here that I got to meet Ellis' colleagues who he often talked about. John Noden, Harold Howard and John Norman come to mind.

Ellis earned his Fire Brigade Long Service and Good Conduct medal after 20 years exemplary service, and in 1977 he was presented with the Queen's Silver Jubilee medal. Ellis was one of eight members of CFB to receive this medal, which was eligible to personnel who had served since Queen Elizabeth II came to the throne in 1952.

Before his retirement in 1978, Ellis found himself working alongside our son Steve at a few road traffic accidents in South Cheshire. Steve, by now, had become a Paramedic, while Ellis was the Sub Officer on White Watch.

Alongside the fire station was Macon House, where people with disabilities attended. The firemen were always receptive towards the individuals from this Centre, who often visited the fire station. One in particular became very friendly with Ellis and he even attended Ellis' funeral in 2007. After Ellis had passed away I continued to feel part of the fire brigade's family and remained in contact with some of Ellis' former colleagues and occasionally attended their functions. I also received newsletters from the National Association of Retired Firefighters (NARF).

Looking back, the fire brigade brought much satisfaction to our family and in Ellis' case; he was passionate about a profession that he was proud to be part of.

Sub Officer Ellis Moss.

BARRIE LUNT

Former Railway Fireman Barrie Lunt enrolled as a volunteer with the Crewe Auxiliary Fire Service (AFS) in 1962 before becoming a part-time (retained) fireman with Cheshire County Fire Brigade. His desire to serve as a full-time fireman was fulfilled a couple of years later, and after completing his basic training, he continued his firefighting duties in his home town of Crewe. Barrie received three commendations for courageous action and dedication during his career and he remained at Crewe until he became a driving instructor at the Brigade's Training Department.

My joy of becoming a fireman soon changed after I realised that I'd signed up for the AFS and not as a part-time fireman as was my intention. Despite this, volunteering for the AFS gave me a better awareness of the work of firemen. The AFS was part of the Civil Defence Corps and had been set up following the Cold War threat.

The AFS in Crewe comprised of 10 personnel at the time, all with a local background. The weekly training sessions with the Bedford RLHZ Green Goddess was often delivered by the Civil Defence, and on occasions, weekend courses took place at Washington Hall in Chorley, Lancashire. The UK Fire Brigades prepared for the Cold War during the 1950s and 1960s. Full-time Firemen were sent to Morton-in-Marsh in Gloucester to take part in communications and water relay training. It was here that fire appliances, with a pumping capacity of 1000 gallons of water per minute were set up at intervals to deliver huge quantities of water over several miles. Fire Officers were also sent to RAF Woodvale, near Southport to carry out surveillance training.

A gasmask was always carried in person in readiness for a nuclear attack, and preparations for these attacks involved taking part in training exercises throughout the county. A large-scale exercise was held at the Crossley Sanatorium in Frodsham, when multiple buildings were intentionally set on fire and then extinguished by members of the AFS, before they were finally demolished. Members of the AFS were also shown hands-on methods of rescuing people from collapsed buildings and given instructions on the use of a range of equipment, which included a RIB boat.

After several months of AFS training, I had a discussion with Bill Moorhouse, the Officer-in-Charge at Crewe Fire Station, about the possibility of becoming a part-time fireman. Fortunately this conversation paid off and I soon joined up. I received a retaining fee and was paid for turning out to incidents. I soon realised this was the career for me, and after a couple of years, I passed the entrance tests to become a full-time fireman.

I returned to Beech Street Fire Station after completing my full-time basic training in 1965. The four-bay fire station, located towards the end of a cul-de-sac had served the town for almost 60 years. It incorporated a watch room, cellar, boiler room, kitchen, toilets, showers, dining room, dormitory, recreation room and a hose-drying tower. The fire prevention and C District administration offices were located in buildings across the Municipal yard. Three garages stood at the very end of the cul-de-sac, which were used to store ancillary equipment and support vehicles.

The fire station had limited space for training, although full use was made of the appliance room, cellar and boiler room to practise with our equipment. The owners of local scrap yards kindly allowed us to break up their vehicles on their premises to train with our rescue gear, and visits were made to the Electricity Works for deep lift testing on our pumps. Fire hydrants were regularly tested and we visited buildings and workplaces of high risk to familiarise ourselves with their risks, the layout of the building and the location of the nearest supply of water, in the event of a fire. This was also at a time when we carried out all types of maintenance work at the fire station, such as painting, decorating and cleaning windows.

Moving to the new fire station at Macon Way in 1966 was met with open arms as it offered ample training area with a purpose built drill tower and a Breathing Apparatus training facility. It was located closer to the industrial risks at Lancaster Gates, the Royal Ordinance Factory in Radway Green and the M6 Motorway. Over 50 firemen took part in the opening ceremony of the new fire station. As well as parading in front of the dignitaries and the many onlookers, a batch of new recruits displayed their skills, which included rescues from the drill tower, using hook ladders and a wheeled escape ladder.

The additional space at the new fire station allowed the AFS to have their own storage to house their fire appliance and equipment. The double garage at the rear of the fire station became their base and was known as the AFS garage for many years, even after the AFS was disbanded in 1968.

It was at Crewe that I spent all my operational service and attended all manner of incidents. Turning out to incidents always brought on an adrenaline rush. However, there was one turn-out with a difference. Bill Moorhouse, my first boss, sadly died in November 1964, while still serving. He was given a fire brigade funeral as his coffin was taken to the cemetery on the back of a Pump Escape. It was Bill's 'last turnout' as the cortege followed from Beech Street Fire Station with two escort firemen standing alongside his coffin.

Turning out to an emergency 300 miles away was a rarity for a Crewe Fireman, but in March 1967, I attended an environmental disaster in Cornwall with my colleague and good friend John Yardley, after the Torrey Canyon Oil Ship struck rocks between the Cornish mainland and the Isles of Scilly. This involved a huge clean up operation alongside members of the armed forces and other fire brigades from all over the UK. Our base for the two week duration was at the RAF base at St. Mawgan.

Another unforgettable incident involved a fire at the New Brighton Tower on 5 April 1969. Fireman Bob Sweeney and myself turned out to the 'towering inferno' to deliver supplies of petrol. No, it wasn't to add fuel to the fire! Our task was to replenish fire appliances and portable pumps with petrol after they had endured hours of pumping. The tower was the tallest building in Great Britain when it was built in the late 19th Century, and at the height of the fire, there were 25 fire appliances in attendance. As well as re-stocking fire engines at major fires, the petrol carrier regularly visited part-time fire stations throughout Cheshire to keep fire appliance fuelled up.

It was members of the Crewe FBU who were fuelled up in 1977, as they added fuel to their own fires to keep their braziers burning during the first National Fireman's Strike. It commenced on 7th November and lasted for nine weeks. It was a difficult period for the FBU members as the Army was brought in to fight fires with their Green Goddesses. Crewe's Territorial Army Centre in Myrtle Street was the Army's base and their appearance in the streets of Crewe was a reminder of my AFS days. Despite considerable hardship by the FBU members, who I represented as Branch Chairman, their solidarity held out through the winter months to eventually bring better pay and conditions and job opportunities for thousands of firemen.

Despite the difficulties during the strike, those dark days could never be compared to the devastation that we sometimes dealt with at road and rail accidents. Sadly it's the tragic incidents that are often remembered. One such incident was a horrific train crash at Gresty Lane, Crewe, in November 1980 when a diesel locomotive ran into the rear of a freight train. The impact caused the derailment of the locomotive and the rear wagon of the freight train. Freeing the rail workers from the wreckage in the confined space of the locomotive's cab was extremely challenging and sadly resulted in the deaths of the locomotive's driver and guard. Despite being seriously injured, the driver's assistant survived the crash.

One of my passions in life was driving, so when I was given the opportunity to become a CFB driving instructor, I jumped at the chance. The instructor training course in West Yorkshire was set to Police's driver training standards, so my expectations from firemen that I taught to drive were also high. I got to know the county of Cheshire like the back of my hand after teaching countless numbers of firemen to drive. The surrounding counties of Staffordshire, Shropshire, Derbyshire, Merseyside and Greater Manchester County were also familiar, as was North Wales, where the 'L' plated fire engines often ventured. The vehicles used for teaching firemen had 'retired' from their operational duties. They included a Dennis F8, Dennis F38 and an ERF. A flat back lorry was later used and light vehicle training was taught in a Vauxhall Cavalier Sport.

After completing a minimum of 20 hours of non-emergency driving to further develop their driving skills, firemen attended an Emergency Fire Appliance Driving (EFAD) course, where they were given instruction on how to drive safely at high speed on a variety of roads, and how to react in slippery conditions at the skid-pan at Manchester's Bus Training Centre. On reaching an acceptable standard, they were given the green light to drive to emergencies under blue lights. As driving instructor I was also tasked with familiarising firemen with new appliances when they were introduced. During the early-1990s, Mercedes fire appliances became part of the fleet, so every driver in Cheshire had to be given hands-on training on the specifics of these vehicles. I also gave guidance to firemen on the operating techniques of specialist vehicles, such as aerial appliances and 4x4 Off-Road vehicles.

Occasionally, some 'sweeteners' came my way as the driving instructor. There was none better than a dealership seminar I attended at Sleap Aerodrome in Shropshire to give demonstrations and promote a Dennis F45 fire appliance (powered by a Rolls-Royce engine). I was given first class hospitality by Rolls-Royce Motors who hosted the event.

Another event I appreciated was held in the executive lounge at Crewe Alexandra Football Club during a summer's evening in 1996. It was when I called time on my career. There was plenty of reminiscing about my fire brigade adventures with past and present colleagues as they were entertained by four Crewe Firemen, whose music band went by the name of 'Standpipe, Key and Bar'...It was certainly a night to remember at the disco inferno!

Crewe Fire Station 1965

Fire Officers

Station Officer Noel Lightbody, Sub Officer John Blenkinsop.

Red Watch

Sub Officer - Harold Howard. **Leading Fireman** - Colin Tyrrel.

Firemen - Marsh Carwright, Bill Harding, Jim Mellor, John Norman, Bill Taylor.

Blue Watch

Sub Officer - Sam Caruth. **Leading Fireman** - C. Cope.

Firemen - Bill Hare, Pete Larcombe, Barrie Lunt, Derek Mellor, John Yardley.

White Watch

Sub Officer - E. Moss. **Leading Fireman** - Tom Wharton.

Firemen - Paul Grimshaw, Don Meredith, John Noden, Jack Rowley, Cliff Stanley.

C District Personnel

Divisional Officer Thompson, Assistant Divisional Officer Fenton.

Sub Officer Dave Apps (Fire Prevention), Leading Fireman Eric Taylor (Staff Officer).

Fire Station Vehicles

Pump Escape, Water Tender, Land Rover, Petrol Carrier, Bedford Green Goddess, Austin A35 Van, Hillman Husky, Hillman Saloon.

*(**Above**) Barrie Lunt.*

KEN GARDNER

Ken Gardner first encountered the fire brigade in the mid-1940s when as an energetic youngster he was entertained by members of the National Fire Service. Later in life, he sometimes became a 'sheepdog' while riding his motorcycle with the green convoy of Auxiliary Fire Service (AFS) fire appliances and on one occasion he guided several AFS fire appliances to a quarry in Milton Keynes. So it was no surprise that he opted for a career in the fire brigade in the mid-1960s. After serving as a fireman with Hertfordshire for a couple of years, Ken re-located to Cheshire and was based at Crewe Fire Station in Beech Street.

Cheshire's Chief Fire Officer (CFO) when I joined up was Archie Warren, a well respected fire officer, who knew all his men and always stood up for them. He unexpectedly paid a visit to the fire station one morning to give us a 'test turnout' to ensure our response times were up to standard. This was quite normal in those days. The Pump Escape (PE) was brought out into the street and we all lined up behind it to await our orders. The CFO pointed to the big wooden doors at the end of the street and stated that there was a fire behind them. He then asked what we were going to do about it. At that moment one of the older firemen, who was coming up to retirement, broke ranks and ran to the hose locker on the fire engine and pretended to unroll the hose. He then mimicked actions of connecting a nozzle into the hose coupling and squirting water. The CFO looked on in amazement and asked what was going on. One of the other firemen replied that he was unrolling his imaginary hose and putting imaginary water on the imaginary fire. All the firemen burst out laughing. The CFO spluttered something to himself amongst the laughter and swiftly disappeared. That was the only time I ever saw our CFO lost for words!

At the rear of the fire station was the local Council builder's yard. Unfortunately for me, I was at the wrong end of a prank one morning, when some of the stock from the builders' yard ended up in my possession. At times I stored my BSA 350cc motorcycle in the engine house when on duty. It was a solid bike with a front shield and fitted with panniers. It was my pride and joy. I left work one morning after a night shift, and by the time I'd gone past Nantwich, I felt that the bike wasn't behaving itself. It was leaning too far on corners. I stopped, tapped the tyres with my feet and quickly checked the frame and engine. Lastly I checked the panniers, only to find that both had been filled very neatly with bricks. There were no bulges in the panniers and both had been kept exactly to the same size. Feeling a little red faced, I left the pile of bricks on the pavement and simply went on my way. I never found out who the prankster was, but it had to be the work of one of my dear brothers at the fire station. I guessed it was either John Norman or Jack Rowley, as both firemen were 'funsters' at that time. There was an inquisition by the local council as to where the bricks had gone, but of course, no one knew anything!

The PE was a great motor and a joy to drive, although it could be a bit of a beast when it came to double de-clutching when changing gear. It was a sad day in 1965, when the PE plunged down an embankment as we headed towards Basford Hall Sidings along the shale covered roadway to carry out an industrial risk visit. The narrow road was embedded with rail sleepers, which had been soaked in oily preservatives. These sleepers had become slippery due to the rain and as the PE's wheels came into contact with them, the vehicle slid and bounced over the edge and toppled 15 feet down the embankment. Fortunately it was prevented from landing on the railway by the girder framework of the gantry, which supported the 25,000 volt overhead electric cable. As the PE rolled down the embankment, the metal first aid box was thrown from its seating and its sharp corner hit a bone in my right shoulder. I escaped from the wreckage in much discomfort and made my way onto the roadway. It was striking how small the fire engine looked with its feet in the air and so sad to see the superb wheeled escape in ruins. Firemen Eric Fisher, Colin Tyrrel and myself were taken to Crewe Memorial Hospital, where I was treated for a chipped bone in my shoulder, while my colleagues received treatment for minor injuries.

A few years after moving to the new fire station at Macon Way we started to play a more prominent role at road traffic accidents. Fire brigades originally attended these incidents in case vehicles caught fire, but as time went by, our presence was utilised in assisting to free people trapped in their vehicles. The Emergency Tender (ET) at Crewe was kitted out with a range of special equipment for use at road traffic accidents, and on occasions, I undertook courses to train my colleagues in the use of oil and compressed air cutting equipment. This involved hands on applications to simulated crashed vehicles followed with sessions in the lecture room. The courses had been straightforward until I took on one of the Crewe watches. I'd spent over an hour scaling down and chalk drawing the interior of the Ripper Gun and the Compressed Air Cengar Saw in fine detail on the blackboard. Prior to commencing the lecture, I was called away to the telephone. After returning and apologising for my absence some 10 minutes later, I turned to see that the blackboard had been wiped blank. I was not too evenly tempered in those days, and to the delight of my audience, I 'blew my top'. When all had quietened down, the joker stood up and turned the blackboard over to reveal my drawings. Yes, I'd been 'well and truly had'. The joker, Paul Bickerton, was young, tall and quietly spoken with a positive disposition, who always insisted on eating really black and crusty burnt toast. He was destined to fit in as a fireman with his sense of humour!

The social evenings, which were held at the fire station, were very popular as the engine house was turned into a venue of entertainment and dance. To make the evenings more amenable, we borrowed greenery and flowers from the local Council's Parks and Gardens Department. They were used to decorate the open spaces and the tables. However it came as a big surprise to everyone that the three foot high healthy looking green plants were believed to be pure cannabis plants. Imagine it, cannabis grown under cover at Crewe Park. The Council staff must have been laughing up their sleeves at us. Little wonder the social evenings went down so well.

Playing pranks and enjoying amusing moments was often a way of life on the fire station. It also served as a means of coping with devastating incidents, whether it was recovering bodies out of burning buildings or from crashed vehicles. One such incident involved an early morning house fire in Peel Street, Crewe on 20 September 1971, which resulted in two brothers in their 30s, losing their lives. Another brother, who escaped the blaze, was treated in hospital for burns. Although two brothers had originally escaped the blaze, one went back inside the house to rescue his brother, but was sadly overcome by smoke. The ferocity of the fire, which started in a downstairs room, left the house so badly damaged that no concrete reason as to its cause could be determined. The brothers who died stood no chance of survival and were recovered from the first floor of the terraced property by myself and my colleague Don Meredith. Other crew members included: Harold Howard, Barrie Lunt and Colin Tyrrel.

JOHN ROBERTS

John Roberts began fighting fires in 1966. He was posted to Ellesmere Port Fire Station after completing his basic training, before heading back to his home town of Crewe, where he remained at the sharp end of firefighting for the remainder of his career. This was at a time when it was traditional for firemen to spend much of their time perfecting their practical skills on the drill yard, keeping their fire appliances and equipment spotlessly clean, preventing fires and relaxing with a game of snooker.

Working at Ellesmere Port gave me a good grounding into the work of firemen with its range of industries especially the Oil Refinery, one of the highest industrial 'risks' in the UK. Ellesmere Port Fire Station was in the Brigade's D District when I joined. Other fire stations in the District included Heswall, Hoylake and Bebbington.

I varied the routes on my daily drive from Crewe to the Ellesmere Port that took me across the Cheshire countryside. To this day I can still remember those journeys, especially during the Foot and Mouth epidemic in the winter of 1967/68. Orange glows of fires with plumes of smoke and a strong smell of burning flesh from the mounds of carcasses lingered in the countryside, as a reminder how serious the outbreak was. Diggers were drafted in to excavate trenches on farmlands where slaughtered cattle, sheep and pigs were buried. However, as the ground became swollen after their burials, it was decided to incinerate them first. The fire brigade's roles during the epidemic were to power-wash Lorries at farms and disinfect machinery. Over 1000 Cheshire farms were affected and the plague continued for over seven months.

It was during my Ellesmere Port days that I was first introduced to playing snooker. Recreation rooms were built alongside dining areas in fire stations to encourage the playing of games and competitive sport. Sport was taken seriously and regular contests in a variety of sports were held between fire stations. The tradition of taking part in sport boosted morale and created a good spirit among the workforce. My passion for playing snooker continued when I transferred to Crewe Fire Station, and like other firemen, I took great pride in maintaining the snooker table, which was the property of the Firemen's Sports and Welfare Association. The table was regularly brushed and ironed to keep it in top condition and its cover only came off at break times and during stand-down periods. As well as playing snooker during our stand-down time, this period was utilised to practice our hobbies or study for promotion exams.

One fireman I worked alongside practised playing his ukulele during his stand-down time. Pete Larcombe was the fire station's George Formby, who was often heard into the early hours of the morning strumming his instrument. On his promotion to Leading Fireman, Pete transferred to Chester Fire Station where he sustained a serious facial injury, after a cylinder exploded and a fragment shattered the window of the fire appliance door as they arrived at a fire involving a workman's hut. Pete was badly shook up following this incident and shortly left the fire brigade to pursue a career in showbiz.

The 1970s was notable for a vast number of property fires in Crewe. One fire in particular was memorable in August 1971. We were by Mornflake Oats in

Gresty Road returning back from a shout at about 11.00pm when we were re-directed to a house fire. As the Con-Op relayed the address of 13 Drury Close, Crewe, over the radio, I was suddenly overcome with horror. The address was my house. To make matters worse, it was a 'person's reported' shout, which indicated that someone was trapped in the fire. I remember shouting out. "Bloody hell, that's my house." My colleague Bill Hare drove with the urgency of a 'grand prix' driver, while Ellis Moss and Jack Rowley reassured my anxieties, which were building up as every second ticked away. By the time we turned into Drury Close, my heart felt like it was coming out of my chest. My head was moving in all directions in an effort to locate my family as I scrambled off the fire engine. At that moment I could see my burning TV laid out on the lawn and I suddenly caught sight of my wife and daughter. To my relief they were safe. I was elated with joy and fortunately the damage in the house was minimal. I then learnt that the next door neighbour, Alan Berry, was on hand to save the day before we arrived. Regardless of his own safety, he dragged the burning TV out of the house. It was a lucky escape for my family after my wife was alerted to the smell of smoke after coming downstairs to use the bathroom.

Another late evening blaze on 12 March 1976 in Derrington Avenue, Crewe, caused severe damage to the Starline Discount Warehouse. Fire appliances from Cheshire and Staffordshire were directed to the scene of the fire. Crewe's new Pump Hydraulic Platform (PHP) appliance was used in anger for the first time. Meanwhile, firemen who had initially been sent inside the building to tackle the fire had a close call when an almighty explosion occurred as a result of a flashover from the build up of heat. This forced everyone to make a hasty retreat and scramble away from the building as the blaze suddenly took hold. The flames were then hit from outside of the building with jets of water. The PHP was set up as a water tower to fight the fire from above and to protect the surrounding properties. Two firemen sustained minor injuries at the blaze and all the contents in the single storey building, which had an asbestos roof and was approximately one third the size of a football pitch, was destroyed.

One of the largest fires in Crewe for many years was at the BR General Offices in July 1983. At the time I was heading back to Crewe from Devon when I noticed plumes of smoke blackening the sky over Crewe. As I came off the M6 motorway I headed towards the heart of the town centre to witness the fire ripping its way through the derelict building. Although I was off-duty, I was given the green light to get close to the fire to take some photos, and fortunately I had enough film left in my camera to take some dramatic photos. I was the unofficial fire brigade photographer that night!

A serious blaze at Underwood Court Elderly Persons Home in Underwood Lane on 8 December 1985 gave cause for concern as we frantically searched the building in a bid to lead the residents to safety. Although the flames were kept to a minimum, 35 firemen attended the incident and the vast quantity of smoke resulted in 39 residents being admitted to hospital with smoke inhalation.

Attending incidents brought out the serious side of firemen, as life on the fire station was often jovial with plenty of banter at times. Playing volleyball, as part of the daily keep-fit sessions, brought out the competitiveness in some, while others (that includes me) guarded their hands and arms for the snooker table! Sadly though, volleyball was eventually outlawed by 'the powers that be' as injuries were often sustained. The keep-fit programme was eventually overhauled to avoid contact sport, in a bid to reduce accidents, although to our surprise, five-a-side football was introduced!

An incident one Sunday morning, while standing-in on another watch to cover a colleague's shift, almost turned into embarrassment as a fire was lit at the rear of the fire station. Old engine oil, which had been deposited into a rectangular metal tray (two metres in length by one metre in width) from fire appliances while undergoing a service, was set on fire with some cardboard boxes. Everything was under control until a gust of wind drove the flames towards the red wooden door of the BA chamber. The intense heat blistered the paint on the door and threatened to spread through the building. Fortunately the fire appliance was nearby to save the day, as a water jet killed the flames. A mad panic followed to find red paint, so no questions could be asked.

I called time on my career in 1996 having made many lifelong friends, some sadly no longer with us. I felt that I'd seen it all, and done it all as a team player at the sharp end of the fire brigade. If asked to do it all again tomorrow, without doubt, I would. For me, it was the best job in the world. All kinds of memories are embedded in my head from the day I joined, from humorous moments to rescuing people from vehicles and buildings. And of course, not forgetting the pleasure when potting those snooker balls!

DAVE HOLMAN

After completing his initial training at Heswall in February 1967, Dave Holman was posted to fire stations at Ellesmere Port and later Bebbington on the Wirral. A keen angler, Dave returned back to South Cheshire in 1969 following his transfer to Crewe Fire Station. After a spell riding fire engines alongside some of Crewe's colourful characters, Dave opted for a specialist role in the Fire Prevention Department where, apart from a two year stint at HQ (1992-94), he worked the remainder of his career at Crewe.

After two years I was pleased to leave the Wirral, but glad of the experience. My flatmates and I had endured a total of seven robberies and one thief took all my work shirts from the washing line. Like a fool I went to work next day in my only clean shirt - a pink one!

I should also explain that there was very little scope for freshwater fishing near Birkenhead and my only outings were to the River Mersey. I would sit in the sidecar of my motorbike on the river embankment at New Brighton watching the rod-tips for a bite and taking my catch of flat fish back to the Mess Manager at the fire station, who would give me credit on my mess fees. The fabulous aroma from the fire station kitchen as the fish were deep fried was so inviting, but I always resisted any offers of a share, as I had seen (and smelt) just where these fish had come from.

At my own request, I was transferred to Crewe Fire Station and arrived for my first shift with only a slight scouse accent and full of the joys of being able to go 'proper' fishing again. I joined Blue Watch with Sub Officer Ellis Moss in charge. Ellis had been a Sub Officer for many years and was good at his job, always fair, consistent and although no one would ever admit it, he was well liked and respected. Ellis was also a fellow angler. The main man on the watch was a certain Barrie Lunt, who was so much fun. At the start of one night shift after checking the fire engines and having a quick brew prior to the dreaded drill session (Ellis so loved his drills), I got into conversation with Barrie. Looking up at the clock, Barrie asked me, "Dave, when you go fishing for barbel, just how do you set up a ledger rig?"

Never needing a second chance to talk fishing, I explained that I immediately start off on a standard swim feeder rig. Ellis firstly just listened and then joined in with the talk. Message pads arrived from the watchroom and sketches were drawn up as the conversation went from River Severn barbel to chub. As the minutes ticked-by, fellow firemen tip-toed away to leave us with our fishing talk. I was in my element and happily rambling away until Ellis realised it was 7.30pm. "Bit late for drill now. Wet the drill yard in case the boss comes back, we'll drill tomorrow." said Ellis, as he headed to his office. Barrie had scored yet again!

In 1974, I was promoted to Leading Fireman and joined John Blenkinsop, John Lewis and Dave Apps in the fire prevention office. The brigade had just taken over the Petroleum Licensing for the Cheshire area and we had 600 sites, mostly farms, to inspect. CFB wrote to each one of these to say we would inspect them all within the next 12 months. This was indeed a tall order and we very quickly started to get behind. The original idea was for two Fire Prevention Officers to conduct an initial visit; this was quickly altered to one, then finally to anyone who could lift a pen.

I qualified in that Department and to assist there was a four page aide-memoir. I was sent to the Wilmslow area and I remember clutching the appropriate paperwork while inspecting a small roadside garage/workshop near to Redesmere. I was ok with the first part of the form and then I came to the section headed 'possible sources of ignition'. Just then, there was a loud honking din as overhead geese took off from the nearby lake and flew over the building. The garage guy immediately stepped inside the workshop, took up a loaded shotgun, went onto the road and blasted off both barrels at the geese. Fortunately for the birds he missed them all and not even a single feather fluttered down to us. I looked at my aide memoir. Not a mention of shotguns! I turned over the page and carried on with the next section.

I was still working out of the fire prevention office as we approached the great drought in 1976. Throughout the spring and into the summer, little or no rain fell. It was so hot. This led to almost empty reservoirs, dried out rivers with little or no flow and severe water restrictions in place. Firemen throughout the country faced a difficult period with tinder dry grass, heath and peat likely to catch fire with the slightest spark. Cigarette ends thrown from vehicles were a major cause of fires, and it wasn't just the fire crews who came under pressure. The Control staff got a hammering as stress levels went through the roof, dealing with all the fire calls. At Crewe an additional fire appliance was manned by mostly part-time personnel and I was drafted back onto the front line in a bid to help out. With the exception of property fires and major incidents, radio messages were cancelled with the aim of reducing 'radio traffic'. The only messages heard on-air were appliances booking available and Control transmitting addresses of fires.

In the mornings we checked our appliances and then loaded them with our 'extras' as there was little opportunity to return to the fire station. Ample supplies of drinking and washing water were stored in all sorts of containers along with flasks of tea/coffee, cool boxes loaded with food and spare clothing. Top of my list was money for ice lollies. The one advantage of the dry weather was that we could confidently head our appliance across any field without the fear of getting bogged down. The ground was rock hard. This allowed us to get closer to fires, although topping up the appliance with water proved difficult at times. I remember emptying several cow troughs around one field to supplement our water tank. Fire beaters were also used to knock down and smother grass fires, although this method was totally exhausting, especially later in the day when fatigue had set in and our enthusiasm had started to dwindle. Railway embankments were by far the worst, as when dealing with one side of the track, we would watch helplessly as the flames spread to the opposite side. It was never ending, hard and dirty work.

One Saturday in September, I was on a fishing trip at Whitemere, Ellesmere (Shropshire) Fisheries, a lake where the water was six foot lower than normal. Suddenly the sky darkened and rain began to fall. It rained and rained for days on end. Shortly afterwards I was transferred back to the fire prevention office. It was a year never to be forgotten!

In 1977, I was promoted to Sub Officer in charge of a watch. This time I was in the front seat of the fire engine. It was a great job keeping the watch from any major mutinies. I truly loved it. The watch was full of characters and none better than Barry Axon; he was a delightful guy, always full of fun with a great smile and sense of humour. At the start of one night shift, I had the watch on formal parade. I was reading everyone's allocated duty for the shift when Barry arrived late. "Fireman Axon why are you late?" apologetically Barry replied, "Sorry boss, I was held up at the level crossing." "But you live at Haslington, there's no level crossing there." "Ahh that's it then, I must have gone the wrong way." replied Barry. With the watch in hysterics, I backed down. "Best not go that way again then Fireman Axon."

For all his good points Barry had one major failing - his driving. Perfectly adequate in normal conditions, but put Barry behind the wheel of a ten ton fire appliance, switch on the blue lights and the two-tone horns and the roads of Crewe became Barry's racetrack. Everyone quickly strapped in when Barry was driving. One evening as I was catching up with the paperwork there came a knocking at the office door. "Could I have a word with you Sub Officer?" said Barry. "Certainly, come in, what's the problem?" "You never put me down to drive the first fire appliance, all the others get regular goes; are you avoiding me?" asked Barry. "That's just not true Barry (I lied!)."

Next time Barry drove to a shout we were approaching a roundabout when I yelled at him. "Slow down Barry, we're only going to a shed on fire, and try keeping to the road." Moments later, I was screaming. "Watch that cyclist...have we hit him?" One of the lads in the back stuck his head out of the side window and said. "No, he's ok, well at least he's got two good fingers."

Later that day I entered the Station Officer's office. "Could I have a quick word about Fireman Axon's driving boss?" The boss appeared concerned and said. "I know, I followed you on that job this morning. Do you think we could get him on a H.G.V. refresher course?" I scratched my head. "He's only just come back from one sir!"

Now it is often the smaller jobs that linger in the memory and one such incident was at a junior school where an unfortunate cleaning lady was locked in a store room. As we rolled up I asked a member of the crew to bring the tool kit and then I strolled across the playground towards the head teacher, who seemed unconcerned about the incident. On reaching the storeroom I inquired. "Are you ok in there?" "Yes" said a meek voice with several sobs. Eager to get her talking and calm her down, I asked what her name was. "Shirley" she said with further sobs. "We'll soon have you out Shirley." The crew got to work with a screwdriver dismantling the lock. Then as an afterthought, I asked. "How long have you been locked in there Shirley?" "Two hours." followed with a further wail of crying. All eyes were turned to me. After a long pause, I looked at Fireman Keith Stubbs. "Two hours...Keith...door!" Now some say that

Keith's tunic turned green and his shirt began to tear at this point. All I remember is Keith lining up the door lock with his size 10, followed by a single blow, which sent the solid half-hour fire door and part of the frame crashing with a shower of hinges and screws to the floor. As the dust settled someone at the back said in a low voice "I wouldn't mess about with him!"

On January 1979, I was promoted to Station Officer at the Crewe Fire Prevention office, working a 72 hour week on the 'residential system' which later became the 'flexible duty system'. The duties included fire prevention visits, operational duties, training at part-time (retained) fire stations and later fire investigating. My part-time station training was mainly at Holmes Chapel, which was expertly run by Sub Officer Pickles, whose full-time job was as a Fireman at Manchester Airport. My task was made easier, because without doubt, he was one of the best at his job and his crew loved him.

With many repeated inspections at the larger sites in South Cheshire, I soon built up a good rapport with Fire and Security Officers in the area. These included: Malcolm Smith (Rolls-Royce), Chris Thorley (Crewe Railway Works) and Aussie (to my shame I have forgotten his surname) at Fisons in Holmes Chapel. Aussie was a giant of a man and former Sergeant in the Guards Regiment. As you would expect he was always immaculately dressed; I'm sure he went to bed in permanently creased pyjamas. No matter how much I bulled up, I always felt scruffy when I went on a visit to Fisons. All their inspections were carried out within a cooperative and friendly atmosphere.

This was not so at my nemesis and often visited, Peckforton Castle though. I can clearly remember what happened on my first inspection at the Castle. It started badly, then it became very bad and then it got even worse. The building had been derelict for a number of years before being taken by a group known as Dungeons and Dragons, where members dressed up in the characters of J.R.R.Tolkien, staying in their costumes for the entire weekend. Approximately 70 people were taking part as they ate and slept throughout the Castle building. There were camping gas stoves everywhere, large steel drums full of combustible rubbish on every staircase level and the basement was full of hay and straw. Bundles of this were set alight to give a smoke effect throughout the building. The only means of lighting was a few hand lamps and candles. I arrived home late that night!

Some months later I got a phone call from the architect asking if there was a possibility that the building could be adapted to become a hotel. "Send your plans and I'll have a look." Sometime later and clutching the plans I arrived at the estate office and was told there was no one who could show me round, but I was quite welcome to take the keys and help myself. I drove up the narrow lane and into the main courtyard; it was indeed an impressive building. Opening the solid oak doors I ventured inside, it was freezing cold and very dark, so I went back to my car and dressed in my fishing jacket and boots. Although I was much warmer, it still felt eerie. Checking my plans by torchlight I was suddenly aware of a presence carrying a shotgun. It was the gamekeeper. He looked angry and demanded to know what I was doing. I had a difficult time explaining that I was here legitimately before he stormed off to check with the estate office. Much later I started driving back towards the main road when a pheasant ran in front of the car. There was a bang as the poor unfortunate bird flapped off into the undergrowth. Not wishing to leave it suffering I chased it into the bracken, he was in a bad way and I decided the only thing to do was to finish him off. I was just in the process of ringing the bird's neck when who should appear? This time the shotgun was angled towards me! "Sorry about that." I struggled and I just ran over to him, then handed over a well blooded bunch of feathers and quickly headed for my car.

It was clear that to upgrade a 19th Century Grade 1 listed building into a hotel was going to take a great deal of time, effort and money. Many visits and proposals were forwarded including a suggestion that if we could evacuate the residents in the event of an emergency onto the battlement, they could drop the 20 feet into the moat below. Not a solution in any of my hotel fire prevention guides! For the owners to eventually achieve their ambitions was indeed a great achievement.

Over the years there was a big upgrade in our operation and personal protection equipment, but I believe the real game changer in our ability to save lives came with the introduction of the 'Hurst' rescue equipment. As a trial, two sets of the kit were sited at Warrington and Knutsford Fire Stations. It immediately received rave reviews by all personnel using it. Cheshire Fire Brigade (CFB) decided to purchase further sets as the budget became available and one Saturday morning a delivery of the kit was made to Crewe Fire Station. The Watch Officer, Cliff Simpson, invited me to join them in trying it out. We all congregated on the drill yard and were in the process of unpacking when the alarm sounded. It was a road traffic accident with persons reported trapped at Doddington, near the roadside lake. Still unpacked, we loaded up the new rescue equipment into the crew compartment and headed to the scene. On arrival we found a single female severely trapped having been involved in a head on crash in patchy fog.

I checked over the scene and taking a chance I ordered the crew to "get the Hurst." I then sent a message to control reporting that the crew would be engaged for approximately one hour. The crew were all practical guys and my reservations about using untried kit were soon overcome. Spreader went into the door jamb and immediately the door flew out, next the posts were cut through. A check-over by the paramedics and within a few minutes, the young lady was en route to hospital - wow we were all stunned with the new rescue equipment.

Some weeks later the lady wrote to the Brigade HQ's thanking us for helping her, although she feared the worst at one point when she heard someone saying "get the Hurst." I was always careful to call it the rescue equipment after that incident! To their great credit many part-time fire stations including, Holmes Chapel, Sandbach, and Nantwich having seen how good the kit was, decided not to wait for the Brigade to provide the rescue equipment. They appealed to local businesses and arranged pub and club collections, until they had sufficient funds to purchase, through the Brigade's Stores Department, their own Hurst rescue equipment.

In the final week of my career I attended a similar road traffic accident on the Crewe Industrial Estate; again it was a single lady occupant who was severely trapped having crashed into a wall. I watched in silence as the crews dealt with the incident. The rescue was slick and smooth with everyone knowing their role as the casualty was quickly extricated from her vehicle and taken to hospital. We had come a long way on road traffic accidents since my early days, using limited equipment, like hacksaws and panel beating equipment. Many lives have been saved thanks to the upgrade in gear and improved tactics. It's called professionalism and we can all feel very proud of ourselves.

My dad, a former Army man who survived Dunkirk and later the jungles in Burma during the Second World War, taught me to never volunteer for anything. Despite his advice, I volunteered to become a Fire Investigation Officer, and although it turned out to be a very interesting part of my job, it was also very demanding. There's nothing quite like being chopped apart by some defence barrister; you are in their territory and they know all the rules, a shredding machine would be a more delicate way of doing business.

The Home Office decided that too many fire reports were being returned with the 'cause of fire' recorded as 'unknown'. As a result fire brigades were required to set up specialist teams to undertake more detailed investigations. Although I wasn't in the Brigade's initial investigation team, I decided to give it a go and was assisted along the way by Dave Greatorex and Alan Coles. Alan was later to lecture on the subject at the Fire Service College in Moreton-in-Marsh.

Many of the investigations turned up in court one way or another. One late evening in Winsford a house fire had resulted in a wife accusing her husband of pouring petrol over her and setting her on fire. She was in hospital and her husband was in custody facing an 'attempted murder' charge. On my arrival, I was met by Sub Officer John Yardley (Yadder). John was a terrific guy, a real rough diamond; he was also the best firefighter I ever came across. "Strange one this boss" he said. "Can't quite figure it out." The two storey house was full from top to bottom with hundreds of empty 'Tennent's Extra Strong' lager tins, so many in fact that you weren't able to walk without stepping on them. Here and there were black plastic buckets full of liquid. "Sniff that John. Does that smell like petrol to you?" I inquired. All the crew were sniffing away trying to detect the smell of petrol fumes until we all hit on the solution at the same time.

With vast quantities of Tennent's lager being consumed, frequent visits to the loo were required. At the risk of falling downstairs it was much easier to provide a number of buckets and cut down on the risk factor and travel distance. So they were both well oiled when the wife's clothing accidentally caught fire from a portable electric heater. He saw what was happening and reached for his life-saving fire extinguisher - a bucket of piss! Happily we were able to get this guy off his attempted murder charge. However not all fire investigations were that simple.

It was pleasing to see younger Fire Officers volunteering for the Fire Investigation Department, allowing me to step down after seven years in the role. I wasn't sorry to hand my investigation kit of a camera and two broken screwdrivers back to the Brigade's Stores Department. To celebrate, I took the wife out for a meal that night, but it was to be two years after I retired that the court cases finally dried up. And one last thing - I have now lost my sense of smell. It must be a Winsford thing!

When I look back on my 32 years in CFB, I feel very privileged to have earned a living doing a very special job and I will always be grateful to a Divisional Officer who interviewed me for the job in 1966. He must have seen something, for when on my final day of employment, Chief Fire Officer Dennis Davis showed me my initial application. Did I really write that on the application form? In all honesty, I wouldn't have taken me on - so glad he did though!

RAY STAFFORD

Ray Stafford became a part-time fireman at Crewe in the late 1960s. His primary work was Director of Operations on Locomotive Power in the Control Room at Rail House. This involved working shifts, which enabled him to serve his community as a fireman in his spare time. Ray was also a leading figure in the neighbourhood as a Youth Leader and a Local Authority Councillor. He was also involved with various charities.

When I joined up we were alerted to call-outs by the sound of a wailing siren, which was fitted on top of the drill tower at the fire station. The rising and falling pitch of the siren was like a Wartime air-raid warning. At the same time an electric bell, which was fitted in the houses of part-time firemen, started ringing. Everyone who lived in the vicinity of the fire station knew a fire was in the making, although the siren didn't sound after 11.00pm and the bell was our only alert. By the mid-1970s, the bells were replaced by personal alerters (pagers or bleepers) and the siren was withdrawn from service.

We trained at the fire station for one evening a week and occasionally during weekends. Familiarity with the equipment and teamwork was vital, so in the event of a fire or road traffic accident, we had the know-how to get things done quickly. There was always a sense of satisfaction when we were turned out to incidents, especially when our services were called upon to help people in distress. We were often turned out to provide back-up for the full-time crew, although there were occasions when we stood alone at incidents, especially during busy times.

I know only too well the devastation that can be caused as a result of fires and road traffic accidents. Memories of some tragedies I attended have remained with me forever. During the afternoon of 17 June 1969 a serious accident involving a double-deck bus at Slaughter Hill, Haslington had an extremely sad outcome, when two people lost their lives and several were injured, after a giant elm tree came crashing down onto the bus travelling from Crewe to Hanley. A ladder was put up to the bus' emergency window to free many of the passengers and two passengers, who were trapped, were released. Many of the injured took refuge at the Whey Products Factory and some were taken to hospital.

A serious fire at Williams Brothers' at Weston Road in Crewe on the 13 November 1969 destroyed most of the warehouse and caused £250,000 worth of damage. I hadn't been home long after a night shift at Rail House when the fire bell sounded in the house. Before I dashed off to the fire station on my bicycle, I noticed my wife Edna's face was full of worry as clouds of dark smoke filled the sky over the Weston Road Industrial Estate. Within about five minutes we joined the full-time crew at the scene of the blaze where the density of the fire became apparent. We immediately attacked the flames with jets of water and were joined by further fire crews from Nantwich, Middlewich, Sandbach and Holmes Chapel. It was several hours later before we finally had the fire under control. One of my colleagues alongside me commented that he was gasping for a fag as the fire eased. Moments later I noticed hundreds of packets of cigarettes amongst the burnt out smouldering rubble. His face just lit up! The warehouse, which stocked furniture, carpets and all types of fancy goods, was burnt to the ground, but fortunately the army of firemen prevented the fire spreading to the office block, where many of the company's documents were kept. Williams Brothers, which was founded in 1934 by brothers Jack and Ray Williams, employed 55 people. After acquiring temporary premises in Richmond Road and in Prince Albert Street, the warehouse was eventually rebuilt at Weston Road.

During the same year on the 16 December, an early morning fire in a maisonette at Broxton Drive, Crewe cost two young sisters their lives. Brave attempts were made by neighbours to rescue the girls but the ferocity of the fire drove them back. Tragically the sisters were found by Firemen huddled together in bed trying to hide from the fire.

Another incident I often recall was when an overhead telegraph cable lacerated my hand and almost severed my artery. The night time house fire in Wheelman Road, Crewe during the summer of 1970, completely destroyed the bedroom and its contents. I was pulling burning wood away from the eaves when the accident occurred and as a result I ended up with 10 stitches in my hand. The scar is a reminder how dangerous the work of firemen could be.

Some fires in Crewe involved historical buildings which suffered extensive damage or total destruction. Fortunately some of these structures re-emerged from their own ashes and were re-built to become places of special interest. These included the Lyceum Theatre and Crewe Hall. As time went by, fewer fires of this nature occurred, thanks to fire safety legislation and the expertise of Fire Prevention Officers who have played a major part in keeping buildings safe from fire.

The fire brigade had a family feel to it. Colleagues helped each other outside work and they often organised events for children. As a youth club leader, I found myself involved with hosting these events. It was also a privilege to support the firemen at many of their fundraising events, especially when I served as the Mayor of Crewe and Nantwich in 1998/99. Although my firefighting days ended in the early 1980s, I'm pleased to say that my links with the fire station continued until 2009.

Serving the people of Crewe has filled me with enormous satisfaction and without doubt my experience in the fire brigade gave me a greater desire to help people, especially those in distress.

ROD BROOME

Control Operators (Con-Op) play a key role in the fire brigade by supporting firemen and co-ordinating their resources at incidents. They are involved with incidents from the moment emergency calls come in, until they finally close

down. Former Crewe Fireman Rod Broome, whose firefighting career was cut short after sustaining a knee injury, became a Con-Op in 1980 and remained in that post for 20 years.

The summer of 1969 was quite eventful in many ways. It was a time I learnt the basics of firefighting, ran out umpteen lengths of hose and climbed ladders (including the dreaded hook-ladder!) on a daily basis, while taking part in my recruits' course. I then joined ranks with the firemen at Crewe, working a three day shift, followed by three nights and then three days off.

The 1970s was a period when dwelling fires were frequently attended. Chimney fires were common in a town that was swamped with rows upon row of terraced houses, many of which housed Railway employees, who dominated the population of Crewe. The hot summer of 1976 was unforgettable, particularly for the numerous grass fires in and around Crewe. The Brigade was stretched to its limits and during the month of August; Crewe attended 180 calls, two thirds of which were grass fires.

Full-time firemen were allowed to double-up as part-time firemen on their days off. This was known as the whole-time/retained system. The life of a fireman, as I knew it, was full-on on occasions, with little time for anything else. The wages were poor in comparison to other semi-skilled jobs, so working whole-time/retained was welcome by some, especially those who had families to support. However, all this changed after the National Strike ended in January 1978, when overtime in the fire brigade ceased.

Unfortunately my return to work became a struggle as my injured knee deteriorated. I was forced to work on light duties, which involved carrying out non-operational duties, such as repairing hose. Sadly, my days as a fireman ended after being medically discharged later in 1978. Despite this set back, I re-joined in 1980 as a Con-Op. I was based at C Division's HQ at Crewe, where I remained until the Divisional Controls were disbanded in 1982. I then re-located to the Brigade's HQ at Walmoor House in Chester, as part of the Main Control team. It was quite a privilege to work at this grade II listed building, built in the 1890s and overlooking the River Dee. However, a few years later the Main Control moved to a purpose built control centre at Vaughan's Lane in Chester, where it remained until the mid-1990s, before moving to the new Brigade HQ at Sadler Road in Winsford.

Cheshire Fire Brigade also had a standby control centre at the former anti-aircraft operations room at Beacon Hill in Frodsham, which had been built in the early 1950s, as part of the UK's Cold War defence. Con-Ops moved into these premises on occasions to check everything was in working order. Entering this eerie bomb-proof building with its steel doors was a reminder of days gone-by, when the threat of War was imminent.

Con-Ops worked a two day and two nights 12 hour shift system, and like full-time firemen, operated with four watches. An understanding of Cheshire's major risks was essential. These included railway routes, motorway networks, and various types of manufacturing industries, petro-chemical sites, Manchester Airport and a vast number of heritage buildings. Although my time as a fireman was short lived, my experience fighting fires was useful in the control room as I could visualise scenes on the fire-ground when messages were sent from fire crews, especially as incidents developed.

Receiving fire calls were usually smoothly handled by the Con-Ops, but on occasions they could be quite challenging, especially when desperate pleas of help were made by distressed callers. Keeping calm and reassuring the callers was vital, as was making instantaneous decisions that might save someone's life. One distressing incident in the mid-1990s had a very sad ending and will probably always remain with me. As my colleague, Jo Cullan, was handing over information at the commencement of my 8am shift, a 999 call came in from a male person in a phone box by the Crewe Bus Station. He was clearly upset and stated that he had poured petrol over himself and wanted to end his life. The Police and Ambulance were informed without delay and a fire appliance was mobilised with instructions to attend the incident on a silent approach. Meanwhile, attempts were made to enter into dialogue with the person to try and keep him talking. Unfortunately, after a few moments the caller shouted, "I am going to do it now". The distressing sound of his voice was relayed to the control room through his dangling handset as he set himself on fire. We were desperate to help, but felt so helpless. Sadly he passed away a day or two later, which left everyone on the watch deeply upset.

Fortunately tragedies of this nature were rare occurrences and the majority of incidents ended with successful outcomes. It was always pleasing to hear messages from fire crews, when rescues were carried out or when people were freed from vehicles involved in road traffic accidents. Hearing the 'stop' message from incidents, which indicated that no further assistance was needed, also lightened the mood at control.

Going 'back home' to the fire brigade as a Con-Op in 1980 proved to be one of the best decisions I ever made, especially after the despair of having to end my firefighting days. I had a sense of satisfaction and fulfilment when I retired in 2000, knowing that I'd played a part in keeping Cheshire safe as part of the control room team. Perhaps my knee injury was destiny after all.

DAVE McCABE

Former RAF Aircraft Engineer Dave McCabe began his fire brigade career in 1973. After his basic training he was posted to Red Watch at Crewe Fire Station. Several years later after spells at Brigade HQ and Macclesfield Fire Station, he returned to take charge of White Watch at Crewe. He later joined the Fire Prevention team at C Division, before returning to HQ as part of the Training Department. After a brief return to the Crewe's Fire Prevention office, Dave ended his career as Station Commander at Congleton.

After nine years in RAF uniform the more relaxed discipline of fire brigade life came fairly easy to me. I enjoyed the basic training despite the freezing weather and actually trained on the iconic wheeled escape ladders, which at that time were being phased out from the front line. The dreaded hook ladder though, was still an important piece of kit on most fire engines. I never used either for real during my career though.

I made my first appearance at Crewe Fire Station during morning 'tea and toast' break time and was introduced to my watch members. "You're not from round here are you then (I was born in Brighton)?" They informed me that they were all locals except for one who told me he wasn't, because he was from Tarporley. That meant nothing to me as I had no idea where that was! As I got to know them though, I soon became impressed at their level of local knowledge.

After fighting fires and dealing with various operational incidents in and around the Crewe area for about 10 years and by now a Watch Commander, I became a Fire Prevention Officer in the Crewe office. This job involved the inspection of all types and uses of buildings across the whole of C Division, which stretched from Audlem in the south to Disley in the north. After a Brigade restructuring exercise I was transferred to the Winsford Central Training Department. My principal role was the training of Fire Safety Specialist Officers with an added responsibility for recruit and apprentice firefighter training. Significant changes in fire safety and health and safety legislation were taking place around this time and I was charged with updating these changes to all operational firefighters as well as the Fire Safety Specialists. I also contributed to the introduction of home fire safety visits, which was a new initiative carried out by operational crews to make people safer in their own homes. I have always found it ironic that most fatalities from fire occur in the premise which are unaffected by legislation - their own homes.

I attained membership of the Institution of Fire Engineers and held the position of Divisional Representative for a number of years. This organisation connects fire professionals from all walks of life and from all over the world. The Cheshire Group maintained an active involvement by hosting meetings, seminars and making visits to a wide range of premises, including the Sellafield Atomic Complex and the Winsford Salt Mines.

As with all firefighters, despite the intervals I spent away from riding the fire engines, I found my years dealing with incidents most rewarding, whether I was on the branch at the end of a line of hose or taking charge at incidents. Obviously some shouts were more arduous than others, but some were quite amusing (with the benefit of hindsight). It is a fact that firefighters generally manage to look at the brighter side of life.

There are a couple of memorable fires that I attended in the 1970s which I recall quite well. A huge pre-Christmas fire in a Crewe fancy goods warehouse, which resulted in the vast majority of local wives, girlfriends and female relatives, all receiving a (slightly smoky) bottle of Musk perfume on Christmas morning. Another large fire, this time at a flour mill in the Nantwich area resulted in all the firefighters being covered from helmet to boots in sticky wet tapioca and their appliances, which had to be cleaned and polished for inspection the following day, needing pressure washing to remove the goo! Then there was the dramatic rescue one Sunday morning involving 12 sheep that had fallen into a sewage farm holding tank in Congleton. Somehow it was left to the Crewe Firefighters on the Emergency Tender (ET) to get stuck in and do the smelly business. Firemen based at Crewe had a relatively wide circle of operational incidents compared with some fire stations, partly because we operated the ET (Bedford TK), which could be called to incidents virtually anywhere, but particularly the M6 Motorway. Incidentally, I distinctly recall driving this underpowered and overloaded vehicle through Wheelock to Sandbach Services one morning, while on a shout, and being overtaken by a young lad on a moped!

Despite feeling embarrassed when driving the aging ET, it was often a pleasure to drive older fire appliances, and back in the day when there was an annual carnival held at Queen's Park in Crewe, myself and another colleague, Kevin Birtles, usually joined in the procession with a vintage fire engine. We were always made welcome despite our habit of gate crashing this event.

JANSSEN BOSTOCK

After serving in the armed forces with the Horse Guards at Hyde Park Barracks in London, Janssen Bostock enrolled into the London Fire Brigade in 1991, where he was based at Belsize Park Fire Station. Two years later he headed to his home county of Cheshire, where he served as a firefighter at Chester, Winsford, and for most of his career at Crewe. Whilst at Crewe, Janssen was part of a delegation that went to Macon on a 'twinning' visit, and in his capacity as a Union Representative, he visit Auschwitz in Poland.

A helicopter crash on 22 October 1996 at Norcroft Farm near Warmingham, when all five passengers lost their lives, was one of the most tragic incidents I attended as a Crewe Firefighter. I recall approaching the scene of the crash in pitch darkness through a wet and muddy field, shinning my torch to see intact parts of the fuselage torn off the helicopter and a trail of debris littering the ground. This included clothes, shoes and travel items such as a toothbrush, which were scattered everywhere. A strong smell of aviation fuel was present as the darkness of the night was broken with shinny glows of light from other firefighters' torches. It would have taken a miracle to survive this accident. The helicopter had crashed on the edge of an area of woodland about half a mile from the nearest housing estate before it burst into flames. Among the dead was Matthew Harding, Vice Chairman of Chelsea Football Club. The helicopter was returning back to London after its passengers had been watching Chelsea playing at Bolton Wanderers in the League Cup.

Fortunately, incidents of this nature were rare. Unlike my time as a London Firefighter, where many of the shouts were to high rise buildings, working in Crewe brought a variety of incidents from house fires in the town to rural and motorway incidents.

Travelling was one of my interests in life, so I was more than happy to represent Crewe Fire Station on a visit to the French town of Macon in 1996 to commemorate the 40th anniversary of the twinning between Crewe and Macon. Accompanying me was Mitchell Clarke, Paul Dunn, Brendan Grant, Rikki Harden and John Lloyd. We travelled to Macon in style as we made the journey in a Dennis Sabre fire appliance, which was showcased in the mile long procession to mark the occasion. Up to 10 fire appliances were housed at the Macon Fire Station, many of which were kitted out with specialist equipment, such as a diving unit. Our hosts gave us a resounding welcome and their hospitality was second to none.

Another adventure came my way in April 2003 when, I visited the former German Nazi Concentration Camps in Auschwitz and Birkenau in Poland. Fire Brigades Union (FBU) officials, including two Merseyside Firefighters and my Crewe colleague Gareth Roberts, were supporting young people referred by the social services and from north west youth services, schools and colleges. Accompanying us was Holocaust survivor Arek Hersh, who despite the pain and trauma he felt on every return to Auschwitz, gave a thorough insight into the hardship he had encountered. Standing in bleak surroundings where millions of people were imprisoned and murdered was a chilling and haunting experience for the adults, let alone the youngsters, who were given an emotional history lesson that can't be taught in a classroom.

The visit to Poland coincided with the lengthy 2002/03 fire dispute, which included a series of strikes, as the FBU fought for more pay for its members. As expected by many of my colleagues, the fire service was reformed following the dispute. Our working shift pattern was eventually changed to 12 hours on both days and nights shifts, which to many firefighters were more desirable, and the increase in pay became more appropriate to our new roles.

We became more active in driving down the number of incidents in the years following the dispute and focused on community safety work, although there was no drastic reduction in our attendance at fires and other incidents. We often turned out as back-up to part-time firefighters from Sandbach, Nantwich and Audlem, with many of these incidents 'out in the sticks'. The Peckferton Castle fire on 19 June 2011 was one such fire. It was fought by 100 firefighters, most of who were from the South and West of Cheshire, and some of the neighbouring fire and rescue services.

It was the turn of part-time firefighters to give back-up to Crewe firefighters on 27 January 2014, as a 200 foot smoke plume at Hutchins Horticultural Supplies in Herbert Street, Crewe, forced the evacuation of nearby homes. Five fire appliances from Crewe, Sandbach, Holmes Chapel and Middlewich attended the fire.

A tragic incident that claimed the lives of four people was attended by Crewe Firefighters on 17 July 2015. The explosion at Bosley Mill near Congleton caused the four-storey building at Wood Flour Mills to collapse as several fires broke out. Fire appliances attended from Cheshire, Staffordshire, Derbyshire, Greater Manchester, and teams of firefighters were at the scene day and night, for almost five weeks.

It was 50 years since the opening of Crewe Fire Station in July 2016, and on 21 August, the public were invited to the Fire Station to observe the duty watch re-enact rescues following road traffic collisions. Chip pan fire demonstrations were also displayed and a smoke tent was on hand to show children how to exit a smoke-filled room.

The following year Crewe Firefighters were part of a pilot scheme responding to cardiac arrests in the fire engine. Although the 12 month trial was abandoned in July 2017, a defibrillator became a permanent fixture on the wall outside the fire station. This was as a result of the British Heart Foundation's 'Restart a Heart' campaign to make defibrillators available for public use.

The neighbouring building to the fire station caught fire during the afternoon of 28 September 2017. With asbestos involved, it forced the closure of Macon Way and Grand Junction Retail Park. The disused building (Macon House), owned by Cheshire East Council, had been used as a day centre for people with disabilities since the 1960s. An aerial appliance and five fire appliances dealt with the fire.

During the last 10 years of my career, campaigns were fought through the FBU as the firefighters' pension came under attack and plans were drawn to downgrade Crewe Fire Station. Both these prolonged battles ended with successful outcomes. Several serious fires took place in South Cheshire to support the argument that downgrading the fire station would be damaging, and in February 2018, a decision was made by Cheshire's Fire Authority to back down from their original plan. The outcome was that Crewe kept both its fire appliances staffed by full-time firefighters. This was a huge victory for the FBU and its supporters, which went a long way to keeping firefighters and the people of South Cheshire safer.

Since my arrival at Crewe it was noticeable that Crewe Firefighters actively worked with the community. After the fire service was reformed following the 2002/03 dispute, huge investments were made to make people safer in their homes. But despite this, a major fire in Crewe resulted in 150 residents having to be evacuated from the Beechmere Retirement Home in Rolls Avenue on 8 August 2019. The fire, which destroyed most of the complex, was fought by 70 firefighters with 16 fire appliances, two aerial platforms and a high volume pump, that delivered water from the water-main near Leighton Hospital. Heroic rescues were made by the public and members of staff at the retirement home, as comparisons were made to London's Grenfell Tower fire in June 2017, when 72 people lost their lives. Fire crews were at the retirement home for several days before the fire was finally extinguished. This devastating fire coincided with my retirement from the fire service and it was ironic that the most frequent question asked after the fire was: 'Why wasn't the retirement home fitted with sprinklers to protect its residents?' Despite public safety being at the heart of the work of firefighters, the public were astonished when they found out that it wasn't mandatory to have sprinklers in this building, despite the high risk to life!

Crewe Firefighters 2019
Red Watch
Watch Manager - Barry Earndon. **Crew Managers -** Dave Jackson and Phil Smith.
Firefighters - Kerry Blease, Leigh Bowen, Dave Brightwell, Adrian Dunning, Paul Gresty, Dan Huff, Joel Olszewski, Tom French and Daniel Gray.

Blue Watch
Watch Manager - Hannah Caulfield. **Crew Manager**s - Rich Douglas and Steve Parker.
Firefighters - Janssen Bostock, Iain Dunne, Adrian Fiske, Mark Huxley, Mark Latham, Don Page, Neil White, Ryan Younger, Theo Burgess and Matty Lyon.

White Watch
Watch Manager - Kristian Clowes. **Crew Managers -** Mike Warburton and Gareth Lewis.
Firefighters - Dan Cope, Phil Cornes, Dan Mistreanu, Phil Moorcroft, Ted Perry, Chris Ryan, Gaz Walker, John Ashby and James Silver.

Green Watch
Watch Manager - Rob Carney. **Crew Managers** - Ashley Brown and Adrian Dewsbury.
Firefighters - Dave Jones, Nick Regan, John Angier, Steve Benbow, Matt Hole, Mike Hubbard, Paul Leigh, Kenny Wong and Sam Woodcock.

Fire Station Vehicles
Scania *(PO11 FZR)* Water Ladder, Scania *(MX67 JUE)* Water Ladder,
Leyland DAF *(J781 HCA)* Breathing Apparatus Command Unit
Dennis F7 *(LFM 200)* - CFRS Heritage Society.

SHOUTS

A selection of incidents in Crewe and the surrounding area as reported in local newspapers and news bulletins through time, courtesy of: *Crewe Guardian, Crewe Chronicle, Chester Chronicle, Staffordshire Sentinel, John Bull Publication, Cheshire Observer, Staffordshire Advertiser, Evening Sentinel, Liverpool Echo, Chester Courant, Manchester Courier and Lancashire Advertiser.*

October 1844 - A fire broke out in an outbuilding of the Holly Sheaf Farm, in the occupation of Mr. Furber, which had originated by a practice too much in fashion among farmers, and to which may be attributed, no doubt, many of those fires which are, from time to time, recorded in glowing language in our daily and weekly journals, as the work of incendiaries, Mr. Furber had been amusing himself by shooting sparrows in his farmyard, and some of the wadding having ignited and fallen upon a thatched outhouse, or lair, set fire to it, and almost immediately the whole was enveloped in flames. On it being made known to Mr. Allen, at the Crewe Works, he promptly despatched a posse of the men under him with two engines. They played energetically upon the surrounding buildings and combustible materials to preserve them from the flames, and we are happy to say that their efforts were effectual. A brick fell upon the head of a little child and injured it very severely, but happily, Mr. Stephen's, surgeon, was on the spot, and he rendered such assistance that it is hoped the life of the little unfortunate will be preserved. We do hope that our agricultural friends will be more cautious in the use of firearms in their farmyards. *(Chester Chronicle).*

August 1851 - One of the third carriages of an up train from Liverpool caught fire when near Crewe, and the communication of the flames to the other carriages could only be prevented by taking out the ignited carriage, from the roof of which the burning luggage was quickly hurled, the carriage itself being entirely consumed. *(John Bull Publication).*

November 1858 - A thatched cottage belonging to the executors of the late Mr. William Kannerley, situated at Haslington, near Crewe, was observed to be on fire, but which was fortunate not of a serious character. It is supposed that the fire commenced in a beam near the chimney, and had it not been speedily subdued, mainly through the praiseworthy exertions of a man named Aaron Moses, a blacksmith, at Haslington, the whole cottage would have been entirely destroyed. *(Chester Chronicle).*

September 1861 - A fire broke out in the outhouse attached to the farm of Mr. Barnett, of Rope, near Crewe. It appears that about the time, one of Mr. Barnett's servants, named Richard Austin, and who had not been in the house since supper time the night before, awoke his master and informed him about the fire. Austin's story was to the effect that after supper he went out, and not returning till all the other people had gone to bed, he went into one of the outhouses, intending to sleep there. He had not been there long before he was conscious of a suffocating smell, and looking about he found the place on fire. The fire spread to the building near to it, and spread so rapidly that it was soon evident that there was no chance of saving anything. The buildings contained a quantity of wheat, a quantity of oats, and about six or seven tons of hay. All this with the buildings was destroyed. A messenger was then sent to Nantwich for the fire engine, but the Board of Health would not let it go. The same messenger was then sent to Crewe Works to get the engine from there, but before he could get to his journey's end another messenger was despatched after him to prevent the engine's going, as there seemed to be no hope of saving anything. The damage is estimated at about £300. Owing to Richard Austin having some time ago used threats against his master, some suspicion was entertained that he had been guilty of incendiarism, and he was therefore taken into custody and conveyed to the Nantwich lockup. *(Cheshire Observer).*

January 1862 - A fire in a very destructive character broke out in the corn and flour mills, known as Crewe Mills, in the occupation of Mr. Edwin Whittingham. About one o'clock in the morning Mr. Whittingham was awoke by a noise as of falling glass on the housetop. He at once arose, and found to his dismay that his mill was on fire, and the flames had reached such a height as to have broken several of the windows, and the falling glass had opportunity awakened him. Mr. Whittingham at once despatched a messenger to Crewe for engines. Intelligence of the fire reached Inspector Wilson, of the Crewe Police, about a quarter past one, and he promptly procured an engine belonging to the London and North Western Railway Company, and was at the scene of the fire in little more than twenty minutes afterwards. This engine the Inspector got to work, and also another which arrived from Crewe Hall soon after. A good supply of water was obtained from the mill pond, but all efforts to save the mill proved unavailing. The mill and contents were destroyed and the bare walls only left standing. The dwelling-house which adjoins the mill, was somewhat damaged, and would probably have been destroyed had the wind blown in that direction. The furniture was hurriedly removed, when some villainously-disposed persons, taking advantage of the darkness and confusion, actually carried off a portion of the goods. Two men who were bearing away the clock, on being pursued, tossed it over a hedge and escaped; but one man, with some of Miss Whittingham's property in his possession, was captured, and lodged in the Crewe lock-up. The fire is surmised to have originated from the carelessness of one of the millers, either from being unguarded in the use of his light, or by allowing the mill stones to run empty. He had left the mill in safety, as he thought, only three quarters of an hour before it was discovered to be in flames. Mr. Whittingham's loss is estimated at over £2,000, but his insurance in the Royal Exchange office will nearly cover it. The buildings, which are the property of Lord Crewe, are, we understand, insured for £800. *(Staffordshire Advertiser).*

January 1866 - The Crewe Hall stately mansion, situate about two miles from the railway station of Crewe, was unfortunately destroyed by fire. It appears that shortly after Lord Crewe and the visitors in the mansion had retired to rest, the attention of his lordship was arrested by a strong smell of fire, and he rang for his valet, to whom he communicated his suspicions. The servants were aroused, and an examination was made of the premises, but the seat of the fire was not then discovered, and the domestics were about to retire, when, on a second alarm being raised, a fire was ascertained to be raging on the top part of the eastern wing of the noble mansion. Special messengers mounted on horseback were instantly despatched to Crewe and Nantwich for assistance, and a telegram was forwarded to Chester requesting the immediate help of the fire brigade. Meanwhile two small engines belonging to the Hall were brought out, and attempts were made to arrest the flames, which, fanned by the strong breeze then blowing, quickly enveloped the eastern wing of the building, but from some unexplained cause they could not be used. It is supposed that in the excitement of the moment the means of turning on the water, which is communicated to the house from the lake, was overlooked, and consequently the fire continued its career of devastation entirely unchecked.

At the moment that the telegram reached Chester, requesting the aid of the fire brigade, a portion of that body was engaged in attempting to extinguish a fire in a shop in Northgate Street, but with as little delay as possible Superintendent Noblet and a party of his men in charge of an engine started for the scene of the conflagration. Engines from Nantwich, and one form the Railway Works at Crewe also arrived on the spot, but the latter was unable to render effective service until extra lengths of hose had been procured. From the moment the fire was discovered its progress was extremely rapid; and before anything like combined efforts were made to arrest its destructive career, the flames spread along the marble hall, picture gallery, drawing room, and the chapel on the north side of the mansion, the ceilings and walls of which were adorned with most valuable paintings, and enveloped them all. A magnificent stained glass window, over the communion table, was also completely destroyed.

Soon after the fire broke out it became apparent that the new portion of the mansion would be sacrificed, and all parties present laboured most assiduously to rescue some of the valuable property with which every room in the mansion was filled. The picture gallery contained a magnificent collection of paintings by ancient and modern artists, several of which were exhibited at the Great Exhibition of 1862, and though some of the valuable contents of this part of the mansion were saved, we regret to learn that many of the best pictures were entirely destroyed, which will be the more deplored because the loss is irreparable. The grand staircase, with the costly statuary which adorned it, is also involved in the ruin. A considerable amount of furniture and valuables was removed from the mansion into the park beyond the reach of harm, but the domestic servants have suffered very severely, and in some instances have lost everything they possessed.

The fire continued to burn with uncontrolled fury throughout the morning, and by mid-day the Hall, with the exception of a very small portion, was a mass of ruins, nothing but the tottering walls remaining to indicate where but a few hours previously had stood one of the most stately mansions in England. The erection of the hall, from the designs of Inigo Jones, was commenced in 1615, but it was not complete till 1636; in 1837 the present Lord Crewe restored the structure at a cost of £50,000, so that it was comparatively a modern erection. At the time of the outbreak of the fire Lady Houghton, sister to Lord Crewe, and other distinguished visitors, were staying at the Hall, amongst whom, it is needless to say, the disastrous event occasioned great excitement. It is, however, matter for congratulation that the timely discovery enabled all the inmates of the Hall to affect their escape before either life or limb was jeopardised.

It is said that provision was made against fire by hydrants placed at certain distances round the house, supplied with water from the lake, and also by taps in the rooms communicating with an immense reservoir on the top of the house; but whether the domestics were panic-stricken or had forgotten these arrangements will probably be a matter for future inquiry. It appears that the taps were not thought till access to them was cut off by flames, and during the early part of the conflagration by hydrants shared the same amount of inattention.

The damage is estimated at upwards of £100,000, but we understand that the Hall was insured for about £40,000 in the Exchange, Phoenix, and Sun Fire Offices. It will therefore prove a serious loss to his lordship; but the loss can scarcely be estimated by pounds and shillings, for many of the works of art cannot be replaced by any outlay of wealth. The fire, it is thought, was occasioned by the overheating of a flue.

It is due to the labourers, farmers, and inhabitants of Crewe who were present at the fire to say that they exerted themselves in the most praiseworthy manner to arrest the flames; but the conflagration defied all human power, and only ceased when all the material of the Hall had been consumed. Great sympathy is felt with Lord Crewe by the inhabitants of the district, his lordship's benevolent spirit and kindly manner having won for him the esteem of all classes of the people amongst whom he lives. *(Cheshire Observer).*

January 1873 - A large booth used as a theatre, situated in High Street, Crewe, took fire. The company of Messrs. France and Loone were rehearsing a piece, and just as they had got to the last scene some sparks from a passing engine chanced to alight on the canvas roof, which was quickly ablaze. An alarm was given, and in a few minutes the burning canvas was torn from the frame. When the fire was extinguished, a detachment of the Volunteer Fire Brigade arrived with the hose and red cart, but their services were not required. *(Guardian).*

July 1874 - The clanging of the firebell about midnight brought a large number of persons into the streets. On inquiry it was ascertained that a man named Owen had brought intelligence that a couple of hay stacks, owned by Mr. Clarke, a butcher and farmer, of Church Coppenhall, were then in full blaze. The majority of the men belonging to the Crewe Volunteer Fire Brigade were in attendance, the horses harnessed, and, in a very short time, the engine was bowling along to the scene of the conflagration, about two miles distant from Crewe. The engine had to be taken across a field to the stacks, and then the men commenced to play on the flames from a couple of pits, partially filled with water, close at hand. In a short time the dense volume of water poured into the stacks had a visible effect, and in about a couple of hours all danger was over. A quantity of the fire was cut out by hay-knives, and, although considerably damaged, the stacks, valued at £50, are not wholly lost. The engine remained on the spot for several hours, and did not leave until all danger was over. *(Chronicle).*

December 1875 - The Railway Company were engaged in widening Liverpool Bridge in Crewe when a fire broke out as the road surface was covered in asphalt. The Crewe Volunteer Fire Brigade were soon on the spot and dealt with the fire. *(Guardian).*

May 1876 - The loud ringing of the Crewe fire bell proved a fruitful source of excitement, for from all quarters of the town came men, women and children trooping thither and eagerly enquiring, "Where, oh where is the fire?" And while the bell pealed out its alarming notes there was seated on horseback opposite the Market Hall, a young man named John Sumner, whose mission in ringing of the fire bell was of course accomplished, while he was courteously leaning over his horse replying to inquiries. It was an interesting sight to watch the gathering of the Crewe Volunteer Fire Brigade and to their credit be it stated that within a few minutes after the first alarm note had startled the town they had nearly all assembled, some donning their uniforms on the way and others with their helmets under their arms. Captain Watson and Mr. Wood, High Street, were among the first to arrive. The fire engine and apparatus were got out in an incredibly short space of time and barely had this been done when Mr. Irving, of the Star Inn, at a smart trot came with his two horses. All things in readiness, the fire brigade started at a swinging gallop for the scene of the fire. They passed rapidly through the principal streets - the Captain blowing his whistle - on into the green hedgerows and past the blossoming orchards of Gresty. It boots not to tell of the hopes and fears of the fire brigade, but it was evident from their temper that deeds of daring would be performed, if needed. Before the burning house was reached the gallant captain told off his men for action. "You are" said he, "to take charge of the sucker and put it into the water" and to another, "you are to run out the hose" and so on. Twenty minutes after the alarm bell was rung, the fire brigade with their apparatus, had reached the burning farmhouse, which is about three miles from Crewe, and is called "The Finger Post Farm" at Shavington, the owner of which is Mr. Ralph Edwards, of Snape Farm, Weston, and the tenant of which is Mr. William Simpson. Mr. Sumner still led the way on horseback, and halted at a wayside pool of water fed by a tiny stream about 220 yards from the farm. There the "sucker" encased in a wicker basket, was speedily lowered into the water, the hose run out, and within a few minutes a strong jet of water was poured over the burning roof.

It is now necessary to explain that the premises which had caught fire was an ancient building, half-timber and half-brick, in the Elizabethan style of architecture, not many of which are scattered throughout Cheshire. In comparatively recent years there had been added to it a brick and slated building entered from the old building by internal communication. It had been thatched at many successive times to a thickness of at least half a yard. This was the cause of the fire. Under the fierce rays of the May sun the thatch had become as dry as tinder, and the mere falling of a spark upon it had set it on fire. There is an oven a short distance from the thatched building, and the good people of the farm had lighted a fire in it with wool, and it is conjectured that a spark was carried from the oven chimney to the thatched roof by the wind, and in an instant set the thatch on fire. Mr. Simpson's little son William, about four or five years of age, first noticed the burning thatch. He told James Wilson, a servant lad, who at once gave information to Mr. Simpson, and he immediately got onto the burning roof, where he was speedily joined by a man named Johnson, who was passing, and who was in charge of a threshing machine. Finding however, all their efforts to stop the progress of the flames to be fruitless, Mr. Simpson with his assistant directed all his attention to the removal of furniture, and in the course of half-an-hour they cleared the thatched portion of the building of everything removable. These household goods were all flung down promiscuously in a blossoming orchard, and a most curious spectacle was presented by clocks, cheffoniern, fenders, bed-posts etc. being all scattered about under the trees. It was at that, moment when the rooms had been cleared that the fire brigade arrived at the scene. The fire, after covering the entire extent of the thatch, attacked the wooden eaves of the Elizabethan gables, and had descended to the tile-covered junction or doorway, leading to the more newly erected portion of the building when the fire brigade opposed the further progress of the fire in this direction. In fact Sergeant Porter, who handled the jet, speedily extinguished the flames here and also at, the wooden eaves, after which he played upon the thatch, while Mr. Herd, Secretary, Mr. Wood, High Street, Mr. Collier and others of the brigade prevented the falling thatch from setting fire to the flooring of the upper stories. This was a work of exceeding difficulty, as pieces of burning wood and thatch were constantly falling in from the roof; but the persistent effort of the firemen, aided by a constant supply of water brought by the inmates of the farm-house, were successful, and in little more than an hour after the brigade arrived at the fire, they had utterly extinguished the flames. Mr. Wood as a finish poured a stream of water upon the smouldering thatch lying upon the ground, the refraction of the sun's rays upon the ground, the refraction of the sun's rays upon the water as it poured across the darkened doorway forming a beautiful rainbow, or rather bringing out all the beautiful colours of the rainbow. Many visitors from Crewe were at the fire, among them were Messrs. Leech, Victoria Street; T.H.Heath, and Thomas Bolshaw, and these gentlemen willingly lent a helping hand. The promptitude with which the brigade were upon the spot and extinguished the flames reflects the greatest credit upon them, and it should be noted in justice to the Nantwich Fire Brigade that they received no notice of the fire. Fortunately Mr. Edwards, the landlord, had the premises fully insured; and therefore the damage, which is estimated at about £100, will not fall upon him. *(Guardian).*

February 1878 - The rising town of Crewe is generally very free from fires, and when a fire does break out it is crushed out on the shortest notice by our energetic firemen. About midnight on Wednesday last the loud pealing alarm bell startled Crewe, and speedily the inhabitants went trooping to the scene of the fire. This was at the house of Mr. Joyce, boiler-maker, Longford Street, on Nantwich Road, where Miss Joyce, before retiring for the night, and whilst downstairs, became oppressed with a sense of heat and difficulty of breathing, upon which, instinct led her upstairs to the bedroom of her three little brothers to see if all was safe. Here there was a suffocating smoke, while the little lads slept on. They were got into a place of safety, and nearly all the furniture removed at the time, when Mr. Bibley, the active manager for the Messrs. Rylands and Son, P.C. Oldfield, and Mr. Laing, secretary of the Crewe Volunteer Fire Brigade, arrived at the spot. Mr. Bibley discovered an intense heat in the ceiling above the bedroom and they soon discovered that the fire had caught hold of the joists or rafters extending from the chimney, which was on fire. Meanwhile Sergeant Porter went to give the alarm and to rouse up his men, who in a very short time gathered at the alarm of the fire bell, and rushed off with their fire-extinguishing apparatus to Nantwich Road. Here, however, there was an immense deal of grumbling, as the men had to stand idle for nearly ten minutes, because although the water was turned on at Station Street, nearly a quarter of a mile distant, yet it took some little time to fill the pipes and reach the waiting firemen. They, however, were not idle, as by a thin jet from the taps, they were able to pour buckets of water in through the roof. At last the water poured through the maize, and in the course of half-an-hour all danger to the property was over. Great credit is due to Mr. Bibley for his prompt and energetic measures; and this, with the praiseworthy and rapid action of the Crewe Fire Brigade, prevented a great and serious fire. The following were the contingent of the brigade who assisted in extinguishing the fire: Sergeant Porter, Sergeant Turton, J. Laing, (secretary), Messrs. Proudlove, Farr, Ollier, Hough, Taylor and Lowndes. Praise is also due to Mr. Johnson, foreman to Mr. Cotterill, who kindly rendered considerable assistance. The damage done is trifling. *(Guardian).*

April 1878 - A startling alarm was raised that the beautiful tower of Christ Church, which has just been finished, was on fire. Information was at once conveyed to Mr. Eardley, and soon a crowd began to gather attracted by the lurid glare of fire thrown from the summit of the tower. A passing fireman hurried to the fire station and got the apparatus in readiness in case of necessity, while Mr. Eardley went to Mr. Baxendale, the foreman's house, and hurried with him to the summit of the tower. Here they found that a workman had left a brazier of coals alight in dangerous proximity to a quantity of pitch and tar; and if there had been a strong wind blowing in that direction some serious consequences might have ensued. The fire in the brazier was soon extinguished, and all danger of a fire removed. *(Guardian).*

November 1882 - Two ricks of hay belonging to Mr. William Allman, of Crewe, were discovered to be on fire and the Crewe Volunteer Fire Brigade had to be called to extinguish the flames. Damage to the extent of £60 or £70 was done. The stacks were five years old, and therefore the fire could not have been caused by spontaneous combustion. The idea is favoured that it was a '5th of November' incident. *(Guardian).*

November 1882 - A fire broke out on the premises of Mr. Leech, broker, Victoria Street, Crewe. The fire had got such a hold that it caught some portion of an adjoining house and considerably damaged it, but the fire brigade being promptly on the spot, it was got under, and the progress of the flames stayed. The damage done is estimated at several hundred pounds. The cause of the fire is said to have been the leakage of paraffin from a cask which flowed down to the cellar and became ignited. *(Guardian).*

January 1884 - A fire, which broke out through the over-heating of the stove pipes, was discovered at Scotch School, Heath Street, Crewe. The Volunteer Fire Brigade were promptly on the spot, and extinguished it before a great deal of damage was done. *(Cheshire Observer).*

August 1885 - A serious fire broke out in a house in New Street, Crewe, the property of the London and N.W.R. A man named Taylor was boiling some tar over the fire when the bucket upset. The room was immediately in flames, an alarm was given, and the town and railway company's fire brigades were promptly on the spot. After a time the fire was subdued, though not until considerable damage was done. *(Liverpool Echo).*

October 1885 - A little boy named Walter Fotherby living in Ramsbottom Street, Crewe, was burned to death. He had scarlet fever, and was lying in bed with a fire in the room. During the temporary absence of his mother he got out of bed, and his night-shirt caught fire. Dr John Atkins was promptly in attendance, but the poor boy died in half-an-hour. *(Cheshire Observer).*

October 1886 - The Crewe fire brigade were called to a fire in the market ground, Crewe. The fire had broken out in a tent with hobby horses belonging to a man named Collins, of Chester, and before it was extinguished damage estimated at £250 was done to the hobby horses. The fire was supposed to have been caused by the engine. *(Cheshire Observer).*

July 1887 - An alarming fire broke out at the South Cheshire Brewery, Wistaston Road, Crewe, which belonged to Mr. E. S. Woolf, and before it could be extinguished the contents of the building were completely destroyed. It appears a workman was in the upper storey of the brewery grinding the malt for the following day's brewery, and it is supposed that a flint was in the malt, for suddenly an explosion occurred, and the room was set on fire. An alarm was given, and the fire bell was rung. The Crewe Voluntary Fire Brigade under the command of Captain Fineberg and Lieutenant Green, were soon on the spot, but on account of combustible nature of the contents the fire had then gained a strong hold upon the building, and the roof gave way with a crash just as the brigade came up. The Crewe Works Fire Brigade, under the direction of Superintendent Kerr and Captain Kenyon, also promptly arrived. There was happily a plentiful supply of water close at hand, the town brigade engine drawing its supply from the Valley Brook, whilst the Works Brigade drew theirs from the railway hydrants, the pressure from which was sufficient to carry the water over any part of the building. It was found that the fire had obtained such a hold upon the brewery that there was no possibility of saving any portion of its contents, and therefore efforts were directed towards the protection of the back building, which was in danger. This was saved altogether. The fire burned fiercely for about three hours, and it was at one time feared that the intense heat would cause the outside walls, upon which rested two heavy chimneys, to give way, but a plentiful stream of water served to cool the masonry and keep the walls intact. There were two large tanks in the building, and during the process of the fire one of these at the top of the building gave way and fell down with a terrible crash. The other tank seemed securely fastened into the walls. The fire smouldered during the greater part of the day, and the volunteer firemen remained pouring water upon the ruins till afternoon, when all danger was over. The building was entirely gutted, and the damage is estimated at about £2,000 which is fully covered by insurance. A force of police, under the direction of Inspector Oldham and P.S. Batty, were on duty at the fire, and kept the crowd from approaching too near the building. *(Chronicle).*

August 1887 - A blaze broke out in a haystack on the farm of Mr. Arthur Cooke, at Weston. The flames ignited a corn stack close by, and on account of there being no water near there was danger of it spreading to some cottage property. A messenger was despatched to Crewe Hall for the fire engine belonging to Lord Crewe, and when this arrived the fire was got under and extinguished. It is not known how the fire originated. (*Cheshire Observer*).

January 1889 - A serious fire occurred at the United Methodist Free Church, Hightown, Crewe. As the children were assembling in the Sunday school, smoke was observed issuing from the windows at the chapel adjoining. In an entrance being affected the building was found on fire. The fire brigade were quickly summoned, and every effort made to prevent the flames spreading. Ladders were raised against the building, and a plentiful supply of water was poured in through the windows. The organ, a fine instrument just presented, fell, and the orchestra was burnt out. The fire was confined to the west end of the building, and before it was extinguished two vestries, the organ and choir seats, and a portion of the side galleries were destroyed. Two men who went into the chapel were overcome by smoke, and one was hurt by a falling window. The chapel was one of the finest structures in Crewe, and had only just been erected at a cost of £5,000. The damage done amounts to considerably over £1,000. The fire is supposed to have been caused by the overheating of the apparatus used for warming the chapel. *(Chester Courant).*

April 1891 - Some excitement was caused at Crewe by the fire alarm from the North Western Railway Company's extensive works. It was thought that the fire had broken out in the works, but it was found to be in an old carriage shed in Britannic grounds near Crewe Station. Besides burning the shed, the fire caught a sleeper fence, which was also destroyed. The shed was occupied by some footballers during the afternoon. *(Cheshire Observer).*

April 1891 - A fire broke out on the farm of Mr. Fellows at Wistaston. With commendable promptitude a staff of eighteen men, under Superintendent Lumb, proceeded with the engine to the farm, and found that a stack of twenty tons of hay was burning fiercely. A couple of branches were brought into play, the water being pumped from an adjacent pit, and after some hours' hard work the flames were got under. By clever manipulation of the limited supply of water Mr. Lumb saved a large portion of the stack, which, it is believed, is insured. *(Chester Courant).*

June 1891 - Two constables discovered a fire in a building belonging to Mr. Laycock, Casson Street, Crewe. An alarm was given, and the fire brigade turned out and directed a plentiful supply of water on the premises. Four horses in a stable were rescued with difficulty, one of them being badly burned. A quantity of hay and straw and some machinery were destroyed, and the building was destroyed. *(Cheshire Observer).*

November 1891 - Elizabeth Barnes, a little girl, aged five years, of Bowling Green, Crewe, was burned to death. Her father is on tramp for work, and while her mother was out charing the child lighted a candle and held it to her mouth like a cigar. The fire caught her clothing, which was instantly a mass of flames. Her screams attracted the neighbours to the house. The child was shockingly burned, and died soon after. *(Manchester Courier and Lancashire Advertiser).*

March 1892 - The most disastrous fire that had ever been witnessed in the history of Crewe occurred at night on 28th March 1892 in an important part of the great railway works known as the Deviation. The terrible conflagration first originated in the outdoor department of the works, which is situated at the extreme end of the Deviation. The fire must have been raging for some time before it was discovered, and although there is an open space on either side of this large workshop, no one seems to have perceived anything of the flames until just before they burst forth in a tremendous volume through the long roofing. Immediately the conflagration was perceived an alarm was raised, and in less than three minutes after the Works' 'fire buzzer' had sounded the members of the Works Fire Brigade had assembled in Eaton Street, and were speedily on their way to the scene of the terrible outbreak. The fire broke out in that part of the works where most of the material is kept for the repairs of the whole of the out-door department, and in which is contained an enormous quantity of valuable machinery for the construction of water columns, stationery engines, and other important appliances in connection with this special department, which is under the superintendence of Mr. W. Adamson and a staff of foremen.

Within a very few minutes of the alarm being given, the fire brigade arrived with several hand engines, and were under the command of Superintendents Kerr and Oke, Captain Kenyon, and Lieutenant Gibson. It was at once seen by the officials of the brigade that it was impossible to battle with the fiery tyrant at the end of the out-station nearest to the chain-making department, which was by the time, one mass of flames, and for upwards of an hour all communication with this part was entirely cut off through the intense heat. Most of the chief officials of the railway company at Crewe were on the spot almost as soon as the fire brigade, and amongst them was Mr. F.W. Webb, Superintendent of Crewe Works. Mr. Webb superintended the arrangements, and under his directions strenuous efforts were made to prevent the adjoining pattern shop and joiners' establishment being enveloped - a most arduous task for those assisting in getting the flames under control. Finding that no headway could be made in the vicinity of the out-station shop, the greater portion of the roof having fallen-in in less than a quarter of an hour after the alarm had been raised, the firemen directed their attention to the millwrights' shop, which soon presented a burning mass. A fire-proof wall divided the millwrights' department from the pattern shop, and several firemen mounted the roof with a view, if possible, of limiting the area of deviation. The men ran considerable risk, but despite this fact, they battled with the flames in a vigorous manner, and after working for upwards of two hours, it seemed as though they had been successful in confining the fiery element to the out-station shop, the chain-making department and the millwrights' shop. Had the flames once obtained a hold on the pattern shop nothing could have prevented the most important block of buildings in connection with Crewe Works being burnt to the ground, besides meaning the utter destruction of a considerable number of houses, situated in close proximity to the joinering department. Through the strenuous efforts of the brigade, together with the company's officials, what would otherwise have been a more frightful calamity was happily averted.

While a portion of the fire brigade were guarding the pattern shop, the other members of the brigade were busily engaged in checking the progress of the fire towards the testing department of the chain shop, at the other side of which there is a very large chimney. Once or twice it seemed as though the flames were going to spread in this direction, but the firemen and the officials worked bravely. Frequently they had to retreat in consequence of the flames, and the dense volumes of smoke, but as soon as they had sufficiently recovered, they returned to their post, and fought hard to master the destructive tyrant. By eleven o'clock, one half of the Deviation, including the out-door department, the chain-making and millwrights' shops, was all ablaze, and the sky was lit up for miles around. The fire had so far spread with alarming rapidity, and the onlookers, who had congregated in thousands on the outside of this particular portion of the works were completely terrified to witness the alarming proportions which it was assuming. For fully two hours great excitement prevailed, which became more intense as minute by minute portions of the roofing gave way and fell with a loud crash into the burning debris below. It is fortunate that the anxious crowd were unable to get too near the scene of the fire, for they would only have proved a hindrance to the brigade at so critical a time.

The origin of the fire is not known, but judging from the alarming proportions it had assumed before the alarm 'buzzer' was blown, it is evident that it had been raging in the interior for an hour or two before it was discovered. It is difficult to estimate, even approximately, the amount of damage done. In a certain sense some of the injury is almost irreparable and nothing like a complete valuation can be made for some days. But rough computations that have already been made lead us to suppose that the damage is most excessive, and will probably be about £40,000. Several hundred hands will be thrown out of employment for many weeks in consequence of the serious disaster. *(Guardian).*

September 1892 - As a goods train was leaving Crewe Station for Liverpool, one of the vans laden with barrels was noticed to be on fire. The train was shunted, and the van was detached and placed under a water tank, but on account of the inflammable nature of the contents, great difficulty was experienced in extinguishing the fire. The van and contents were destroyed. The origin of the fire is unknown. *(Cheshire Observer).*

April 1893 - A serious fire broke out on the farm of Mr. Thomas Cliffe, Crewe Gates. The fire was observed in one of eleven stacks of wheat, barley, clover, etc and soon spread to the whole of them, which was quickly ablaze. There was a strong wind, which blew straight in the line of the outbuildings which adjoin the farmhouse. The Crewe Fire Brigade were on the spot in a few minutes; but the flames had got such a hold on the stacks that it was useless to try to save them. Efforts were made to prevent the fire spreading to the buildings, and these were successful. The fire burned for several hours, and the whole of eleven stacks were completely destroyed, the damage being about £1,000 which is covered by insurance. It was ascertained that the fire was caused through a child playing with matches near the stacks. A number of trees in Lord Crewe's park were scorched by the heat. *(Crewe Chronicle).*

September 1893 - A constable passing the Euston Coffee Tavern, Crewe, early this morning noticed volumes of smoke coming from the cellars. The fire bell and the railway buzzer alarmed the Crewe Works Brigade and the Borough Brigade, who found some waste material on fire in the cellars, having evidently been smouldering all night. The fire was promptly extinguished. The property belongs to the North Western Railway, and adjoins the town hall and library. *(Liverpool Echo).*

November 1893 - A disastrous fire broke out on the premises of Mr. Jones, farmer, of Woolstanwood, near Crewe. The fire was first observed in the hayloft, where a large quantity of fodder was stored. The flames spread with alarming rapidity. The Crewe Fire Brigade attended, and did their best to extinguish the flames, but the premises were gutted, the damage being estimated at £500. The fire is believed to be the work of incendiary. It is somewhat singular that several similar conflagrations have occurred near Crewe within a few months. *(Chester Courant).*

January 1895 - An alarm of fire was raised at Crewe and the town bell was rung. Several members of the Corporation Fire Brigade quickly assembled at the Central Fire Station, where they were informed that a fire had broken out in the establishment of Mr. Leeming, tobacconist and hairdresser, Liverpool Bridge. They proceeded to the shop, but the fire, which had been confined to the window, had by this time been extinguished by Mrs. Leeming and a number of helpers. The cause of the outbreak was the dropping of a window blind on a gas jet, the blind being burnt away, and damage was also done to the contents of the window, a large glass shelf on which some fancy articles were placed being smashed. *(Guardian).*

April 1895 - Another fire broke out at Bank Farm, belonging to Mr. G.F. Whittacker, and situated on the Crewe Hall estate, near Haslington. The Crewe Fire brigade, under Lieutenant Grieves and Captain Harding, and Crewe Hall Fire Brigade who were captained by Mr. B. Dunkley were quickly on the spot and found the fire confined to an out-building which contained a large quantity of oats, hay, straw and other farm produce. A plentiful supply of water was obtained from a pit near, and efforts were made with a view of preventing the spread of the fire. The cattle, horses, fowls etc had all been got safely out of the building, but the other contents were all destroyed, and the roof was dismantled. The damage was estimated at about £400, which was fully covered by the Royal Exchange Assurance. The fire is supposed to have been caused by someone smoking in the building. (*Chronicle).*

April 1895 - A fire was discovered in the carpenter's and joiner's shop, a building in close proximity to Crewe Hall, the Cheshire seat of Lord Houghton. The Crewe Hall fire bell was rung, and the estate Brigade, under the direction of Mr. Dunkley, arrived, and were soon ready to work. They had some difficulty, however, in starting, as the hydrants were in the building that was on fire. Another hydrant was found, and a plentiful supply of water was poured into the building. The contents were of a rotten inflammable character, and the building had got well ablaze, and threatened the stables. It being thought that the local Brigade might not be able to get the fire under control a mounted messenger was despatched for the Crewe Corporation Brigade. These were soon on the scene, under the command of Lieutenant Grieves and Captain Harding. The Crewe Hall Brigade had, however, in the meantime got the fire well in hand and the Crewe brigade stood by to render service if necessary. The horses had all been got out of the stables and away from the building. Fortunately there was no wind (it was a clear frosty night), and therefore the Hall was not endangered. The carpenters shop and contents (including the tools of the workmen) were all destroyed. Much praise is due to the Crewe Hall Fire Brigade for the energetic way in which they worked to extinguish the flames, and no less credit is due to the Crewe Corporation Brigade for the promptitude of their arrival ready to give whatever assistance was required in case of emergency. How the fire originated cannot definitely be ascertained. The damage is estimated at several hundreds of pounds. *(Chronicle).*

May 1896 - The Crewe Works Fire Brigade were called to an outbreak of fire in one of the offices of the Cattle Traffic Department at Crewe Station. The building was used as a store for correspondence etc. connected with the department, and among the mass of papers the fire appeared to have originated. Superintendent Warneford and Captain Kenyon were soon on the scene, and there being a good supply of water the fire was prevented from spreading to the adjoining building. The office in which the fire started was however gutted, and the papers were destroyed. The flames from the office scorched the side of the privilege ticket office. They also caught some tar fencing which divided the Britannia Ground, and the clouds of dense smoke from this caused people to think that the fire was one of considerable dimension. The damage to the building is estimated at about £50. The cause of the fire could not be ascertained. *(Chronicle).*

May 1896 - The Crewe Fire Brigade were called to 66, Chetwode Street, occupied by Mr. Walley. The fire was confined to the back portion of the house, being in fact the door and frame leading from the kitchen to the back kitchen, which was in flames. The fire was promptly extinguished before much damage was done. The fire is supposed to have been caused by some matches in a coat behind the door having become ignited, for the coat appeared to have been first burnt, and this caught the door. *(Chronicle).*

January 1898 - A fire broke out in a house in Smallman Road, Crewe, occupied by Mr. Boag, photographer. The occupants were away. The fire raged and spread to the adjoining house occupied by Mr. Thompson, and involved the roof of a third house, but was checked by the Fire Brigade. Messrs. Boag and Thompson's houses were gutted, and their furniture destroyed. The fire is supposed to have been caused by a spark from the kitchen grate. *(Liverpool Echo).*

October 1899 - Crewe Fire Brigade were summoned to a serious outbreak of fire at Eardswick Hall, Minshull Vernon, occupied by Mr. Charles B. Davies, secretary to the Cheshire Chamber of Agriculture, and a member of the Cheshire County Council. The conflagration originated in the middle portion of a large block of buildings which are in the shape of a quadrangle. The flames rapidly gained a strong hold on this portion of the building, which contained tons of unthreshed oats, and several farm implements. The Brigade directed their attention to saving the remaining portion of the building, in which valuable implements were stored, and also a large number of stacks which were only a few yards away from the burning mass. The buildings are of modern design, fitted with fire-proof walls throughout, and to this must be attributed the fact that the fire was practically confined to the central portion of the building, in which the outbreak originated. The damage is considerable. It is supposed the fire originated through someone smoking in the buildings. *(Cheshire Observer).*

November 1900 - An alarming fire broke out in a warehouse in Gresty Terrace, Crewe, in the occupation of Mr. Turner, boot and shoe manufacturer. The occupants of an adjoining house - a young couple named Davenport - had their attention attracted by a strong smell of fire, and on getting up they discovered that the street was full of smoke and that flames were proceeding from the roof of the warehouse. Mr. Davenport made speedy tracks for the Corporation Fire Station, and having given the alarm, the members of the Corporation Fire Brigade were quickly summoned by means of the electrical communication attached to each fireman's house. In about six minutes the brigade with Captain Harding and Lieutenant Roberts in command had arrived at the scene of the conflagration with the reel cart. They promptly ran out a length of hose, but to their utter astonishment they found, on coupling up to the hydrant in Hungerford Road that the water was off. Mr. Eaton-Shore, the superintendent of the brigade, who lives in the same locality, was immediately fetched, and it then transpired that the water in this part of the town had been cut off from eleven o'clock the previous night, owing to the fact that a number of workmen in the employ of the London and North Western Railway Company were engaged in laying a new water main along the Liverpool line. The operations of the firemen were, of course, greatly hampered through there being no water and nearly half an hour elapsed before they were able to play upon the flames. While a messenger was despatched to instruct the railway officials to turn the water on to the Earle Street mains, several of the firemen returned to the engine house for the manual. As two of Messrs. Ward's horses were in readiness, no time was lost in running the engine to a large pit in a field close to the Manchester line, but some considerable distance away from the burning building. From this pit a good supply of water was obtainable, but owing to the serious delay which had been occasioned, the warehouse was by this time all ablaze, and the flames were shooting upwards in great masses.

For quite three-quarters of an hour the spectacle was a grand and imposing one. Aided by a rather strong wind, blowing from the direction of Hungerford Road, the fire raged furiously, until the entire roof became a roaring mass of flames, throwing showers of sparks high into the air, some being carried by the wind into the field where the pumpers, who worked manfully under the direction of Sergeant Jervis, were engaged with the fire engine. The fire burned with such fierceness that at one time the building presented the appearance of a huge furnace, and so intense was the heat that the work of the brigade was rendered exceedingly perilous. The fact of the fire assuming such serious proportions caused the utmost alarm in the neighbourhood, and scenes of great excitement were witnessed, terrified women and frightened children anxiously watching the efforts of the firemen as they desperately fought to obtain the mastery of the flames, and to prevent the spread of the fire to the adjoining property. The house in which Mr. and Mrs. Davenport reside, and which, as we have already stated, is next door to the factory, was for a while in imminent danger of becoming ignited; so much so that it was deemed advisable to carry all the furniture into the street. The walls became red hot, and had it not been for the roof of the dwelling being considerably higher than that of the factory, which was only a one-storey building, nothing could have prevented the house from falling a victim to the flames.

Under the able guidance of their officers, the firemen worked strenuously with a view of checking the spread of the fire, and by about half-past three o'clock they succeeded in getting it fairly under control though they continued to play upon the smouldering debris until close upon six o'clock. The building was practically gutted, and a quantity of valuable machinery, including a gas engine, was considerably damaged by fire and water. The fire proved to be the most disastrous that had occurred in Crewe for quite a number of years, the loss being estimated at upwards of £1,000 and we understood that it is only partially covered by insurance. How the fire originated is a mystery.

The premises were built several years ago, and were originally used as a football factory. They were subsequently converted into a sweet manufactory, and for some months past had been rented by Mr. Turner in connection with his business as a boot and shoe manufacturer. *(Guardian).*

November 1903 - A serious fire was discovered on the farm of Mr. Samuel Brerton at Weston, near Crewe, the estate of Sir Delves Broughton. The outbreak occurred in an outbuilding in which was sorted a large quantity of hay, and the mass was soon well alight. The Crewe Corporation steam fire engine, the Crewe Hall Estate Fire Brigade and the Weston Fire Brigade were quickly on the scene, and a plentiful supply of water was thrown on to the fire, but most of the contents were destroyed. The fire is supposed to be due to an incendiary. *(Manchester Courier and Lancashire Advertiser).*

July 1904 - A fire was discovered in the stackyard at Moss Farm, Warmingham, occupied by Mr. Levi Stubbs and belonging to the Earl of Crewe. The Crewe steam fire engine was dispatched to the farm, but the scarcity of water for some time impeded the efforts of the brigade to extinguish the fire. The fire was prevented from spreading to adjoining property. The stackshed, however, was gutted and the contents destroyed, the damage being estimated at about £200. The brigade worked for 14 hours on the burning mass. The origin of the fire could not be ascertained. The loss is partially covered by insurance. *(Staffordshire Advertiser).*

March 1905 - One of the largest fires for many years took place in the Cabinet and Joinering Works of the Crewe Co-operative Friendly Society, at the rear of Market Street. The Co-operative Society have centralised many of their industrial departments in Market Street and here also are stored the bulk of the goods which are in constant demand by their patrons. Great extensions of the premises have of late years become necessary, and a cabinet department and timber store have been provided at the rear of the boot and shoe department, forming, with the bakery, almost a square block of buildings, extending from Market Street to the back of Old Whitegates.

It was in the rearmost of these buildings that the fire occurred. The dimensions of the buildings affected were 40 yards by 10 yards, and containing two storeys. In these buildings were the cabinet manufactory, the wheelwright's shop, the dynamic sheds, stables providing accommodation for nearly 40 horses, and a harness room.

The premises were locked up securely at 5.30 the previous night, at which hour the employees left off work. It was seen by employees of the society about an hour before midnight, and then appeared to be perfectly secure. Constable Evans, who was patrolling the district, passed the building as late as one o'clock in the morning, and it then appeared to be all right, while pedestrians passing in close proximity did not perceive anything wrong.

During this time it was conjectural that the outbreak, which is supposed to have been caused by a fusing of an electric wire in the office of the cabinet department, must have been smouldering and making rapid progress. Suddenly the smouldering materials were wafted into flames, and spread with amazing rapidity. A baker named Coffin, who was proceeding to work at this time, became alarmed on seeing such an intense glare issuing from the building. On raising an alarm, Coffin encountered Constable Evans, and the two made their way to the fire station, which is immediately opposite the scene of the fire.

The brigade quickly arrived on the scene, and with the new steam engine they soon got the hose into play. Their operations were, however, greatly hampered owing to the limited supply of water which was available, it being customary to shut off a considerable amount of water during the night. A messenger was despatched to the residence of the Borough Surveyor, Mr. G. Eaton-Shore, in Hungerford Road, and in about twenty minutes a full supply of water was coursing through the mains.

Meanwhile the conflagration had been spreading with remarkable rapidity, and the sky was lit up with a lurid light, visible miles distant. A large number of horses, stabled at the far end of the building, were fortunately taken from the building, although not without much difficulty, and much assistance was rendered by the employees of the society. The Brigade, continuing to work with an ardour well worthy of such a cause, succeeded in effectively choking the further spreading of the fire, which was now raging fast and furiously.

About three o'clock the onlookers were startled by the collapse of the uppermost part of the building and many of the bystanders had narrow escapes from the falling debris. Fireman Collier was injured by some falling masonry, although fortunately his injuries were not very serious, and he continued to work with his colleagues.

A number of iron girders supporting the upper part of the building were twisted into all manner of shapes by the intense heat, while the paint on buildings in close proximity was blistered and burnt. The firemen were still engaged in the work of quelling the flames, which after causing havoc on every hand began gradually to subside. Great fears were entertained owing to the close proximity of a huge cauldron of petroleum, which the flames at one time threatened to envelop. Had this become ignited, the result would probably have been the destruction of the whole block of buildings. Happily this was prevented by the strenuous exertions of the firemen, who at length effectively quelled the outbreak in this portion of the building.

At nine o'clock nothing remained but a pile of smouldering ruins, with debris scattered on every hand. A large quantity of valuable machinery and plant were destroyed, while of the furniture and timber, which the building had previously contained, nothing remained but smouldering embers. The damage is estimated at no less a sum than £2,000. The building and effects were, however, fully insured. The departments destroyed gave employment to about 30 men. *(Guardian).*

December 1907 - A serious fire was discovered on the premises of Mr. Coppal, a grocer and provision dealer, carrying on business in Oak Street, Crewe. The shop was locked at the time of the outbreak, as Mr. Coppal was away at Stafford where he had a stall in the market every Saturday. Smoke was seen issuing in great volumes from the premises and an alarm was raised. The Corporation and Works Fire Brigades were speedily summoned, and, upon arrival found that the front room above the shop was well alight and the contents, consisting of a large quantity of miscellaneous goods were burning fiercely. Several lengths of hose were run out, and, although there was a plentiful supply of water, the room and its contents were practically destroyed, and serious damage was done by fire and water to other parts of the house and shop. On arrival of the brigades the smoke was so dense that several of the firemen were almost overcome in attempting to enter the room where the fire originated. *(Staffordshire Sentinel).*

March 1910 - One of the most disastrous fires that have occurred in Crewe for many years broke out during the early hours, resulting in the entire destruction of the Opera House in Heath Street. The company occupying the boards for the week was Mr. D. Thomas's pantomime in 'Dick Whittington.' They had had a very successful week up to Thursday night, and when they left the theatre about 11.15 everything appeared all right. Mr. Ambrose Fischer, the manager of the theatre, remained behind with his wife and child and shortly after twelve o'clock as he was about to leave the building he made, as was his custom, an examination of the premises. Proceeding from his office to the pit-stalls below he noticed a strong smell of something burning. He at once rushed to the entrance of the stage door, which had been locked up by the staff. He then noticed smoke issuing from underneath the stage, and without losing a moment he hurried and gave an alarm. At first he rushed across to the fire station, which is only a few yards away, and returning he made a gallant attempt to get onto the stage, where a number of hydrants were kept. He broke down a door, but was met with a great volume of smoke. This drove him back for a while, but after recovering somewhat he made a blind rush into the building. He almost reached the hydrants, when he was overpowered, and fell to the ground. At this point a fireman appeared on the scene, and seeing Mr. Fischer's perilous position he with commendable promptitude dashed on to the stage and succeeded in dragging him out. A minute later flames shot out right and left across the stage, and had it not been for the fireman's timely rescue the manager would have undoubtedly perished in the flames. The fire proof curtain, which had only recently been erected, was drawn after the night's performance, and this kept the flames confined for a time to the back part of the theatre. The brigade attempted to concentrate them here, but the property on the stage was of such an inflammable nature - consisting of canvas scenery and tons of light wood work - that their task was impossible. The fire had got such a firm hold that the destruction of the whole building seemed inevitable, and the adjoining property was in imminent danger. Mr. Eaton-Shore with Captain Harding and Lieutenant Roberts were in charge of the Corporation Fire Brigade, and in view of the serious outlook they deemed it advisable to call out the L. and N.W. Railway Fire Brigade. They responded to the call with remarkable promptitude, and aided by the high pressure main, which belongs to the railway company, and under excellent supervision of Captain Earp rendered valuable assistance. The fire spread with lightening like rapidity. From the apartments beneath the stage the flames forced their way through the platform, and into the wings, where all the gorgeous and valuable scenery belonging to the pantomime company was stored, and after devouring this they shot up into the roof, which was nearly 100 feet from the bottom. Notwithstanding that there was a tremendous volume of water being poured on to the flames the fire raged furiously.

The fall of the roof over the stage caused the safety curtain to collapse, and then the flames shot out into the auditorium. The orchestra, where many of the musicians had left their instruments, was rapidly enveloped in the flames and consumed and in turn the pit stalls fell victims. In half an hour the whole place was like a red hot furnace. The circle and the galleries fell with a thud, and then the other part of the roof crashed in. The flames lit up the skies, and the reflection could be seen for a radius of twenty miles.

At Nantwich Captain Thistlethwaite, of the Nantwich Brigade, saw the illuminated skies, and he set out on his bicycle to be of service if required. He did useful work; in fact all the firemen worked manfully. When they found the hopelessness of saving the theatre they directed their attention to the adjoining property, and to keep the high surrounding walls of the theatre cool by spraying them with a good supply of water. Had these walls collapsed the adjacent property would have not only suffered great damage by the fall, but they would have been in great peril of the flames. As it was the high walls confined the fire to the building alone, and it was the splendid work of the firemen in this direction that saved the other buildings. At half-past two the fire was at its fiercest, and the heat from the blazing furnace was intense. Hundreds of people turned out to witness the sight, but in view of the dangerous condition of the walls, which were out of plumb to the extent of one to one and half feet, the police, under the personal command of Superintendent Pearson and Inspector Sudlow, kept them at a safe distance. It was a magnificent sight when the fire was at its height. Nothing has been seen in Crewe to equal it since the great Deviation fire, when one portion of the works was completely destroyed.

It was not until about six o'clock that the firemen had the flames perfectly in hand. With the exception of the manager's office, and one side of the Dutch bar belonging to the circle, and one or two steel pillars, which held the circle together, everything had collapsed. Under the stage there is a well many feet deep and into this almost everything had fallen. The frame of the piano in the orchestra had buckled up, and lay amongst the debris. It was scarcely good enough for scrap iron. The brass rails and piping had all melted away. To view the picture at six o'clock one could scarcely believe that a few hours previous a pretty theatre stood on the site. The fire had done its work completely; in a marvellously short space of time it had wrought havoc. So rapidly did the fire obtain a hold that it was practically impossible to save anything. Had it originated in the auditorium it might have been possible to have saved some of the things on stage.

It was well into the afternoon before the firemen ceased to play on the smouldering debris. They had been hard at work for twelve hours. They had failed to save the theatre, but their splendid work had been the means of saving the property around. It was due to Captain Earp and his men that the fire was prevented from spreading to Miss Rogers' tea rooms next door. The rooms adjoin the two theatre bars, and at some points only a wooden partition separated the two buildings. The gallant captain, despite the dense volume of smoke, stuck to his post heroically. For upwards of an hour he never moved away form the circle corridor, and he must have poured tons of water on to the flames to keep them in check.

The cause of the fire is unknown. Judging from the firm hold which it had obtained when first perceived by Mr. Fischer, there can be little doubt that it had been smouldering for some considerable time. It is supposed that it originated in one of the dressing rooms on the east side underneath the stage. It can only be conjectured that somebody must have dropped a lighted cigarette in one of the rooms. The damage is estimated at about £6,000. This does not include the personal effects of Mr. Dan Thomas' company, which were very considerable. Neither does it include the quantity of valuable scenery belonging to the Crewe St. Paul's Institute. There was also a considerable quantity of beer and spirits destroyed. The building was covered by insurance to the extent of £4,000, but the majority of the other things were not insured. *(Chronicle).*

May 1912 - A warehouse in Chestnut Grove, Crewe, a small cul-de-sac off Richmond Road, was discovered to be on fire on a Sunday morning at 10.30am. The Fire Brigade was summoned and arrived on the scene with all possible haste, only however, to find that the building was blazing like a huge furnace. The flames burst through the windows and eventually through the roof. The heat was so intense that it could be felt quite fifty yards away and for a time the residents of the property in close proximity were very anxious as to the safety of their houses. The line posts in the back yards nearest the building caught fire and to quote some resident's description, they were burning like torches for a time. The Fire Brigade under Captain Harding and Lieutenant Roberts stuck manfully to their task, but they were somewhat handicapped by a poor pressure of water. The contents of the warehouse consisted of toys, dolls, fancy goods, baskets, celluloid articles, children's picture books, picture and photo frames, packing cases and large quantities of enamel and tin ware. When the combustible material was properly alight, there was no hope of saving the stock.

The building was practically gutted, only the four walls, which fortunately were of a very substantial character remaining. Although the Brigade got the fire under control within about an hour, it was not considered wise to leave the building until six o'clock in the evening. The building was stocked with goods from floor to ceiling and only a small quantity was saved in addition to the books of accounts, which were rescued by the manager, Mr. Skidmore.

The cause of the fire is unknown. The damage is estimated at between £2,000 and £3,000 and we understand is covered by insurance. The warehouse was formerly a tailoring factory, and having been in the hands of several firms was taken over on a tenancy by Messrs. Whiston and Co. in October 1910. *(Guardian).*

December 1914 - The Crewe Corporation Fire Brigade were called out to a fire on the farm of Mr. Davenport, at Gresty, near Crewe. A stack of hay, about 20 tons was well alight, which a strong wind rendered dangerous to other stacks near, and a bay and some farm buildings. Captain Harding was in charge of the brigade, Sergeant Jervis assisting. A plentiful supply of water from a pond near was thrown on the burning stack, and about four tons of hay was saved. The Brigade was successful in preventing the fire spreading to the other stacks and farm buildings. The police arrested a man named Thomas Harry Price on suspicion of being the cause of the fire. One or two stack fires have occurred in the same district recently, the origin of which has been mysterious. *(Chronicle).*

January 1917 - A fire broke out at a farmhouse, known as Ragged Castle, in the parish of Haslington, near Radway Green, and occupied by Thomas Bennion. It appears that about two o'clock Mr. Bennion's son, Bertram, was aroused by volumes of smoke, which filled the bedroom. He wakened the occupants of the house, and they got up and went outside, but failed to discover any signs of fire on the exterior of the house. They then made an examination inside the premises, and found that the roof was on fire. A messenger was dispatched for the Alsager Fire Brigade, who arrived on the scene about three o'clock. By this time the fire had got a good hold on the building, fanned as it was by a strong breeze. Mr. Bennion became alarmed about the safety of a considerable quantity of produce in close proximity to the house and he took the precaution to send for the Crewe Volunteer Fire Brigade. The brigade proceeded to the farm with all possible haste, and worked hard with the Alsager men to extinguish the fire. Mr. Bennion and his family succeeded in getting to a place of safety most of the household furniture and effects, but the flames made such headway that it was impossible to remove everything. A quantity of bedding and furniture were destroyed. The building was a very old one, and it had a thatched roof covered with corrugated iron. Connected with the chimney there were two large oak beams. It is supposed that these beams had been smouldering for some time, and that the strong wind caused them to break out into flames and to ignite the old thatched roof. A large portion of the roof was destroyed and the house and furniture were insured. Both fire brigades worked strenuously, and owing to their exertions the fire was prevented from spreading to the produce. *(Guardian).*

February 1917 - The Baptist Church in Union Street had a narrow escape of destruction by fire. During the severe weather the heating apparatus has been kept going. About six o'clock in the evening the caretaker visited the place, and there was no evidence of anything wrong. Just before seven, however, there was an alarm of fire, which appeared to have broken out in the basement underneath the school buildings in Lord Street at the rear of the church. The fire seemed to have got a hold of the wood work of the minister's vestry and the classroom, and was spreading to the Sunday school, which is held in the top room. The Crewe Corporation Fire Brigade, under Captain Harding arrived promptly on the alarm, and the pressure of water being good every effort was made to save the buildings. These fortunately were very largely successful. At one time it was feared the chapel was doomed, but through the strenuous exertions of the firemen, the fire was confined to the school buildings. The minister's vestry, a large classroom, and the furniture were practically destroyed. The school was damaged by fire and water, and the church slightly. There is much pitch pine in the church, and had the fire caught this, it would have been impossible to prevent the interior from being burnt out. The fire, being in the heart of the South Ward, and a most populous district, lit up the surrounding area and for a time there was considerable alarm. Crowds visited the place, but Superintendent Thompson, Inspectors Swords and Whiteley and a force of police were on duty, and everything was done to expedite the work of the fire brigade. Councillor A. Jervis (chairman of the Corporation Water Committee) was also present to see that the fullest pressure of water was available for use. The damage is estimated at some £200 or £300. The buildings are insured. About ten years ago a fire took place in the same area of the building, and practically burnt it out. Much sympathy is felt with the Pastor (Rev. J. Thomas) and the church officials in their additional loss. The Baptist Church in Union Street is one of the best buildings in the neighbourhood, and is closely associated with the names of many of the leading members in Crewe and District. *(Chronicle).*

February 1917 - The Crewe Fire Brigade were called to an outbreak of fire at Mirion House, Earle Street, Crewe, the residence of Dr. Atkinson. The staircase was found to be on fire, but prompt action prevented the flames making much headway, and by the time the Brigade arrived all danger was practically at an end. *(Guardian).*

June 1923 - Crewe Corporation Fire Brigade were called out to a serious outbreak of fire to a cottage situated off Warmingham Road, Coppenhall, opposite the White Lion Hotel. The brigade found the building a mass of flame, and the roof was almost about to collapse. Efforts were made to save some of the furniture in the lower rooms, but the fire had obtained such a firm hold that practically the whole of the contents of the house were destroyed, the building being gutted. It is supposed that the origin of the fire was due to a faulty flue, which caused an accumulation of soot, thus igniting the woodwork of the stairs. The fire, which broke out during the absence of Mr. Martin, the tenant, was first discovered by a neighbour, who was startled to see flames issuing from the roof. He at once raised the alarm and before the arrival of the brigade was successful in enlisting the aid of a number of people in the neighbourhood, who valiantly attempted to cope with the conflagration. The premise had been recently purchased by Mr. Martin who had stripped the old thatch roof and converted the building into a modern dwelling. The damage, which was considerable, is covered by insurance. *(Chronicle).*

September 1925 - Crewe Fire Briagde were engaged for 54 hours continuously at a farm at Old Hall, Barthomley, on the Marquis of Crewe's estate. Twelve stacks of hay were destroyed, the damage being estimated at £2,000. The cause of the fire is unknown. *(Liverpool Echo).*

August 1926 - Mr. and Mrs. Cecil Wilkinson, of 36 Samuel Street, Crewe, were motoring from Shavington to Crewe when the car caught fire and crashed through a fence into a field, near Mr. Hughes' residence in Gresty. Mr. and Mrs. Wilkinson jumped clear of the car, and in doing so Mr. Wilkinson sustained a fractured collar bone, and his wife suffered from shock. Dr. Wilson was sent for and the Crewe Corporation Fire Brigade were summoned and found the car a mass of flames. But they managed to salvage the chassis, engine and a tin of petrol. The body of the car was completely destroyed. *(Staffordshire Sentinel).*

May 1927 - The Crewe Corporation Fire Brigade were called to the farm of Mr. James Moseley, Church House Farm, Warmingham. Within a few minutes of the alarm they were on their way with the new motor engine. Arriving, they discovered that the roof of the homestead was well alight. Some of the slates were quickly removed, and the first-aid extinguisher brought into action, with the result that the flames were subdued in a few minutes. At the time there was a strong breeze blowing, but fortunately, this fanned the flames away from the roof. Had it not been for the prompt response to the call - the fire might have extended and much damage been done. It is supposed that a spark from a chimney set fire to a bird's nest in the spouting of the roof. The damage is estimated at about £20. *(Chronicle).*

December 1927 - The Crewe Corporation Fire Brigade received a call to an outbreak of fire at the residence of Mr. J.W. Palmer, Victoria Street. When they arrived under Chief Officer Collier they found that a beam under the floor of the upstairs sitting-room was ablaze. The brigade soon got to the seat of the fire by taking up the hearth tiles and a number of floorboards. A plentiful supply of water soon extinguished the flames. *(Chronicle).*

June 1929 - A serious fire broke out at Crewe's Town Hall during the early hours of a Sunday morning. The property was owned by the L.M.S. Railway Company and was part of a triangular block of buildings known as the Mechanics' Institute. The fire had secured a firm hold by the time the Works Fire Brigade and the Crewe Corporation Fire Brigade were on the scene, and as a result, the hall, science class room and the staircases were completely gutted as the roof collapsed and tons of masonry and heavy beams crashed onto the ballroom floor. Fortunately the newsroom, library and social club were not affected by the fire although the contents, which included valuable paintings, were damaged by water and smoke. This was the second serious fire at the Mechanics' Institute in Prince Albert Street. It had suffered partial destruction in 1869 after a blaze. *(Chronicle).*

October 1929 - The Crewe Mechanics' Institute and Social Club were threatened with destruction for the second time this year when an outbreak of fire occurred in a warehouse at the rear of a grocer's shop in Earle Street, Crewe. The shop is in the island block of property of which the club and Institute form a part. The fire was discovered when a porter at the club noticed a smell of burning. He looked through a window to see if anything was wrong, and saw the warehouse blazing. He immediately sounded the alarm that connects the L.M.S. Deviation gates, at which centre warnings to the L.M.S. Fire Brigade are given. The brigade, on arrival, found the shed burning fiercely. Papers, books, and a quantity of firewood were destroyed, and, but for the prompt action of the porter, the flames would have reached the club. Already they were attacking a roof under the club premises, but the brigade limited the affected area. Aided later by the Crewe Borough Brigade, which was called out by police officers, the firemen extinguished the fire. Two men were kept on duty throughout the night in case of a recurrence of the outbreak. *(Evening Sentinel).*

Otober 1930 - Combustion underneath an oven is stated to be the cause of an outbreak of fire at Messrs. F. W. Whiston's Toy Factory, Mill Street, Crewe. Mr. J. Boatwright, an engineman employed at the factory, was going on duty when he noticed smoke coming from a large building at the rear of the premises, known as the gilding department, and which is a fire-proof structure. Immediately he opened the doors to investigate the cause and was met with dense fumes. He summoned the fire brigade, who fought their way into the building to reach the seat of the outbreak, which was concentrated under one of the ovens used in the gilding process. There were no flames; otherwise the whole of the building would have been endangered. In close proximity was a large quantity of highly inflammable liquid, which was used in the gilding process. This was moved into the street out of all danger. The firemen had to scrape out the ovens before they could quell the outbreak. They had the situation in hand a few minutes after their arrival. Damage was done by water to a number of picture frames. It did not, however, throw any of the girl employees out of work. *(Chronicle).*

September 1932 - The reserved stand on Crewe Alexandra's football ground, which extends the whole length of one side of the ground, was gutted by fire early morning on 22nd September. The outbreak was discovered shortly after five o'clock by officials on Crewe Railway Station, who called out the Railway Company's Fire Brigade. Almost at the same time residents of houses adjoining the football ground also noticed the blaze and called out the Corporation Fire Brigade.

By this time, however, the centre portion of the stand had been almost burnt down, and the fire was spreading rapidly to the wings. The Railway Brigade tackled the outbreak from the railway end, while the Corporation Brigade attacked the other end, but they were unable to prevent the entire stand being burned to the ground. Only a few charred uprights remain.

The firemen were successful, however, in saving the secretary's and directors' offices and the visitors' dressing-room. The intense heat scorched the grass on the playing pitch for a considerable distance.

The stand was in use last night, when the semi-final of the Cheshire Bowl competition between Crewe and Tranmere was played, and it is thought that a cigarette dropped by one of the spectators was the cause of the outbreak. The stand was capable of seating 2,000 people, and the damage is estimated at £2,000. *(Liverpool Echo).*

January 1933 - When a fire broke out in a Crewe garage, a saloon motor-car was destroyed; the garage was badly damaged, and a nearby clothing factory luckily escaped. The garage was in Buxton Drive, Crewe, and the motor-car belonged to Mr. T. Joy. The damage is estimated at several hundred pounds. (*Observer).*

July 1935 - There was an unexpected thrill for the audience at the Palace Cinema, Crewe, when a fire in the operating box caused the abandonment of the programme for the remainder of the evening. The evening programme had been in progress about half an hour, when the film suddenly ceased and flames were reflected on the screen. Almost immediately pungent fumes from the burning film permeated the hall, causing alarm among the spectators. There was a rush for the exits, but fortunately, there were fewer than a hundred people present, and after the first alarm had passed, there was a quiet and orderly exit. Meanwhile Mr. D. Jackson, the chief operator and his two assistants, were fighting the flames with fire extinguishers, and they quickly had the outbreak under control without calling upon the Corporation Brigade for assistance. The film was completely destroyed and damage was done to the projectors. The outbreak is thought to be due to an electrical fault. *(Chronicle).*

January 1936 - Crewe Fireman, Mr. Bert Johnson of Albert Street, Crewe, answered a call to his own home. He was engaged upon Corporation work when the fire siren was sounded and hurried to the fire station where he learned that the outbreak was at his own home. When he arrived with the remainder of the brigade they found that some workmen had put out the flames. The outbreak was of a minor character. It appears that Mrs. Johnson was airing a bed in front of the fire when it caught alight. The floor was also affected by the flame. *(Evening Sentinel).*

January 1939 - As a heavy lorry was being driven in the neighbourhood of Weston near Crewe, something went wrong with the ignition and before the vehicle could be brought to a standstill the petrol tank containing nearly ten gallons of petrol exploded and enveloped the lorry in flames. The driver, J. Evanson, Henry Street, Haslington, jumped from the cab and escaped injury. The Crewe Fire Brigade were summoned and the flames were soon extinguished. The lorry belonged to Messrs. Mulcaster of Haslington. *(Chronicle).*

May 1939 - A father rescued his three children from a smoke filled bedroom when an outbreak of fire occurred at a house in Oakley Street, Crewe. It appears that Mr. Harper, the tenant of the house, was at home with three of his four children, who had gone to bed. Shortly before 10 o'clock Mr. Harper went to place money in the gas meter when there was an explosion and the room became enveloped in flames. Mr. Harper dashed from his home and gave the alarm to passers-by in Victoria Street. When he returned to the house there was dense volumes of smoke issuing from the living room and a section of the stairway was on fire, cutting the escape of the children in bed. Mr. Harper secured a ladder from a nearby hotel, climbed to the bedroom window and rescued his children. The three children, Derek, Ivor and Brian, were taken care of by neighbours. The firemen found furniture and clothing in the living room well alight, and suffocating fumes had spread to the other parts of the house. Several of the firemen donned gas masks before entering the house and with a plentiful supply of water they were able to get the outbreak under control. Mrs. Harper was not at home at the time of the outbreak and it was a shock to her when she returned to find her home seriously damaged by fire and water. It was a relief, however, when she discovered that all her family were safe in the custody of neighbours. *(Chronicle).*

May 1939 - The Crewe Corporation Fire Brigade turned out to a fire at the Rolls Royce Works, where a hut containing workmen's tools was destroyed. The hut was situated near the entrance to the works and being used by the men engaged in the erection of the works. When the firemen arrived it was impossible to save the hut, and they concentrated their efforts in saving surrounding property, including a petrol pump. In this they were successful. *(Chronicle).*

July 1939 - Two fires in Crewe have been caused by the fusing of electric wires. The first occurred at Crewe Railway Station when a small department adjacent to the left-luggage office on No.1 platform was damaged by fire. The room, in which there are hundreds of telephone connections, in addition to the mechanism which controls the electric clocks on the station, is kept locked, and the alarm was not raised until flames were seen issuing from the door. The Station Fire Brigade were summoned and quickly had the flames under control, but not until considerable damage had been done to the electric wiring. It was first thought that I.R.A. sympathisers might have been responsible for the outbreak, and the police officers and C.I.D. men rushed from Crewe Alexandra sports ground, where the police were holding their sports. After the examination they were satisfied that the outbreak was caused by an electric fault. Considerable inconvenience was caused through the station clocks being put out of order, but workmen got them going again before midnight. They were engaged for several days, however, in replacing all the electrical connections, during which time there was only a temporary telephone service. The second outbreak was when a shed and tools belonging to Mr. S. Allen, 55, Earle Street, were extensively damaged by fire. The prompt arrival of the Corporation Fire Brigade prevented flames spreading to adjoining property. It is estimated that the damage amounts to £100. An electric fuse is held responsible for the outbreak. *(Chronicle).*

January 1940 - Fears that an outbreak of fire in the Progress Office attached to the Railway Erecting Shops of the L.M.S. Works at Crewe may have been due to sabotage have now been dispelled, and the authorities are satisfied that the cause of the outbreak was an accident. The fire occurred at midnight and the entire office - a wooden structure in close proximity to the Erecting Shops - was gutted. Plans of work in progress in the shops were destroyed. Apart from the office staff, who had to move into new quarters, there has been no dislocation of work. The fact that the fire was discovered only a short time after the office had been visited by a night-watchman, who then found everything in order, and that it followed the receipt of a warning that there was a danger of enemy action against the railways, gave rise in the first place to the suspicion that the fire might have been the result of sabotage, and officials were cautious in giving information on the subject. A close investigation has now revealed the true cause. Railway workers have been warned to keep a look-out for unauthorised persons, either on the permanent ways or other railway property. Day and night, close watch is being kept to guard railway centres. *(Chronicle).*

June 1940 - Two motor-cars have been damaged by fire in Crewe. The first outbreak was near the entrance to Crewe Railway Station when a car from which the passengers had just alighted burst into flames. The flames were confined to the engine, and little damage was done. The second outbreak was in West Street, where the driver of a Post Office van saw flames issuing from under the bonnet of a small car. He stopped his van and put out the flames with a fire extinguisher. *(Chronicle).*

September 1942 - Members of the NFS from Crewe and Nantwich fought a stack blaze at the farm of Mr. Charlesworth, of Hough, near Crewe. Two stacks, one containing about 15 tons of this year's hay, and the other a similar amount of unthrashed oats, under a courtyard iron shed in the farmyard, were involved. Most of the oats were destroyed, but the greater part of the hay was saved. *(Staffordshire Sentinel).*

March 1946 - Crewe NFS were summoned to an outbreak at 91 West Street and when they arrived they found three of the occupants of the house huddled together on the roof over the first storey bay window. Their retreat from the house had been cut off by the dense smoke and they were rescued with the aid of the fire escape. The fire brigade, under Column Officer Ball soon had the outbreak, which had occurred in the living room, under control. It is assumed that a spark from the fire ignited a chair in the room and the fire spread to other furniture. The chief damage was to the furniture in this room, but it was fortunate that the smoke penetrated into other rooms of the house to give the occupants timely warning of the danger. *(Chronicle).*

August 1947 - Crewe Fire Brigade were called to an outbreak at Heath Farm, Chorlton, when a spark from a passing engine is believed to have started a fire, which affected about half an acre of stubble. The tenant, Mr. A. E. Proctor, and his men, isolated the flames by ploughing round them. Crewe N.F.S. put out the flames. *(Chronicle).*

February 1949 - Fire which broke out in a stock of clover at Snape Farm, Weston, near Crewe, caused damage estimated at £500. The farm is the home of Mr. J.R. Williamson. Forty one bales of clover were damaged and firemen from Crewe were kept busy for several hours. *(Chronicle).*

November 1949 - Fire broke out at Kelvinators Ltd. Crewe, makers of refrigerators. Four fire engines were used to check the blaze. Flames were first noticed in an oil-cooling tank. Within half an hour of the alarm the fire was under control with only slight damage to the plant. *(Manchester Evening News).*

May 1950 - Heat from the sun rays caused explosions in a small arms ammunition dumping ground at the ROF Radway Green Factory. Exploding bullets flew in all directions in an area of 300 square yards. Fortunately the efficiency of the Factory's Firemen, who were backed-up by Firemen from Crewe and Kidsgrove, prevented the spread of fire and salvaged many of the phosphorous incendiary bullets stored in cases. *(Staffordshire Sentinel).*

April 1953 - Alsager Hall, the home of Lady Joseph, widow of Sir Francis Joseph, was wrecked by fire in the early hours as the fire swept through the house. The housekeeper, Mrs. Flora Turner and her 10 year-old son, Timothy escaped through a back bedroom window by climbing 20 feet down a rope of knotted bed-sheets. (*Cheshire Observer).*

August 1954 - A ten-wheeler petrol lorry with 3,000 gallons of petrol overturned while passing through Shavington, on its journey from Ellesmere Port to Hanley. The lorry ran off the road onto the grass verge and overturned, the petrol flowing in a stream into the ditch at the side of the road. The lorry driver and his mate jumped clear and were uninjured save for a few scratches. The petrol did not catch fire, but the Crewe Fire Brigade were called out to stand-by until a breakdown vehicle put the overturned lorry back on its wheels. *(Liverpool Echo).*

February 1956 - Damage estimated at several thousand pounds was caused by a fire which broke out at the premises of Messrs. E. Charlesworth and Son, builders and undertakers, of Bradfield Road, Crewe. The fire was discovered as a result of a motor horn sounding continuously. This actually was on a car which caught fire and was one of two concerned in the outbreak. Both were burnt out. A large building was also involved, together with machinery and timber. The Crewe and the Nantwich Brigades were called to the scene and fought the blaze for nine hours. The call was received shortly after one o'clock in the morning and they returned to their depots at 10 a.m. *(Chronicle).*

September 1956 - Damage estimated at several hundred thousands of pounds was caused when fire swept through the Pyms Lane, Crewe, plant of Nash Kelvinator Ltd. It was the biggest fire in Crewe's history and the biggest for some years in Cheshire. Within a few hours a large part of the home of one of the town's new industries was a smoking ruin. Modern buildings which had contained valuable materials were laid waste, walls sagged and bulged, roof supports, twisted and buckled, stuck out at crazy angles, charred timbers lay on the sodden floors, debris, much of it unrecognisable, was strewn around. That was the scene after the flames had swept their fiery path through the workshops, resisting the efforts of employees and officials and ninety firemen from Cheshire and Staffordshire with fifteen pumps.

It was a grim episode in Crewe's industrial life, an episode which will long be remembered. The story began soon after noon. At 12.09 p.m. came the first flash to Crewe Fire Station: "Fire at Kelvinators!" The blaze broke out in the plant's paint shop. About seventeen men - half the maintenance staff - were at the plant at the time. Within a few seconds flames spread to barrels of paint, and soon the south end of the workshop was an inferno. Tanks full of bitumen, thinners and white spirit caught fire, and thick black smoke plumed from the buildings. The smoke, fanned by an east wind, could be seen ten miles away.

Three Crewe fire units, helped by others from Nantwich, Sandbach, Congleton, Holmes Chapel, Winsford, Middlewich and Kidsgrove, went into action. As firemen entered the buildings, oxy-acetylene cylinders and barrels of paint were exploding. Soon twenty jets were playing on the flames and the yards became a criss-cross of hoses. Workers from Rolls-Royce Works, which adjoins Kelvinators, helped to roll barrels out of reach of the flames, then moved equipment at their own Works out of the danger zone. Fourth Avenue was a base for most fire engines. Because telephones were out of order, all fire messages had to be sent via radio transmitter in one of the engines.

There were other dangers for the firemen. Arcton, a liquid gas used as a refrigeration agent, was piped through the factory and there was a risk of it exploding. There was also the danger that a 1,000 gallon petrol tank might explode. Dense smoke affected several firemen and hampered operations, the acrid fumes stung their eyes and a number had particles of grit extracted in First-Aid treatment at the factory. Workers took large cans of drinking water round to the smoke-blackened firemen, and an emergency canteen was set up in one of the yards.

Rolls-Royce Fire Brigade joined the other fire-fighting units, all of which were directed by Mr. A.H. Warren, Assistant Chief Officer of Cheshire County Fire Brigade. It was nearly four hours before the outbreak was brought under control; even then there were small pockets of flame which had to be doused. Then, when the fire was apparently out, firemen kept a vigil which lasted throughout the night and most of the next day. In case there should be another outbreak. A fire officer said no men had been seriously injured. The firemen had not been able to stop the fire enveloping the assembly lines. Their work had been made difficult by bitumen from the roof-covering dripping on to the floor and forming small streams of fire. Breathing apparatus had been found to be unnecessary, he added. About five foam jets had had to be used.

Mr. G. F. Staples, Works Manager, said that at least 50 per cent of the factory had been gutted. Of the total floor area of 236,000 square feet, over 120,000 had been destroyed. It is believed to have been started by a spark caused when paint was being scraped off the floor of the workshop. *(Chronicle).*

July 1956 - Houses in Oakley Street, Crewe, had their woodwork blistered and charred and their windows cracked and shattered, in a blaze which enveloped a merchant's yard. The fire was fought by three brigades from Crewe and one from Sandbach, with Nantwich 'standing by.' It was twelve hours before the firemen, directed by District Officer C. Gorrie, returned to their stations leaving behind the gutted remains of a building and masses of fire-damaged sacks and woollen and cotton materials.

The fire was at the yard of W. Houston and Sons. It began shortly after 9 p.m. and within minutes was 'a blazing inferno'. Firemen were quickly on the scene and they fought without respite to save what they could from the yard and protect a row of eleven houses, directly opposite the fire and a few yards from the blaze.

At daybreak, a gaunt scene met the eye. In the yard, a brick chimney-stack stood alone like a silent sentinel to the night's havoc. Around it were the remains of what had once been a two-storied shed blackened, charred timbers. Strewn over the ground were sacks and coloured garments, a few untouched by the ravaging fire. Across the way, the houses are evidence of the intensity of the heat, Upstairs and downstairs windows cracked and here and there no windows at all. Carefully painted doors and window frames burned to look like charcoal. Bedroom doors blistered. *(Chronicle).*

June 1958 - Firemen took two hours to bring a fire under control at ROF Radway Green. The fire involved packing cases, small arms ammunition and ammunition machinery in a workshop. The ammunition threatened to explode during the early stages, until the Factory's Firemen and fire crews from Cheshire and Staffordshire were able to pull ammunition packing cases clear of the flames. Over 50 Firemen dealt with the blaze under the direction of Cheshire's Chief Fire Officer A.H. Warren and Crewe Station Officer H. Whalley. *(Chronicle).*

October 1959 - A fire which broke out in the window of Riley's Wool Shop in Queensway, Crewe's new shopping centre, was soon brought under control by Crewe Firemen. They confined the damage to a small part of the window. *(Liverpool Echo and Evening Express).*

August 1961 - Crewe Corn Exchange, the town's civic social centre was badly damaged by fire a few hours after a bingo session. Alderman Frank Roberts said that the building was beyond repair and not worth wasting money on. It would be better to build a new hall. Fire chiefs are of the opinion that bingo tickets thrown in heaps on ash trays caused the fire, which damaged the roof and stage, hundreds of chairs and the hall's piano. *(Liverpool Echo).*

September 1961 - Thunderstorms swamped many houses in Crewe and its district. They disturbed telephone and electric services, partially blocked a number of roads and gave Crewe Fire Brigade its most hectic day since the wartime blitz. All the Brigade's pumps were out on bailing operations as a stream of calls came from houses, a farm, a public house and a garage, mostly in the rural areas surrounding Crewe. The newly installed flood sewer in Nantwich Road saved a lot of calls. But one block of houses it did not save at the town end of Lockitt Street. There, four householders and their families actually had a torrent swirling straight through their homes as they ate their dinner - and the houses have special flood barriers bricked two foot high across their doorways. Several tons of hay were destroyed and a stable damaged when lightning caused fire at Old Hall Farm, Betley, the property of Mr. J. Sutton. It was dealt with by Crewe Fire Brigade. Livestock were not endangered. Lightning also disrupted electric services in and around Crewe and cut off 200 subscribers on the Alsager exchange when it struck a pylon. Electric current was off for several periods and church services in the Willaston and Wistaston areas had to be cut short when power failed. The Fire Brigade were called to a flooded cellar at the White Lion Hotel, Barthomley and also pumped water out of Hough Garage, which was swamped. The main Crewe to Macclesfield Road was partially blocked at the junction with Sydney Road; and Ivy Lane, Alsager, was also under several inches of water. Householders on the nearby housing estate at Alsager were forced to move into upstairs rooms as the water flooded their ground floor quarters. Water rose to a depth of three feet at Wybunbury and residents were forced into temporary evacuation until it subsided. There were no reports of personal injuries caused by the storms. Lightning struck several houses in Minshull New Road, Crewe, but only the home of Mr. and Mrs. T. Robson was extensively damaged. The roof of Mr. Robson's house was also struck and several tiles came falling to the ground allowing a substantial hole to appear. Water and soot then began to gush through the hole into his front bedroom. *(Chronicle).*

November 1961 - A fire broke out at the Belle Vue Inn, Earle Street, Crewe, destroying nearly 10,000 cigarettes and eight dozen bottles of beer and lemonade in crates. Timber shelves in the bar were also badly charred. The outbreak was discovered by Mr. Basil Sydney Webb, who fortunately had occasion to leave watching TV in the living room at the rear of the premises to fetch a newspaper from the bar. He was met by a smoke filled room, fire spreading along the shelves and exploding bottles. Together with his wife and their gardener he managed to get the blaze out before the Fire Brigade arrived a few minutes later. The seat of the fire was a plastic bucket under the bar into which bar sweepings apparently containing a lighted cigarette end had been placed, which set alight wastepaper and other combustible material. It was opening time as usual in the evening, but customers had to find other sources for their cigarettes. *(Chronicle).*

June 1962 - A cigarette end carelessly dropped underneath a double seat on the back row of the balcony of the Ritz Cinema, Crewe, is believed to have been the cause of a fire. A three-foot square hole was burned in the cinema floor before an automatic fire extinguisher gushing out 60 gallons of fluid a minute put out the fire. The first performance of 'Carry on Cruising' went on at the cinema last night after mopping-up operations by the staff in the afternoon. The manager, Mr. K. Shepperson, said: "We were very lucky. The cinema could quite easily have been burned down. Usually the back row is booked by courting couples and I think one of these must have been responsible for the damage. There is a no excuse, ash trays are provided on every other seat." *(Liverpool Echo and Evening Express).*

April 1963 - It was a case of bringing a fire to the fire station rather than the Fire Brigade going to the fire at Crewe last week. The Fire Brigade had an unusual call when a Corporation refuse lorry with its load blazing was driven up to the Fire Station. The flames, caused by hot ashes setting light to paper, were put out in no time at the station doors. *(Chronicle).*

June 1965 - Rolls-Royce firemen fought for an hour alongside their colleagues from Crewe, Nantwich and Sandbach fire stations, to control a fire which broke out in the extractor plant. *(Chronicle).*

June 1967 - Crewe Fire Brigade were called out 11 times within two hours after a sudden downpour of rain caused extensive flooding throughout Crewe. Special service calls, involving pumping-out operations, included Crewe Railway Station, where flood waters had swamped the G.P.O. station subway. Other areas affected were in Casson Street, Evans Street, Bradfield Road, Broughton Road and Sandlands Park. (*Chronicle).*

May 1968 - Crewe Fire Brigade were called to Manley's Cattle Market, Gresty Road, Crewe, after a quantity of hay and straw caught fire in a single-storey shippon. Altogether, about three or four tons of straw was damaged, and flames also damaged part of the roof of the building. *(Chronicle).*

June 1969 - Crewe Fire Brigade dealt with a small spillage of cyanide, giving off toxic gas in the laboratory at Calmic Ltd in Crewe. Using breathing apparatus, two firemen diluted it with chemicals provided by Calmic and the poisonous gas was safely dispersed. (*Chronicle).*

January 1970 - The clubroom at Crewe Golf Club was destroyed by fire. Firemen fought for five hours and managed to prevent the blaze from spreading to the ladies' locker room and the professional's premises. They were alerted by the Club Steward, Mr. John Sutton, who spotted the blaze from his nearby cottage. Mr. Sutton and members were mystified as to how the fire started. He said no members had been there during the day and he was taking his day off. Plans for a new £25,000 clubroom were recently approved. *(Chronicle).*

April 1971 - About 70 per cent of the waste paper plant at Crewe Corporation's Refuse Disposal Department at Pyms Lane, Crewe was destroyed by fire. Mr. Reginald Platt, Chief Public Health Inspector, said that damage to machinery, which was installed at a cost of £10,000, had yet to be assessed. Three plant employees have had to be put on other duties. It took Crewe Firemen about two hours to bring the blaze under control. It is not known how it started. *(Chronicle).*

September 1972 - Firemen rescued a homeless man from a derelict house in Edleston Road, Crewe, after fire broke out in a ground floor room which he was occupying. A Brigade spokesman said the fire damaged floorboards and filled the house with smoke. The man, 76-year-old George Ollier, was brought out by firemen. Later, a spokesman at Leighton Hospital said that Mr. Ollier had been treated for head and hand injuries and then released. *(Chronicle).*

December 1972 - The Jubilee Pavilion, the Victorian landmark of Queen's Park, Crewe, has been gutted by fire. A senior fire officer told the Chronicle that possibly an electrical fault was the cause of the fire. He pointed out that there was no forced entry into the building. The pavilion was opened in 1887 at the same time as the Park which was given to the town by the L. & N.W.R. Company. It commemorated the Golden Jubilee of Queen Victoria. The pavilion was used as a cafeteria. In the blaze, its fittings, including three refrigerators, two cookers, tables, chairs and other equipment, were completely destroyed. The structural damage was estimated by a Crewe Corporation official at £15,000. And a further £1,500 to £2,000 can be added to that for the furnishings. The official added: "We shall never get another building like that." Shortly after the alarm was raised two appliances from Crewe Fire Station arrived at the scene to find the building "blazing from end to end." Firemen were occupied at the scene for nearly seven hours. The water main along Victoria Avenue was frozen and water was eventually pumped from the park lake to extinguish the fire. A spokesman for Crewe Corporation said later that the matter would be discussed at a future meeting of the Amenities Committee when consideration to the question of a replacement for the pavilion would be given. *(Chronicle).*

February 1975 - A major fire involving 95 drums of waste magnesium swarf and a battery operated stacker was averted at ROF Radway Green. The blaze was fought by the Factory's Firemen with assistance from Cheshire and Staffordshire Fire Brigades. *(Chronicle).*

August 1975 - A serious fire involving two passenger train coaches on platform two at Crewe Railway Station caused much fire and smoke damage to the coaches. *(Chronicle).*

April 1976 - Severe damage was caused by fire to a single storey shed (20ft x 40ft) in Beech Street, Crewe. The fire involved an asbestos roof, timber doors and a large quantity of cardboard. The building formed part of the old Crewe Fire Station. *(Chronicle).*

March 1976 - A large warehouse fire occurred in Derrington Avenue, Crewe when the Starline discount warehouse was ablaze. The structure of the building was severely damaged and most of the contents were destroyed by the fire. Fire appliances from all over Cheshire and Staffordshire fought the fire and two firemen sustained minor injuries. *(Chronicle).*

March 1980 - Six Rolls-Royce cars which were in for repair at the Crewe factory were involved in fire after fire causing £200,000 worth of damage spread through the body shop. Two workers were using cutting equipment on a car, which was set away from the body shop building. Despite there being Rolls-Royce firemen standing by, the flames spread quickly and the six cars belonging to customers, were badly damaged. Four fire appliances were sent to the incident. *(Chronicle).*

July 1983 - A major probe was under way after part of Crewe's railway heritage was devastated by a huge fire. About 100 firemen from a wide area of Cheshire and Staffordshire fought a blaze which gutted about 90 per cent of the former British Rail General Offices on Chester Bridge, Crewe, which had been vacant for about three years. And ironically, it was revealed today that the 106-year-old building was, in a few days' time to be made a listed building of special architectural merit. The blaze broke at about 8pm and residents of Tollitt Street, Betley Street and Dorfold Street whose modernised former railway cottages are close to the General Offices building, were evacuated from their homes for about three hours, while firemen using 15 pump appliances, two emergency tenders, two hydraulic platforms and various other back-up vehicles and eight sets of breathing apparatus, fought the fire which lit up the sky for miles around as darkness closed in. By the time firemen arrived on the scene, the fire had a real hold. It got into the roof space and spread rapidly, engulfing the old building with its distinctive curved frontage built to align with the old Chester Line which one ran past.

"We could see a pall of smoke and flames shooting into the air as we turned out from the fire station a mile away," said a senior fire officer at Crewe Fire Station. Firemen from Crewe were joined by colleagues from as far north as Wilmslow in fighting the blaze which started in the middle of the long, narrow building which was up for sale with a price tag of around £100,000. The building hadn't been used since it was vacated by a computer peripherals firm about three years ago. The building was erected in 1876, the same year as the formation of the London and North Western Railway Company, and continued to be used as railway offices for 100 years, until 1976.

The fire was one of the most spectacular, and devastating, seen in Crewe for years. Mr. Harry Almond, of Betley Street, told the *Sentinel*: "It was an inferno. It just seemed to go whoosh. The heat was terrific and the cars in the street had to be moved; they were red hot with heat. Mrs. Ethel Webster, of Betley Street said: "It happened so suddenly. I looked outside at five to eight and there was nothing happening. Then I saw a reflection on my windows and saw the fire. It was frightening." Both Mr. Almond and Mrs. Webster and other residents in the street spoke of their wish to see the building pulled down. They feel it is now an eyesore and a place which children have been getting into. A spokesman for the British Raid Property Board said: "We have a responsibility to make the building safe and we shall have to consider whether to demolish what is left. We had intended to sell the site as it stood, lock, stock and barrel." *(Evening Sentinel).*

December 1985 - Eight fire appliances attended a blaze at Underwood Court Elderly Persons Home in Underwood Lane. Many of the 39 residents were taken to hospital having inhaled large quantities of smoke. *(Chronicle).*

March 1986 - A Sunday morning gas explosion completely flattened the house at 402 Underwood Lane. Miraculously no one was injured. *(Chronicle).*

August 1986 - A major blaze which gutted one Crewe council flat and badly damaged four others was caused by a piece of newspaper used to light a cigarette, fire experts said today. The fire was spotted and the alarm raised shortly before 1 a.m. when passers-by spotted smoke and flames pouring from windows of a first floor flat in Fanshawe Walk, Crewe. Families asleep in flats were roused from their beds and most escaped without injury. One 67 year-old was rescued from his smoke filled home by firemen using breathing apparatus and two other people suffered minor cuts and bruises in their flight from the blazing property. All three received treatment at Leighton Hospital together with a fireman who needed five stitches to a gash in his knee. The fire started in one flat and went through the ceiling to spread through the roof space and affect other flats in the same block. It was quite a spectacular blaze and five pumps were on the scene to tackle it. One of the flats is completely gutted, the ceilings have collapsed and the others are badly damaged. Firemen spent several hours damping down smouldering timbers before an investigation team could move in to search for the cause of the blaze. The people taken to hospital were not badly hurt and were not detained for further treatment. *(Evening Sentinel).*

August 1987 - Fire Officers were probing the cause of a blaze which ripped through a 200-year-old Cheshire Tithe barn. Twenty firemen from four towns battled to save the building which dates to the days of Queen Anne - at Maw Green farm, Coppenhall, near Crewe. They used water from a nearby duck pond but were unable to save the roof and about eight tons of baled hay and straw in the loft. Mr. and Mrs. Sidney Bona who live at the farm, said they planned to find out whether they could get grant aid to rebuild the roof. The blaze was tackled by firemen from Crewe, Nantwich, Sandbach and Middlewich. *(Evening Sentinel).*

February 1988 - A massive blaze destroyed a South Cheshire School after a suspected arson attack. Firefighters who raced to Gainsborough County Junior School in Claremont Road, Crewe, found signs of forced entry. Crews from all over Cheshire were drafted in to fight the huge blaze which raged for several hours and brought down part of the roof. At the height of the drama more than 60 firemen battled to contain the flames many of them wearing breathing gear. They eventually got the fire under control but not before the building - erected in 1974 - was wrecked. As clearing up operations began, fire investigation experts were sifting through the debris searching for clues to how the blaze started. Divisional Officer Brian French, one of the senior fire officers involved in the firefighting operation described it as 'hazardous'. He said: "This was a very severe and dangerous fire because of its sheer size and the intense heat." One fire officer was taken to hospital with severe bruising after being caught in a 'flash-over' explosion, but he was not badly hurt and was released after treatment. *(Evening Sentinel).*

March 1988 - A toy factory which supplies rocking horses to the top people's store Harrods has been destroyed in a mystery £750,000 blaze. More than 50 firemen battled throughout the night to control the fire at Pegasus Toys on the Weston Road Industrial Estate at Crewe. A passing police patrol spotted smoke billowing from the brick and steel clad building. Fire crews were drafted in from throughout the county with ten pumps and two emergency tenders used to surround the blazing factory with a wall of water. A fireman from one of those first crews to arrive said their main priority was to prevent the huge amount of heat given off by the fire from spreading to other nearby premises. He said: "We sent in men with breathing gear and water jets to try and bring the fire under control. Huge plumes of smoke were billowing out of the roof, and the factory was already well alight when we got there. Suddenly it just seemed to take hold and it was like a fireball. It spread rapidly throughout the rest of the premises, and it all happened in about a minute."

Pegasus employ 65 local people making wooden toys, including rocking horses priced at several hundred pounds each, garden furniture and foam mattresses for cots and prams. As shocked workers arrived to clock-on managing director Mr. Alan Cross gave assurances that no-one would be laid off despite the loss. He said: "Fortunately we have another production unit at Shavington which was due to come on stream next week and we can transfer some of our staff to there. We also have a couple of small warehouses in the area, which can be turned over to production. No one is going to lose their job, and I would hope to have some production going again within the next few days." Mr. Cross was shocked by the extent of damage to the factory. Toys produced at the Crewe factory are sent to top stores all over the world and the company have in the past been commended for their expert achievements. *(Evening Sentinel).*

October 1988 - Crewe Police are investigating the cause of the fire which gutted Crewe Bowling Club's pavilion, doing nearly £2,000 worth of damage. A search of the debris has revealed a crowbar near to the main entrance, and the police are working on the theory that the club was broken into and it was the result of this that the fire broke out. The club, situated on the Crewe Hall estate, is very isolated, and has been broken into a number of times previously. The safe was found intact among the ruins. *(Liverpool Echo).*

March 1989 - A freight train carrying a highly inflammable liquid was brought to a halt when a tanker was found to be leaking. The hundred tonne tanker containing the dangerous substance propylene was spilling liquid gas from the faulty valve. British Transport Police and the fire service were alerted about the incident at Gresty Lane Railway Sidings. Crewe and Nantwich Firemen brought an emergency tender to the scene and monitored the spillage until a Shell engineer arrived. The valve was made safe and the train was allowed to continue on its journey to Shell at Partington. *(Chronicle).*

May 1990 - Firemen blamed youngsters playing with matches for sparking a blaze on a railway embankment. Flames engulfed about 500 square metres of grass in the incident at Wistaston Road, Crewe. Fire Service Officers issued a call for greater care during the current dry spell. *(Evening Sentinel).*

August 1990 - Firemen wore breathing apparatus to enter a smoke-filled kitchen at a house in Darlington Avenue, Crewe, to deal with a blaze caused by overheated fat. A cooker and electrical fittings were damaged. *(Evening Sentinel).*

May 1991 - A bedroom was badly smoke-damaged when a fire broke out at a house in Crewe. Firefighters wore breathing apparatus to tackle the blaze at 58, Alton Street. No one was hurt in the incident, which was thought to have been caused by a faulty electric blanket. *(Evening Sentinel).*

January 1992 - Firemen were called to the town's railway station after a drum of explosive acrylic resin was found to be leaking on a goods train. The chemical was washed away and the drum was made safe. The drum was believed to have been punctured when it was loaded on to the train by a fork lift truck. *(Chronicle).*

June 1992 - A scrap yard blaze devoured 50 cars and spread to an office building before firemen brought it under control. The fire at Moston Lane, near Sandbach, was dealt with by firemen from Crewe, Sandbach, Middlewich and Holmes Chapel. Four main jets were used and a similar number of firemen used breathing apparatus during the operation. *(Guardian).*

January 1994 - Bedding was damaged in a bedroom fire at a house in Leighton Park *(Staffordshire Sentinel).*

August 1999 - Not for the first time, a fire broke out at Maw Green's landfill site involving 60,000 cubic metres of tyres. The deep-seated fire, which started on 28th August, was finally extinguished on 4th September. *(Chronicle).*

November 2002 - At 2019 hrs on 21st November 2002, a call was received indicating that a fire alarm activated at Underwood West Infant School in Crewe. Two pumps were ordered to the school but due to the two appliances from Crewe being engaged at another incident in the Crewe area, the pumps ordered to attend were from the retained stations at Nantwich and Sandbach. Within moments of the pumps responding the two pumps from Crewe became available and were also ordered to the school. On arrival the Officer-in-charge, Sub Officer Rowlands, observed flame and smoke issuing above the central area of the school and requested six appliances together with an aerial appliance. The caretaker was on the scene and able to advice on the location of the fuel oil tank for the heating system for which a spray jet was deployed to prevent the tank from becoming involved. Within minutes of arrival, and before a check all around the premises had been completed, the windows across the front of the building failed. The Officer-in-charge could clearly see that the fire was well developed throughout the main building.

Hydrants outside the school were only 75mm and the supply insufficient to provide the quantity required for a sustained attack using main jets. Use was made of the vehicle mounted data system computer on the fire appliances to identify the locations of additional hydrants and larger water mains to which pump crews were allocated. A message was also sent to the Water Board to request increased water pressure in the area. The fire, which was fully vented and assisted by the materials of construction and moderate winds, was spreading rapidly across the roof area towards the nursery unit and the rear teaching area, both of which had been extensions to the original main building.

The fire weakened the steel structure of the building and it was not safe to commit crews inside the building. The jet from the aerial appliance was used effectively to control the spread across the roof and reach areas in the centre of the building not accessible to crews. Due to the amount of smoke and the school being surrounded by housing, a message was passed to local radio stations advising residents to close all doors and windows. Fire crews to the rear of the premises were instructed to wear breathing apparatus to combat the toxic smoke, whilst using hand held jets to maintain effective fire breaks at the points where the nursery unit and rear teaching area classrooms had been added. Good progress was also made in preventing further fire spread and extinguishment of the fire in the main building.

Pumps were increased to eight to service the breathing apparatus equipment. Gas Board engineers located the underground main and isolated the supply for the fire crews to extinguish the fire in the kitchen area. The 'stop' message, indicating that firefighting operations were complete, was sent at 0807 hrs on 22nd November and all crews left the incident by 0910 hrs. Subsequent investigations by Fire Investigating Officers and Police Officers determined the cause as arson. *(Cheshire Fire & Rescue Service).*

February 2003 - An inferno which destroyed three businesses has prompted fears a serial arsonist is targeting Crewe properties. Crimefighters believe a blaze at Hungerford Road Service Station, which incorporates Mr. Tread, Trade Up Motors and M&S Cheshire Ltd, was started deliberately. They fear it could be the work of the same firebug who last week torched Alec Ross carpets at Edleston Road, a flat in West Street and attempted to burn down Empire Clothing in Hall O'Shaw Street. Eight fire engines were called to the latest fire after reports of tyres ablaze in a storage unit. Firefighters evacuated families from 10 nearby homes and roads around the site were closed as they battled the flames. The fire gutted tyre dealer Mr. Tread and caused substantial damage to Trade Up Motors where several cars were burnt out on the forecourt, and the M&S Cheshire garage was also hit. *(Chronicle).*

July 2004 - A serious fire at the Rolls-Royce factory resulted in two firefighters and two security officers needing hospital treatment for smoke inhalation. Five fire appliances, an aerial platform and a Hazardous Materials Unit dealt with the fire in the plating shop, which was undergoing refurbishment. *(Chronicle).*

June 2007 - A major blaze on an industrial estate in Crewe saw propane cylinders explode, 50 gallon drums of solvent erupted into flames and hundreds of aerosol cans blasted high into the air. The fact that there were no reported injuries is due to a rapid evacuation and the enforcement of a rigid exclusion zone by all of the emergency services involved. The first call to Aztec Chemicals on Fourth Avenue, Crewe Gates Industrial Estate, was received by the Fire and Rescue Service control room at 12.16 on Monday 4th June. This was followed by a further 43 calls from both staff on the site, local residents and nearby businesses. The first fire engine was on the scene in six minutes and more resources were immediately called for. At the height of the blaze there were 25 fire appliances, a high volume pumping appliance, a foam unit, aerial appliances and a hazard management unit. A 200-metre exclusion zone was set up - later, this was increased to 400 metres because of the potential risk of explosion from mass storage cylinders containing 25 tonnes of Liquid Petroleum Gas (LPG), close to the original site of the fire. Fire crews concentrated initially on cooling the LPG cylinders and had to use walls to shelter from exploding aerosol cans as they set up jets. The fire made rapid progress and spread to other buildings on the site and Cheshire Police's plane was brought in to assess the spread from the air. With a specialist high volume pump supplying water to 10 ground monitors - which allows water to be applied safely from higher-risk areas - and a foam tanker being used as a water cannon, crews managed to contain the fire and at 6pm the incident was reduced to 10 appliances. The following morning appliance numbers were reduced to two, and the cordon and roadblocks minimised, although crews had to remain at the scene damping down potential hotspots for a further two days. Investigations into the incident are continuing, with the Service working closely with other agencies including the Health and Safety Executive. Chief Fire Officer Steve McGuirk said: "I have no doubts that the truly courageous actions of our staff and our partners, while not saving the immediate buildings, did stop the fire from escalating further and devastating this important economic area of Crewe. To have brought the fire under control without any reported injuries is a major achievement." *(Cheshire Fire & Rescue Service).*

Fire at the Crewe Opera House (Lyceum Theatre) in March 1910.

Crewe Firemen tackling a fire at a property in Haslington in the mid-1960s.

Two fire appliances at the scene of the Haslington fire.

*(**Above**) Firemen at the Williams Brothers' warehouse fire - 13 November 1969. L to R: Bob Sweeney, Barrie Lunt, John Yardley and Gordon Mottershead. Front: Jeff Goddard. (**Below**) Fighting the British Rail General Offices' fire on 23 July 1983.*

*(**Above**) Attacking the fire from the rear of Dorfold Street and Betley Street. (**Below**) An aerial appliance used as a water tower at the General Offices' fire.*

(**Above**) *The aftermath of the fire.* (**Below**) *Explosion at 402, Underwood Lane, Crewe on 2 March 1986.*

01270
623151
WICH
POLICE

Tetrosyl
DK06 HXF

*(**Opposite page top**) Road traffic accident involving a Morris Minor at West Street, Crewe in the mid-1980s. (**Opposite page centre**) Road traffic accident involving a cyclist and a car in Edleston Road, Crewe in the 1990s. (**Opposite page bottom**) Road traffic accident on the M6 Motorway in the 1990s. (**Above**) Road traffic accident, M6 Motorway on 26 June 2000. (**Below**) Damage caused by lightning strike, Crossway, Crewe on 20 May 2002.*

*(**Above**) Fire damage showing the extent of the blaze at Underwood West Infant School, Crewe on 21 November 2002. (**Below**) Fire involving farm machinery at Hunterston in 2006.*

(Above) *Fire at Aztec Chemicals, Gateway Industrial Estate, Crewe on 4 June 2007.*
(Below) *Cars belonging to the employees at the Chemical Plant gutted by the fire.*

(Top) *The aftermath of the Aztec Chemicals fire.* ***(Above)*** *Firefighters inspecting the damage after the fire.*

(Above) *Fire at Beechmere Retirement Home, Rolls Avenue, Crewe on 8 August 2019.*
(Below) *The aftermath of the Beechmere fire.*

FIRE BRIGADES UNION

In 2018, the Fire Brigades Union (FBU) celebrated the centenary of its foundation as the Firemen's Trades Union. Rechristened in 1930, it has campaigned throughout its existence to improve the safety of both the public and of firefighters. This work has often resulted in the introduction of new legislation, especially in the aftermath of tragic incidents.

Another objective has been improvements to firefighters' pay and conditions. The weekly shift on full-time fire stations during the 1920s and '30s covered 72 hours. This was reduced to 56 hours in the 1950s and '60s, with a later reduction to 48 hours. Although the present 42 hour shift has often come under attack from fire service leaders, the FBU has resisted such changes.

Nationally, the FBU represented about 3,400 full-time firefighters in 1920, with over a third of the membership employed in the London Fire Brigade. During World War II, membership among both full-time and part-time staff increased sharply in line with the influx of firefighters working in the Auxiliary Fire Service and later the National Fire Service. FBU membership has fluctuated over the years:

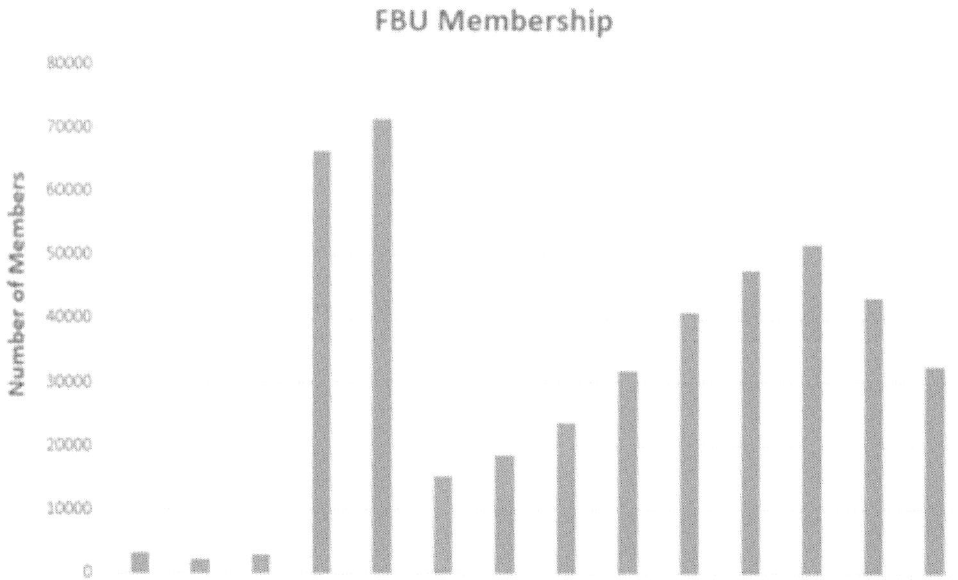

Each generation of firefighters has benefited from the struggles of its predecessors and many lessons have been learnt along the way. A dispute at Crewe Fire Station in January 1952, as detailed in the *Chronicle,* describes the sacrifices that were made by Crewe Firemen after taking part in a 'spit and polish' strike.

The town's Trades Council and Labour Party got involved in the dispute after disciplinary action was taken against the Crewe Firemen by sending the following resolution to the County Fire Brigades' Committee:

'That this Trades Council protests most strongly against the drastic disciplinary action taken by the Chief Fire Officer for Cheshire in respect of the Firemen at Crewe who took part in the recent demonstration. We feel that these men as Trades Unionists took the only course open to them in an industrial dispute and we are of the opinion that the sentences imposed are a gross injustice. We therefore appeal to the members of the County Fire Brigades Committee to give this matter further consideration with a view to annulling the sentences passed on these men, and falling into line with other authorities in various parts of the country. This would remove the discontent which has arisen as a result of the disciplinary awards, and lead to a more efficient service.'

Members of the Crewe branch of the National Union of Railwaymen also asked their head office to support the FBU in an effort to stop the victimisation of some of their members. Their resolution was as follows:

'We are of the opinion that some of the treatment, penalties and fines being inflicted on its members are far too harsh and not justified. We ask our Head Office to raise the matter with the Home Secretary, the Minister of Labour, Secretary of the County Councils Association, the Association of Municipal Corporations and the Clerk to the London County Council.'

Leading Fireman Percy Cooke, Chairman of the Crewe FBU, said to the *Chronicle:*

"Thirteen men had been involved in the 48 hours 'spit and polish' strike, but they all carried on with routine work and actually attended a fire at Holmes Chapel on one of the two days. All they refused to do was clean brasses and undertake drills as a protest against refusal of pay parity with Police. Because of our action we have been fined amounts ranging from £1 to £7 each, amounting in all, to about £30. I was recommended by the Cheshire County Chief Officer to be reduced in rank, but that was withdrawn and changed to six days' stoppage of pay, which amounts to about £6. We do feel that a grave injustice has been done and out of all proportion to the offences with which we were charged. During the ban they had done the same as they would have done on a Sunday or Bank Holiday. The public were safeguarded by the men's guarantee to provide fire coverage. The fines were still subject to endorsement by the county authority, and he hoped that Cheshire would do as many other authorities had done - take no action. If the Chief Officer's decision was upheld, the Union would pay the fines."

The County Fire Brigades Committee heard the appeals by Crewe Firemen at the Crewe Arms Hotel. The barrister acting for the firemen on behalf of the FBU, Mr. P. Payne, made a strong case, contending that the men had carried out all essential duties, and had actually attended a fire during the so-called strike. The Committee upheld four of the appeals and remitted the fines. In the five remaining cases, the Committee confirmed the original action and the men had to forfeit some of their pay, amounting in all to about £15.

A row in September 1954 saw firemen at six Cheshire Fire Stations including Crewe in dispute over duty hours after Mr. A.A. Boulton, the Chief Fire Officer asked them to volunteer for a system of duty in excess of 60 hours without overtime payment. The *Chronicle* stated that the FBU had informed Mr. Boulton that duty systems were the subject of recommendations by the National Joint Council for Local Authority Fire Brigades. At the time, it was waiting ratification in statutory regulation form by the Home Secretary and therefore the Union refused to approve his proposal. In a letter sent to the Clerk of the County Council, the Union's General Secretary stated that, given the existing regulations, Mr. Boulton's actions were illegal.

The FBU were not satisfied that a really determined effort had been made to attract recruits and claimed that the Brigade's serious manpower shortage had not suddenly appeared in recent weeks. Wastage in the Brigade had been building up over years as the Chief Fire Officer's own annual reports clearly demonstrated. Indeed, his most recent report showed that the Brigade was nearly 25% below its scheduled establishment strength. The problem was two-fold: the Brigade was neither attracting new recruits nor retaining experienced firemen. Longer working hours would hinder any solution to either problem. Mr. Boulton commented:

> *"It is true that the position in Cheshire is a very serious one from the manpower point of view, and to meet the situation at certain stations, men are being asked to perform extra hours of duty. In almost every case the response was satisfactory, although the regulations make no provision for payments to be made for such duty. The circumstances are so exceptional that the action taken was unavoidable. The amount of extra duty necessary is being kept to an absolute minimum, but if the position worsens, undoubtedly longer periods of extra duty may be necessary. The legality or otherwise of this does not arise, and the Union's attitude to the problem is deprecated and is totally at variance with the traditions of the Service, which has always been prepared to adjust itself in emergency."*

Demonstrations of this manner gave firemen an education in working-class solidarity as FBU members came to feel that they had a connection with other workers. 'Work to rule' protests were often carried out and the Government scrutinized (Holroyd and Cunningham Reviews) the work of firemen with the aim of overcoming the discontent in the fire service. It is worth noting that the starting pay for a fireman in October 1965 was £740 *per annum* while the average pay for manual workers in 1964 was £915.20 and £1,220 for non-manual workers.

Paul Bickerton, who became a junior fireman in 1968, remembers several pay campaigns during his first few years in the fire brigade. He recalls:

> *"Pay and conditions in the fire brigade were poor in the 1960s and into the '70s and threats of strikes and 'work-to-rule' protests were quite common, when as a way of demonstrating to highlight our discontent, we would only answer emergency calls."*

Firemen of the 1980s became the beneficiaries of the FBU's campaigns to improve pay and conditions after a bitterly fought national strike that lasted from 14 November 1977 to 16 January 1978. Almost 30,000 firemen took part, and over 1.25 million working days were lost. Emergency cover was provided by 10,000 servicemen using a fleet of 'Green Goddess' fire engines.

Why did they go on strike? At the time, a qualified fireman was paid £65.70 for a 48-hour week, while the national average wage was £78.60 for a 42-hour week. The strike had been brewing for several years as promises of pay increases had been regularly abandoned. Firemen wanted a pay formula that would make the qualified firemen's rate of pay equivalent to the national average wage plus 10% to take account of the special skills they needed to meet the hazards they faced. This equated to approximately an additional £20 per week.

Terry Kelly spent many years as the Crewe FBU branch secretary. Nicknamed 'Spike', he was well known in the wider community as a distributor of the News Line newspaper published by the Workers Revolutionist Party. The Crewe branch was well-organised under the leadership of Spike and other representatives, Barrie Lunt and Maurice Higginson. Spike recalls the strike:

"Firemen were being paid poverty wages. Some had to be supplemented by state welfare benefits. So the question of whether to go on strike was simple - if we wanted a fair and reasonable wage, then we would have to fight for it. Despite the harsh winter and the bleak Christmas for our families, the strike remained solid. Crewe Firemen showed firm solidarity during this difficult period. They carried out picket duties and huddled around braziers outside the fire station and the overwhelming public support kept everyone's spirits high. The people of Crewe were shocked when they learned how low our wages were for doing a difficult and dangerous job. A great deal of pressure was put on our members because most of us were the only breadwinners in our families. Firemen had mixed feelings about the subsequent return to work with a 10% pay increase in line with the Government's pay guidelines. The long-term benefits of the index-linked pay formula, however, prevented firemen from drifting back into poverty. A 42-hour per week shift was also introduced, resulting in the creation of thousands of firemen's jobs."

Despite these improvements in pay and conditions, there were further periods of unrest during the 1980s when the government proposed to increase pension contributions. This resulted in further work-to-rule protests on fire stations staffed by full-time firemen. Cheshire's FBU delegation was headed by Keith Davies, Mick Eaves, Ernie Magnall and Mike Maher.

A general feeling of solidarity among FBU members was clear at branch meetings. There was also a noticeable division between members of the FBU and some senior officers and politicians who organised the fire service. The protection of FBU members in the workplace and other health and safety issues were regular topics of discussion.

The FBU played a major part in developments within the fire service and constantly campaigned for safer systems of work. They also resisted lowering standards of fire cover to ensure maximum safety to the public and their members. In addition, they actively supported other trade unions during their own disputes. For example, the FBU supported families of striking miners in 1983/84 with regular donations of food.

A campaign to maintain the safety of the public at road traffic collisions was fought by Crewe Firemen in 1994 when Cheshire Fire Authority proposed to remove the GMC rescue tender special appliance from service. The rescue tender, which had replaced the emergency tender special appliance in 1990, was kitted out to help people or animals trapped in various circumstances (machinery, road traffic collisions - or cows stuck in ditches). Although rescue equipment was upgraded on the Brigade's first-line fire appliances, the FBU claimed that rescuing people trapped in vehicles required an expertise that Crewe firefighters had developed over many years. The rescue tender's off-road capability was another reason to maintain it as a rescue vehicle. Despite the campaign, which was supported by Gwyneth Dunwoody MP and many local councillors, the rescue tender was withdrawn from service and the vehicle itself remained as an operational support unit. One of its functions was to tow an inflatable safety boat, which was based at Crewe for three years.

A hardcore of FBU members from Crewe often supported FBU campaigns in other areas of the country, usually in big cities, such as London, Liverpool, Manchester, Birmingham, Nottingham and Glasgow. FBU representatives were also given opportunities to gain knowledge in health and safety and employment law, by attending TUC courses and workshops.

A pay campaign in 2002 led to further turmoil in the UK fire service. Crewe Firefighter Dave Williams, who was also Cheshire's FBU Secretary, summed up events during the dispute:

> *"The FBU were seeking a £30,000 wage, a new pay formula and full pay parity for part-time firefighters and Control Operators, who were paid 92% of a firefighters wage. The pay was determined by a formula dating back to 1978 and was linked to male manual workers and industries that had since been in decline, such as shipbuilding. As a result firefighters' pay had gradually fallen behind in comparison to other workers' pay. At the same time the work of firefighters had changed in many ways. The new pay formula would link fire service pay to that of employees in the 'Associate, Professional and Technical' group of workers. A series of meetings followed between the FBU and the National Employers group. Little progress was made on pay, however, until 12 November 2002. But just as an agreement was about to be signed, the Government instructed the National Employers to withdraw from it. This led to firefighters taking strike action on 13 November 2002 (48 hours), 22 November 2002 (eight days), 21 January 2003 (24 hours), 28 January 2003 (48 hours) and 1 February 2003 (48 hours). An agreement was eventually reached when the Government were given legal powers to impose a settlement. The dispute ended on 12 June 2003 with acceptance of a pay increase of 16% over three years, linked to changes in working conditions."*

Following the 2002/03 strike, a modernisation agenda was adopted. The changes included lifting an overtime ban among firefighters that had been in place since 1978, and the proposed replacement of existing fire control rooms with nine purpose-built control centres across the UK. Amid spiralling costs, this project was cancelled in 2010 after hundreds of millions of pounds had been wasted.

Crewe Firefighters faced challenges to keep their pension rights following the control centres fiasco and they also protested against the downgrading of their second fire appliance. Cheshire's FBU Secretary Andy Fox-Hewitt, who also served as a firefighter in Crewe describes these challenges:

"Between 2010 and 2020, Cheshire Fire and Rescue Service saw a reduction of more than 180 full-time firefighters. Also during this time we have seen major incidents, huge floods due to the ever frequent extreme weather patterns and also attacks on the profession by the Government. But Crewe Firefighters have stood strong in defence of their conditions, their profession and the local community they serve. In 2012, the Tory-led Coalition Government announced that in 2015 they would impose a series of detrimental changes to firefighters' pensions. These included built-in 'transitional protection' which kept older firefighters on better pension schemes while younger members were moved onto a worse pension scheme with requirement to work until the age of 60. This set in motion a three year campaign by the FBU, which involved several strike days in 2014. In December 2018, the Court of Appeal ruled that this transitional protection arrangement constituted age discrimination and was therefore unlawful. The Government then attempted an appeal to the Supreme Court. This was denied in June 2019, ending their legal challenge. The Government has since confirmed that the court ruling will be applied across all public sector pension schemes. Crewe Fire Station was due to lose its 'second fire engine' in 2018, in line with plans to remove five full-time fire engines that had been approved in 2013. After fire engines were taken from Chester, Runcorn, Warrington and Widnes, the FBU decided to run a full campaign to retain the engines at Crewe and Ellesmere Port. This involved a petition; street stalls and rallies in the town centre; press briefings; presentations at local council scrutiny meetings; a full lobby and demonstration at a Cheshire Fire Authority meeting at the Fire and Rescue Service HQ; and several meetings with MPs at the House of Commons. Alongside local Councillors Damian Bailey and Dorothy Flude, Laura Smith MP for Crewe and Nantwich gave full support to the firefighters. After 12 months of continuous campaigning, the Authority reversed its plan and announced that the fire engines would be saved. Crewe's proud tradition of having two fire engines that can respond to incidents was safe for future generations. More recently, Crewe Firefighters, union officials and local councillors have campaigned for a modern replacement of the outdated fire station on its existing site at Macon Way. Local firefighters opposed Cheshire Fire and Rescue Services' suggestion of an integrated police and fire station. Although this might have saved money, it would have jeopardised the firefighter's roots in humanitarian

assistance rather than in law enforcement. They are trusted and welcome in most people's homes, in schools and in youth groups and their public reputation is invaluable for the continued success of their vital fire prevention work."

Information for this chapter sourced from: Crewe FBU Officials (past and present), Forged in Fire (FBU book 1992), FBU journals, FBU Head Office and Crewe Chronicle.

*(**Above**) Firemen Pete Neary, Eric Taylor and Terry Kelly on the picket line during the 1977/78 strike. (**Below**) Firefighters Mick Clays, Graham Thomas, Kevin Bowen (Retired Firefighter), Leigh Bowen and Frank Bratley on the picket line during the 2002/03 strike.*

Trades Council Officials Andy Sharpe, Nina Hammill, Kathy Clarke and Stuart Crehan supporting firefighters during the 2002/03 strike.

Firefighters during the 2002/03 strike. L to R: Rob Benson, John Roberts (Retired Firefighter), Martin Jones, Ian Swan, Mitchell Clarke, Dave Langer, myself, Ian Selby, John Dunne, Steve Herbert, John Spicer, Bob Hughes, Dave Hanley, Hazel Jones (Station Cook), Lyndon Loweth and Steve Burrows.

A Green Goddess fire engine in Crewe during the 2002/03 strike.

Firefighters on the picket line during the 2014 strike.

*(**Above**) FBU Representative Dave Williams. (**Below**) FBU Representative Andy Fox-Hewitt with Laura Smith (MP for Crewe and Nantwich) during the 2014 strike.*

FIRE BRIGADE COMPETITIONS

It was traditional for fire brigades to compete against each other in the early days. Strict rules were in place as firemen took part in drills involving pumps, ladders and hose. The competitions were organised by the National Fire Brigades Union, which later amalgamated with the Professional Fire Brigades Association to form the British Fire Services Association. Competitors included Volunteer, Local Authority, County and Industrial Fire Brigades.

These competitions encouraged teamwork and served as a useful purpose in the development of firemen, as effective firefighting relies on getting things done quickly. Bringing different Brigades together also gave firemen opportunities to observe different methods and gain new ideas from each other. The competitions were public displays and the firemen competed with high spirits and rivalry. This helped to perfect the firemen's skills, improve moral and develop friendship. Dignitaries attended these events to observe the firemen's skills and present the rewards of cups, shields and prize money to the successful teams.

However, there were the occasional moments of controversy at these contests. In 1876, the Crewe Volunteer Fire Brigade made a strong protest after they were disqualified after winning two first prizes at the Chester Fire Brigade contest. The dispute ended up in the County Court at Chester Castle as the competition adjudicator (Superintendent Copland of the Liverpool Fire Brigade) faced a charge of fraud and dishonesty. After sitting until a late hour the Judge's final words in court were: "It cannot be expressed in stronger terms than these. You must show that he had a bad mind." The Judge then entered a nonsuit.

Details of some of the competitions involving Crewe Firemen as reported in local newspapers are listed below:

April 1879 - A contest organised by the Crewe Volunteer Fire Brigade took place in the grounds of the Royal Hotel in Crewe, with Volunteer Brigades from Carlisle, Barrow-in-Furness, West Derby, Stafford, Aston (near Birmingham), Winsford, Nantwich and Crewe competing. Colonel Sir Charles James Frith, JP, President of the Fire Brigade Association, acted as Judge, assisted by Superintendent Chadwick, of Northwich. A banquet followed the competition at the Royal Hotel. The competition results were reported in the *Manchester Evening News:*

Drill for Four Men with Engine
1. Stafford 2. Nantwich 3. Crewe.

Single Men Drill
1. H. Sparrow (Crewe) 2. Fletcher (Stafford) 3. Bailey (Stafford).

Drill for Eight Men and Sergeant (leather hose)
1. Stafford 2. Nantwich 3. Winsford.

Drill for Eight Men and Sergeant (canvas hose)
1. Crewe 2. Nantwich 3. Stafford.

May 1882 - On Whit Monday, the Crewe Volunteer Fire Brigade was very successful when they took part in a contest at Carlisle. It was reported in the *Guardian* that the competition, took place on the paddock of the racecourse under the auspices of the Carlisle Brigade. The contests were conducted very much on the lines of the successful gathering held in Crewe on Easter Monday, 1879. The Judge Mr. R.W. Vining, of Liverpool, organiser of the Crystal Palace contests, was assisted by Mr. T. Bellfield, Secretary of the Crewe Brigade, Lieutenant J.H. Bell of Carlisle, being the timekeeper.

Five Brigades entered into the competition. The Border City itself contributed four engines, the town of Crewe one, Kendal one, and Darlington one. Punctually at noon they were assembled in Court Square, and shortly afterwards they were arranged in order of procession and paraded the principal streets. Shortly after one o'clock, the engines formed in line with the paddock.

The first competition was a dry drill for four men, and the conditions were that the engine was to be put through working order, the pole and draw bars to be removed, levers to be turned over and secured, fore carriage locked and levers unlocked, 40 feet of leather delivery hose to be run out, branch pipe and two lengths of suction pipe to be attached with strainer and basket. The Crewe Brigade proved themselves long way superior. Their four men - Sparrow, G. Ollier, J. Ollier and H. Green - made 'ready' in 25 seconds, with two added, in consequence of a slack branch. Carlisle was second, Little, Sanderson, Weller and Heywood performing their task in 30 seconds, two being added in consequence of a loose clip on the levers.

The second competition was a dry drill for single men. The competitors had to spring from their engines which were supposed to have just arrived at the scene of a conflagration, and put everything in readiness single-handed. Two men from each Brigade competed. J. Ollier of Crewe was 1st in 55 seconds, with a 'clean sheet'. Sparrow of Crewe 2nd in 59 seconds also with a clean sheet and Garrett of Darlington 3rd, who did his work perfectly in 60 seconds. The first prize was £3, second £1.10s, and third 15s.

A wet drill for eight men and Sergeant was perhaps the most interesting event on the programme from a spectator's point of view. The engine, as in the first competition was to be put in thorough working order but the hose pipes were put in connection with a water tank, and the time was taken when the stream of water struck a mark at the height of 30 feet. This work in the opinion of the Judge was done excellently. The Darlington team was first, getting their hose into play in 27 seconds, with two added for a clip of the levers loose. Crewe were second in 35 seconds, with two added for a loose joint. The Crewe men who took part in this competition were Turten (first Sergeant), Farr (second Sergeant), Privates Green, G. Ollier, J. Ollier, Lowndes, Chatfield, Hough and Sparrow.

At the close the Judge remarked that in the course of ten years' experience he had never seen better work done, the single man drill especially in the case of the Crewe men being wonderfully quick. In the four men drill too, the work was remarkably smart.

After the contests had been brought to a close, a dinner was provided at the Turf Hotel. Lieutenant Bell of Carlisle who presided, proposed 'prosperity to the Crewe Brigade' and said the Brigade deserved credit for coming such a long way to the contest as well as for the very efficient manner in which the Brigade was conducted.

Captain Watson, of Crewe, in responding complimented the Carlisle Brigade upon the progress they had made since the contest held in Crewe, in 1879.

September 1911 - A report in the *Cheshire Observer* stated how the town of Crewe was honoured as the place to be selected by the North-Western District of the National Fire Brigades Union for holding their annual competitions. By the permission of the Corporation the competitions were held on the Goddard Street recreation ground. The entries of the Fire Brigades numbered forty-six. The arrangements of the competitions were made by the local committee, headed by Captain Harding, and the co-operation of Mr. C.J. Bowen Cooke, Chief Mechanical Engineer of the LNWR Company, himself an old Fireman, was much esteemed. The Earl of Haddington is president of the North-Western District, and in that capacity he displays the keenest interest in the work of the Brigades. Enthusiasm was the keynote of Saturday's competitions, and certainly a very encouraging spirit prevailed throughout. The only discouraging factor was the small attendance of the general public to witness the contests. An unusual and somewhat novel incident occurred during the progress of the competitions, the Nantwich Brigade being summoned to an outbreak in their District. A gentleman present, Captain W.B. Barlow, of Helsby, immediately offered the loan of his motor-car, which was gratefully accepted, and the Brigade drove off amid the cheers of their colleagues and the spectators. The results of the competition were as follows:

Four Men Manual Drill (Dry)
1. Nantwich 2. Crewe 3. Hoole.
Steamer Wet Drill
1. Castner-Kellner 2. Bury 3. Nantwich.
One Man Manual Drill
1. Crewe 2. Chester.
Manual Wet Drill
1. Tarporley 2. Nantwich 3. Alpraham.
Hose Cart Challenge
1. Greenall & Whitley's 2. Castner-Kellner 3. Tarporley 4. Macclesfield Volunteers.

May 1941 - An eventful day was held at the King George Playing Fields, when the Crewe Corporation Fire Brigade involved members of the community, including a number of Crewe Girls to take part in the Fire Drill Tests. Councillor Frank Roberts, Chairman of the Fire Brigade Committee, congratulated the 150 competitors on their splendid turn-out and their smartness in carrying out the various drills while presenting the prizes. The winners were:

Stirrup Pump Drill
1. Central 'A' 2. Maternity Home 3. North Street.
Hydrant Drill
1. Central 2. West Bent 3. County Clothes.
Trailer pump Drill
1. County Clothes 2. Wildings 3. West Bent.
Ladies' Stirrup Pump Drill

1. Miss Yoxall 2. Miss Dawson.
Best Dressed Fireman
Fireman E. Harrison.

August 1948 - Crewe Works Fire Brigade were the winners of the Hydrant and Breeching Drill when they competed against Railway Brigades from Holyhead, Heysham, Fleetwood, and Horwich at the Crewe Show and Carnival. Members of the Crewe team included: Sub-Captain H. Rodden, Firemen L. King, J. Jackson, H. Mottram, L. Minshull, H. Metcalf, Sub-Captain Handley and Captain H. Evans.

September 1948 - Firefighting teams serving industries and local authorities from all parts of North Wales and Merseyside took part in the annual Fire Brigade competition at Brymbo (Wrexham). Results were as follows:

Four Men Hydrant Drill
1. Rolls-Royce Ltd (Crewe) 2. BIC Cables Ltd (Helsby) 3. Electro Hydraulic Co (Sankey).
Two Men Hydrant Drill
1. Shell Refinery (Ellesmere Port) 2. Rolls-Royce Ltd (Crewe) 3. Courtaulds Ltd (Flint) & J Bibby & Sons Ltd (Liverpool) tied.
Five Men Hydrant Drill
1. J Bibby & Sons Ltd 2. Courtaulds Ltd.
Four Men Light Trailer Pump (Wet Drill)
1. Colwyn Bay 2. Wrexham.

August 1950 - Local firefighting teams from Crewe (Cheshire County), Crewe Works, Rolls-Royce, ROF Radway Green and Foden's in Sandbach took part in the annual Crewe Show and Carnival. Foden's team were warmly congratulated on their performance against the regulars. The events included: Hydrant Drills, Breeching Drills and Motor Pump Drills.

September 1950 - When Rolls-Royce Fire Brigade was formed in the mid-1940s they also took the opportunity to participate in these events. Standards were high, as was stated by General Sir Frank Simpson, GOC-in-C, Western Command, who presented prizes at the Chester and District Fire Services Competition at Littleton Old Hall. "We in the Services know well how we are backed up by civilian Fire Brigades; the co-operation between them and ourselves, from our point of view, could not be bettered. We are very grateful for it. We are facing difficult times and we never know when we shall have to face times much more difficult. The standards you Brigades have shown in your competitions are very high." The six events, one of which involved the scaling of a wall 10 feet six inches high, as part of the light trailer pump drill, attracted 57 teams from Cheshire, Lancashire and North Wales. *(Chronicle).*

May 1952 - The second Fire Brigade competition of the London Midland Region, British Railways, was held at the Goddard Street Sports Ground, Crewe. Five teams competed from Crewe, Wolverton, Horwich, Derby and Westhouses. The honours went to Wolverton, who won the two competitions. The first competition was a three man Hydrant Drill, during which a team of three ran out two lengths of hose in one line from the hydrant, knocked down No. 1 target, after which the first length was presumed burst and after replacement, the second target was knocked down. The Trailer Pumps Drill was next. A crew consisting of five men placed the pump at the dam, connected suction and one length of delivery hose. After knocking down No. 1 target, they replaced the hose nozzle with breeching and connected two lengths of hose and knocked down targets 2 and 3. *(Chronicle).*

July 1953 - The Chester Fire Service competition was held at the King George V Memorial Fields in Crewe. The competitions included: Hydrant Drills, Breeching Drills (Dry), Motor Pumps Drills (Dry), Hose and Ladder Drills, Light Trailer Pump Drills (Wet) and Large Trailer Pump Drills. A record entry of over 90 teams competed for 14 trophies and £700 in prize money. The 200 Firemen taking part were from Cheshire, Lancashire, Staffordshire, Wales and Yorkshire. Despite the wet and muddy conditions the event was hugely successful and the prizes were presented by Lieutenant General Sir Charles Loewen (GOC-in-C, Western Command) who commented that the competition had shown a great deal of skill and hard work which is needed to make our Fire Services so efficient.

September 1956 - Firemen from Crewe's Rolls-Royce represented the Merseyside Branch at the annual National Industrial Fire Protection Association competition at the Lancashire County Council Fire Brigade HQ in Liverpool's Albert Embankment. Those taking part included: Chief Officer G. Valentine, Sub Officer W. Jones, Firemen R. Best, W. Kirkland, R. Dodd, G. Ford, A. Nicklin, E. Rimmer and R. Shore.

June 1961 - The Rolls-Royce team proved they were among the best when they tied for the first prize in the North West District British Fire Service Association against 24 other works teams. The Crosfield Shield awarded to the team with the highest number of points from five events was shared by Rolls-Royce and the BICC team from Prescot, as was the Nantwich Cup, for the second aggregate prize. The Rolls-Royce team also retained the Reddaway Cup, awarded to the team gaining second place in the dry Whiston motor pump drill event. They also added to their trophies the Leyland Motors Cup by gaining second place in the dry hydrant drill event. The team on that day included: Robert Thornhill, Arthur Pickup, Frank Ollier, William Jones, Walter Kirkland, Robert Dodd and Ronald Best. The ROF Radway Green team was third in the aggregate prize list. Their team included: Messrs. W. George, L. Dale, T. Hassall, A. Walker, J. Rhodes and C. Brockley. The master of the arena was Mr. H. Harding and the assistant master was Mr. G. Valentine (Chief Officer at Rolls-Royce).

September 1962 - Seventy nine teams travelled from all parts of Cheshire to Littleton Old Hall, near Chester for the annual Chester and District Fire Services Competition. Welcoming the competitors and spectators, Mr. W. Mitchell, Chairman of Chester Rural Council, said that since the competition started in 1948, it had become one of the largest in the country.

The most successful competitors were the County Fire Brigade's Hoylake 'A' team, captained by Station Officer A.C. Fenton. They took four trophies including the Challenge Cup presented by Cheshire County Council for best aggregate score.

Motor Pump Drill
1. Hoylake 2. Albright & Wilson Ltd (Widnes) 3. BIC Cables (Helsby).
Hose and Ladder Drill (Dry)
1. Hoylake 2. Morecambe (Lancs FB) 3. War Dept COD (Branston).
Large Trailer Pump Drill (Wet)
1. Albright & Wilson 2. Whiston (Lancs FB).
Hydrant Drill (Dry)
1. Rolls-Royce Ltd (Crewe) 2. Proctor & Gamble B Team 3. Glovers Gable.
Light Trailer Pump Drill with Obstacle (Wet)
1. War Dept FB COD 2. Lostock Works 3. BIC Cables 4. ROF Radway Green.

During one of the events, a spectator, Mrs. Ivy Kitchener, of Dearson Place, Sheffield, was soaked when she got a little too near the target for the jets. She had come with a competing trip on a coach from Sheffield, but her face was saved when the St. John Ambulance Officers came to her rescue. Commander Miss K. Boden said: "We took off her clothes and sent her to the County Fire Brigade Headquarters to have them dried. As Mrs. Kitchener had only recently had an attack of pneumonia, officials were very concerned, but when the time came for her to return to Sheffield she had fully recovered. *(Cheshire Observer).*

These competitions continued until the mid-1960s. A *Guardian* reporter summed up the benefits of these events:

> *'No doubt such competitions, promoting as they do, attendance and efficiency at drill, perfection of appliances for the preservation of life and property from fire, and the cultivation among the members of esprit de corps, and pride in their voluntary organization, are of the greatest value.'*

Information for this chapter sourced from The Chronicle, The Guardian, Cheshire Observer and Manchester Evening News.

CREWE WORKS FIRE BRIGADE

By the mid-19th Century Crewe's railway industry, under the leadership of John Ramsbottom, was equipped with two steam fire engines. They could be fitted to wheeled frames allowing them to travel along the rail tracks with hoses attached in readiness to deal with fires. In October 1861, the *Cheshire Observer* reported that a steam fire engine belonging to the London and North Western Railway (LNWR) was capable of projecting a jet of water 180 feet high. But the Crewe Works Fire Brigade (CWFB) not only dealt with fires on railway property - it was also a major force in fighting fires in Crewe.

Although the Brigade only dealt with one serious blaze in 1872, their efficiency using their firefighting equipment was kept up with regular drilling. Their value to the town had proved itself in fighting major fires at Crewe Hall (1866) and at the Town Hall (1869). Between 4,000 - 5,000 feet of hose was available throughout the Works and the Steam Shed. A reference to 'the Steam Shed Brigade' suggests that it had its own designated fire-fighting team.

By 1876, the CWFB's 16 firemen were led by George Pottie (Chief Officer), W.B. Watkins (First Captain), James Hughes (Second Captain), James Kenyon (Lieutenant), George Thomas (Sergeant) and Jonathan Kemp (Engineman). In addition to their steam fire engines, they also had the use of two hand engines. One of these belonged to the LNWR and was kept at the Works and the other belonged to W.B. Watkins, which was housed for local use at the Royal Hotel in Nantwich Road. Notice of fire was given to James Hughes (Works' Watchman) at the Forge Street Works entrance, or to Charles Welch at the Royal Hotel. The fire alarm was raised by a steam buzzer at the Works.

In July 1876, the loud sound of the buzzer summoned the CWFB to a fire in the proximity of the oil stores. It was feared that the fire involved the company's oil stores located at the old Works, which had been burnt to the ground some years before. Fortunately, this was not the case on this occasion, although a fire was raging from a van wagon containing oily waste that had been collected from different stations on the line. The cotton waste was saturated with oil and grease and the fire was believed to have been ignited by spontaneous combustion.

By 1880, the Brigade was led by Alex Kerr (Chief Officer), James Hughes (Captain), James Kenyon and George Thomas (Lieutenants). It was traditional for fire brigades to hold dinners to commemorate special occasions, and in November 1883, a presentation evening was held at the Imperial Hotel to honour J.C. Peache (Superintendent) who was leaving to take up a management position in Leeds. Members of the CWFB took part, as well as Captain Uke and Mr. Muir of the Crewe Volunteer Fire Brigade.

A disastrous blaze at the Works on 28 March 1892 proved to be one of the worst in Crewe's history. The fire was discovered in the Chain Shop, but it spread to the Millwright's Shop. It resulted in 500 workers losing their jobs.

During the early 20th Century, 16 firemen were enlisted to the CWFB. Their captain of 22 years, James Kenyon, retired in 1903. He was succeeded by Captain Earp. For several years, the CWFB had been serious competitors in many contests against other industrial and local authority brigades. The CWFB also regularly joined in local events such as the annual carnival.

In June 1924, Crewe Town Council reassured Captain Beames of the CWFB that the Crewe Corporation Fire Brigade (CCFB) would give assistance at fires on railway property in the Borough. Although the CCFB had made significant progress since the beginning of the 20th Century, they were in many ways regarded as second best to CWFB, whose oilskin uniforms gave them added protection at fires. The CWFB continued to play a key role in fighting fires in Crewe especially in the vicinity of railway property. One such incident involved a blaze at the Works' Carriage Shed in March 1929. The fire soon took hold after it was discovered by Night Watchman Gresty. The Shed was open at both ends and was gutted as the strong wind fanned the flames causing the roof to collapse. Several passenger coaches were also involved.

In May 1938, the CWFB, the CCFB and a crew of Staffordshire Firemen fought to contain a fire at a locomotive steam shed in Alsager. Six locomotives were removed from the building as flames licked the roof of the shed that was eventually gutted.

The Works was served by the following firemen during the 1930s: T. Allman, J. Barnard, G. Debank, R. Dixon, G. Eckinsley, H. Evans, J. Giles, A. Gilham, S. Glover, H. Gough, F. Hanley, J. Harrop, J. Hazelhurst, J. Hughes, N. Jinks, H. King, H. Mottram (Sr), H. Mottram (Jr), F. Patridge, H. Roddan, T. Roddan, W. Rodger, H. Rutter, G. Trigger and W. Woodhouse.

In August 1936, Captain R. Dixon retired from his duties with CWFB. In his younger days he had played for Crewe Alexandra Football Club and had been a member of the Crewe Engineers, accompanying them to South Africa during the Boer War.

A fire train came into service in 1924, and was brought up to date by the Great Western Railway Company during the 1930s to become a modern firefighting unit. It carried two large static water-tanks behind the fire coach, and enough equipment to fight a serious fire. The train was on-call and was used to fight fires close to railway lines and at railway stations. On 11 June 1937, it provided back-up to firemen from Hanley, Longton and Stoke when a goods warehouse was gutted at Stoke Station. Fortunately, the adjoining buildings were saved.

Three fire trains were brought into service at Derby, Horwich and Crewe where the fire 'coupe' was kept under the Chester railway bridge. During the Second World War, the Crewe fire train was deployed to fight fires - often caused by German incendiary bombs - in cities such as Birmingham, Liverpool and Manchester. In addition, they were on permanent stand-by to the constant threat of bombing in places such as the Sutton Weaver Viaduct which would have affected the rail route to Northern England and Scotland. The crew of the fire train became known as 'the flying squad' during the blitz. Some of the major fires they attended in 1940 as reported in the CWFB log book included:

26 June 1940 - Hanley Railway Station - Fire involving roof and veranda, caused by German bombing.

22 September 1940 - Alexandra Docks, Liverpool - Goods warehouse on fire, caused by enemy high explosive bombs followed by incendiary bombs. Firemen with the Horwich fire train were also fighting the fire. Insufficient water supplies hampered firefighting and this resulted in the whole of the warehouse being gutted.

26 September 1940 - Crewe - Air raid message received at 7.40pm. Incendiary bombs were dropped on various Shops at the Steel Works and were dealt with by the AFS. A detachment of the CWFB dealt with a fire on the roof of the Tender Shop, while another fire team went to the Coal Wharf in Thomas Street, where they found the AFS and the CCFB dealing with a coal wagon on fire. The CWFB were then deployed to examine the Stock Shed Carriage Works, and found that the roof had been damaged by a bomb containing oil. This caused a small fire in the roof which was successfully dealt with.

30 September 1940 - Egerton Docks Goods Warehouse, Birkenhead - A three story warehouse, 300 x 50 feet, was ablaze from end to end. The fire was caused by enemy bombing. CWFB supported fire teams from the Birkenhead Fire Brigade.

3 October 1940 - Chester Railway Line, Crewe - Pumping operations by the crew of the fire train at Chester Bridge, following enemy bombing on the railway line.

24 October 1940 - Victoria Railway Station, Manchester - The fire was caused by enemy action. It covered a very large area, which involved platform numbers 12, 13, 14, 15, and 16. The fire also affected the offices beyond platform 16 and the roof and several parcel trains that were standing in the station. CWFB set up water relays in conjunction with the Horwich Fire Brigade and a unit of Manchester AFS to prevent further fire spread.

29 October 1940 - New Street Railway Station, Birmingham - CWFB worked alongside Birmingham City Firemen and the fire train team from Derby to bring the fire at the parcels office under control.

22 December 1940 - Canada Dock, Liverpool - Enemy bombing set the warehouse on fire, and caused the canal bank to burst and flood the entire goods yard. Although the water had subsided, it left layers of silt. This made it difficult to locate hydrants. The warehouse was gutted and the military dealt with the additional hazard of an unexploded bomb.

23 December 1940 - Fire at Mayfield Railway Station, Manchester - The fire train was delayed attending this incident due to fear of bombs on the railway line on the approach to Manchester.

24 December 1940 - Fire at Victoria Railway Station, Manchester - Caused by enemy bombing. Due to a lack of water supplies, CWFB were involved in water relay with the Manchester AFS.

Many of the Works' fire calls were to deal with burning slags of coal or grass and embankment fires. In a 12 month period during 1941, they turned out to over 100 emergencies. Enemy bombing at railway stations continued, and on 2 June 1941, CWFB were once again firefighting at Victoria Railway Station in Manchester alongside their colleagues on the Horwich fire train.

As well as firefighting and maintaining their equipment, CWFB collected data from other railway stations. This included location and availability of water supplies, hydrants water pressure, building construction of the station and signal box and details of the nearest local authority fire brigade. The following information is from the CWFB log book:

'Conway Railway Station - Passenger Station, built chiefly of brick and stone. Station Master's house on UP platform. Six fire buckets on station. One extinguisher in emergency box fixed in Signal Box about 50 yards from east end of platform. Signal Box is closed at 10.45pm. Council's fire station is about 300 yards in distance, motor fire engine. Hydrant close to station entrance and pressure of water is only moderate. Volunteer Brigade, Station telephone communications. Goods warehouse built of bricks with nine fire buckets.'

A *Chronicle* report during February, 1948 described the role of the CWFB:

'The Railway Firefighters at Crewe are equipped to dash by road or rail directly an alarm is given. They are equipped with a train which carries them to various parts of the country when their aid is sought. Whenever the train leaves its lair at Crewe, the station lights flick over to green to speed it on its property - and possibly, life-saving - mission. Harry Evans, who is the full-time Captain of the Crewe Works Fire Brigade, has had a full share of Fireman's thrills. In addition to being Captain of the two road units attached to Crewe Works, he also has the special train at his disposal. The train, throughout the 24 hours, is kept ready for an immediate journey to any part of the system, and at any time of day or night the volunteer crew of turners, boilermakers and fitters are ready to make a speedy turn-out to any call. Painted throughout in bright red, the fire train (there are others at Derby and Horwich) consists of two tenders of water (8,500 gallons) and a coach, in which the firemen travel. It contains iron rations, a mobile pump of 360 gallons-per-minute capacity, with miles of hose, a foam-making unit for dealing with petrol and oil fires and appliances and couplings which will convert or fit any appliance in use in the country. The Crewe Works road units ('Dennis' and 'Sulzer') are modern machines, capable of attaining a volume of 1,500 gallons-per-minute. They are used chiefly for fires in and around the Works estate, which is also covered by many high pressure mains upwards of 300 hydrants and 130 fire cupboards holding miles of hose and hundreds of fire extinguishers. The Crewe Area Fire Superintendent is Mr. John Wheeldon, who is proud of the keenness and efficiency of his Officers and men, and considers that the Crewe Works Brigade, for speed, efficiency and up-to-the-minute appliances has no unit superior in the country. Last year the Crewe Brigade took first and second prizes at Horwich

in the North West District competitions, and the Superintendent is confident that they will yet make their mark in the National Fire Competitions.'

CWFB's outstanding service was recognised in April 1947, when the *Chronicle* reported that Mr. J. Rankin, Superintendent at Crewe Works presented cheques to 15 of its members. This followed a fire, which originated in the Erecting Shop stores when a number of tanks were in danger. Mr. H. Mottram (jr), a member of the Brigade, discovered the outbreak, and he and a number of men employed in the Department kept the flames in check until the arrival of the Brigade. In handing over the cheques, Mr. Rankin said that had it not been for this prompt action the consequences might have been very grave. They certainly saved fire from spreading to other Departments. Mr. J. Wheeldon, Chief Fire Officer, expressed the thanks of the men to the Company and Mr. Rankin for the cheques. The recipients were Messrs H. Evans (Captain), G. Debank (Sub-Captain), J. Giles, F. Hanley, J. Harrop, W. Woodhouse, H. Mottram (sr), J.G. Jackson, C. Riley, H. Mottram (jr), J.R. Hewitt, L. Minshull, J. Barnard, L. Wood and H. Jones.

Captain Harry Evans retired in 1948 after 37 years in the CWFB. He attended about 2,000 fires and had served as Captain since 1939.

The fire train remained in operation until the late 1950s. Its crews had fought a variety of fires on railway properties, often alongside Local Authority Fire Brigades. They also worked alongside RAF Firemen from Hawarden on one occasion, when they attended a fire at Mold Junction on 13 June 1946. The train was dispatched to another 'over the border' fire on 13 March 1950 after fire broke out at the tubular rail bridge at Menai Bridge.

A ceremony was held at Crewe Works in April 1957 for the opening of the new fire station. Mr. I. C. Forsyth, Manager of the Works, opened the building that had cost £4,500. It was able to house two modern fire engines and trailers and was situated near the Deviation Entrance of the Locomotive Works. It replaced the old timber-built fire station. The Works Fire Brigade was now dealing with an average of 50 fires a year.

One of longest serving firemen at the CWFB was First World War Veteran Harry Roddan. The former boiler-maker, who worked on the railway for over 50 years and as a fireman for almost 40 years, joined CWFB in 1922. In 1952, he became Captain and was sometimes in charge of the fire train. Harry's father, Thomas Roddan, was also connected with the CWFB. He served for over 30 years and held the position of Captain for two years. Harry Roddan was succeeded as Captain by his deputy, Dennis Cotton, who played a pivotal role at the Works from the 1950s until the early 80s. His wife Elizabeth tells us about his time at the Works:

"Dennis took up an apprenticeship in the Erecting Shop as a 16 year old during the early 1940s. He worked on the weed killer trains before moving into the Works' Fire Brigade. At the time he lived in one of the railway houses in Betley Street, which was fitted with an alarm bell, to alert him of fires. It was from here that he would sprint to the fire station, close to Eaton Street when a fire-call came in. He frequently attended 'line-side' fires which had to be tackled. These were caused by the hot soot from steam engines that set fire to the dry grass and shrubbery alongside railway lines. Thursday

evenings were the drill nights, which also involved testing the fire alarms. Some of his close colleagues included: Derek Pover, Harry Cutler, Horace Metcalfe, Reg Tabley and Charlie Whittle, to name a few. It wasn't just the fire brigade that occupied Dennis' time at the Works. He attended weekly classes in first aid and was a lead in treating workers when they sustained injuries. As well as his fire prevention duties, especially with apprentices as they came through the ranks, Dennis also became involved with security work, and also hosted visitors and VIP's on tours around the Works. He was also involved in organising Christmas parties for the workers' families and ensured that Father Christmas had enough presents for every child!"

Robert Wootton worked in the offices next to the fire station at Crewe Works from 1944 until 1988. He remembers how busy the firemen were during his time at the Works.

"Until my latter few years at the Works, the Fire Brigade had been kept very busy. On hearing the sound of the hooter they left their jobs and raced into the fire station, and in no time at all, they were dashing off in the fire engine to deal with a fire. In my early years at the Works they covered an area, which was at least three miles long and when not dealing with emergencies, they often spent time in the larger shops (Erecting, Machine and Fabrication), where they checked fire extinguishers, the exits routes and fire doors."

At its height, over 20,000 were employed at Crewe Works, but as the site downsized and went through several changes of ownership from the mid-1980s, the CWFB was revamped. Responsibility for fire safety was now in the hands of Chris Thorley, who remained in post until 1994. Chris recalls his days at the Works:

"There was nothing pleasant about being covered in asbestos, ash and oil as a 15 year old, when I started working as an apprentice fitter on steam engines in 1954. The only good thing was that you made some great mates and gained a good apprenticeship, especially in the Erecting Shop. At 17 years of age I trained to be an electrician, and seven years later, I became a Railway Electrical Inspector travelling all over the country on test runs to check the electrical 'finished work' on steam engines. As steam engines were phased out in 1967, inspections continued on diesel engines and a bulk of the work involved checking the automatic warning devices. In 1971, I was asked to provide cover for Dennis Cotton, who was in charge of the Works Fire Brigade. After studying the relevant legislation I agreed to take up the position and on Dennis' return to work, I continued to work alongside him. Dennis was passionate about his work as a Fire Officer. He often talked about past fires that had been dealt with by the crew of the fire train and about the Works' fire appliances. Dennis also organised holidays for the Railwaymen's Touring Club. He would arrange everything. All we had to do was turn up. One holiday at the Italian resort

of Alassio was particularly memorable. My wife Margaret and daughter Caroline would cry with laughter as my 10 year old son David accompanied Dennis to the swimming pool. They created mayhem by jumping and diving into the water with one purpose in mind...to splash the Germans! Sadly Dennis passed away in 1985. By now I was responsible for 25 fire and security members of staff at the Park Entrance and seven firemen, who worked in the Maintenance and Erecting Shops. I was also asked to set up a Works Emergency planning team by my Manager, Andrew Gormley. The team's gruesome task was to free the bodies of trapped drivers and their colleagues from locos following fatal incidents when trains had been involved in crashes or fires. The team included: Harry Hardaway, Graham Deeming, Les Skit and Reg Tabley. Harry was tasked with cutting and grinding in very dangerous circumstances as the loco was full of diesel fuel, battery gas and acid. There was also a police officer present during these tasks, usually a woman, who collected and delivered the personal belongings of the victims. These were harrowing moments for the team. I took redundancy after 39 years service. Within an hour of arriving home after my last shift I received a phone call from the Works to ask if I would return to work. I was informed that as I had signed the fire certificates, which was confirmation that the statutory fire regulations had been complied with throughout the Works, then I had to be on site otherwise the insurance cover would be invalid. So after discussions with my wife Margaret, I decided to continue working for a further three months. However, after a meeting with the Works' Managing Director, it was suggested that I set myself up in business as a Fire Consultant and continue with the fire prevention work. The offer was too good to turn down, so with Margaret's assistance, I operated a successful business with responsibility for fire precautions at Crewe, Derby and York Railway Works, until I retired at the age of 66 years. After giving up work I continued to remain active in the community as a Councillor with the Crewe and Nantwich Borough Council and served as the Mayor, as we welcomed the new Millennium in 2000. As a Councillor with a 'fire safety' background, I was duly elected as a member of Cheshire Fire Brigade's Fire Authority Committee, whose role was to oversee policy and delivery of the Fire Service."

The CWFB continued until the mid-1980's and like many industrial fire brigades, they joined forces with the on-site security department.

Information sourced for this chapter from: The Chronicle, The Guardian, CWFB Call-out Log Book, Mrs. E. Cotton, Mr. C. Thorley and Mr. R. Wootton.

*(**Above**) Crewe Works Fire Brigade in 1885. (**Below**) The Works Firemen after winning a Brigade competition in 1926. Among them are: H. Evans, W. Rodger, W. Woodhouse, G. Debank and two members of the Mottram family (father and son).*

(**Above**) *Crewe Works Firemen at Captain Beames' house, 1926 (the Crosville Club occupies this site these days). Back L to R: Harry Mottram, William Woodhouse and Harry Evans. Front: G. Debank.* (**Below**) *Crewe Works Fire Brigade in the 1930s.*

*(**Above**) Crewe Works Firemen with their fire train and fire appliances (Dennis and Sulzer) outside the British Rail General Offices in 1948. (**Below**) Crewe Works Fire Brigade Calls, 1938 - 1960.*

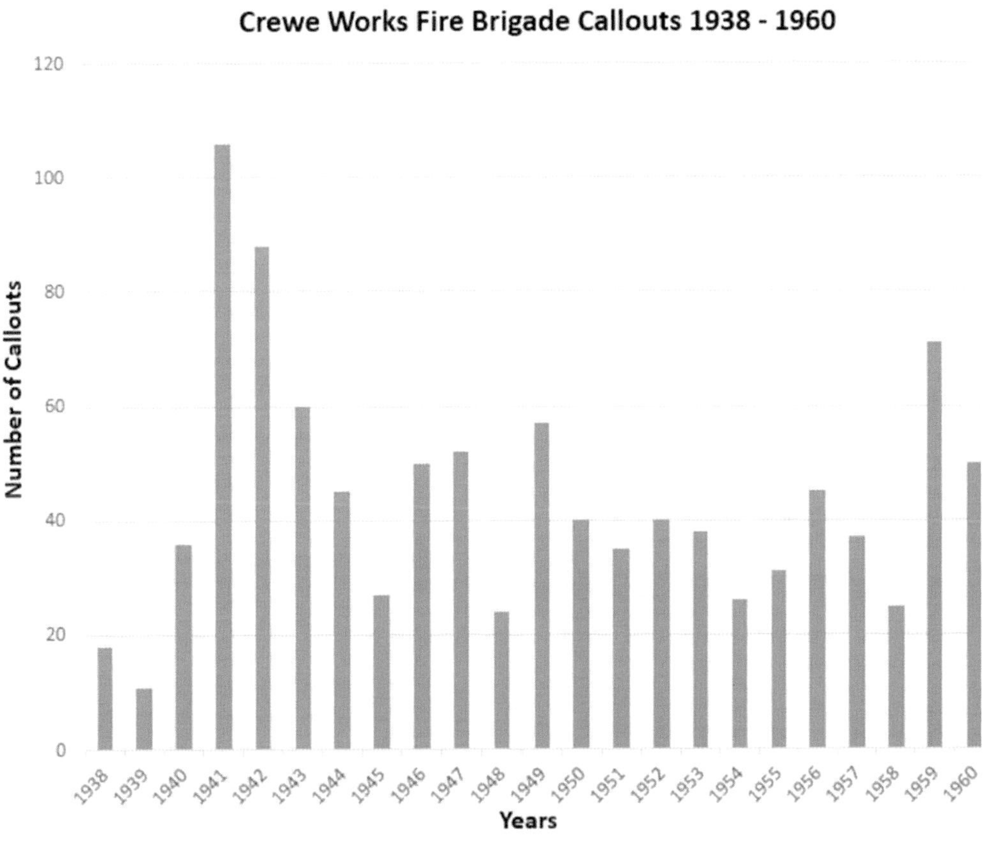

*(**Above**) Fire Officer Dennis Cotton presented with his long service medal by Mr. G. Oldham (Works Manager) in 1970. (**Below**) Firemen from Crewe Works and Crewe Fire Station at Dennis Cotton and Harry Cutler's medal presentation on 20 August 1970. Among the firemen and officers are: Jeff Goddard, Dave Holman, Harold Howard, Geoff Humphreys, Noel Lightbody, Len McIntosh and Ray Mills.*

*(**Above**) Crewe Works Firemen in the 1980s. L to R: Dave Prince, Bob Moores, Trevor Harris, Chris Thorley, Gerry O'Connor and Alf Wood. (**Below**) Fire Officer Chris Thorley in the Works' Land Rover fire appliance during the 1980s.*

ROLLS-ROYCE FIRE BRIGADE

Malcolm Smith's 30 year career with the Crewe Rolls-Royce Fire and Security Department began in 1971. His mentor when he joined was a former RAF Fireman, who once served on the Blue Streak (Ballistic Missile) programme at the Spadeadam Rocket testing site, where safety was of extreme importance. Similarly, safety was at the heart of the Rolls-Royce Fire and Security Department's work, which underwent many changes during Malcolm's career, as new legislation and the influence of market forces, impacted the Factory. For the last 11 years of his career Malcolm was Manager of the Department.

FIRE BRIGADE (1939 - 1968)
FIRE AND SECURITY DEPARTMENT (1968 - 2001)

In 1936 the UK Government began a programme to expand Britain's Air Defences and modernise the Royal Air Force. In 1938 the Air Ministry and Ministry of Labour agreed to build a Rolls-Royce Factory to manufacture and test Merlin aero engines at Crewe. Building commenced on a 60 acre site at the west end of the town that had formed part of Merrill's Farm. The first engine produced at Crewe left the factory in June 1939. This factory and a number of similar ones within the UK became known as Shadow Factories.

Pertinent fire safety legislation at the time would have been the Factories Act 1937. Manufacturing in wartime was clearly a high risk undertaking, even more so to a business providing aero engines for the nation's war effort. The site itself was considered a legitimate enemy target. This prediction was to become a reality when the factory was attacked in an unexpected bombing raid in December 1940 with a number of casualties resulting.

Despite the ever present fear of attack, the workforce continued to produce large numbers of aircraft engines, as did other Shadow Factories. They had always understood an attack could happen at any time. Protection afforded them were blast walls sectioning larger buildings and an extensive network of air raid shelters. An air raid siren fitted on the factory water tower alerted both factory and surrounding area of impending attack and all clear.

The Air Raid Precautions (ARP) set up by Government provided guidance and preparation for war and it created countrywide posts for ARP Wardens whose duties included overseeing and monitoring precautions in case of air raids, these included ensuring lights were not displayed in times of blackout, getting people to air raid shelters and operating warning sirens and whistles. It is believed that ARP Wardens were deployed at the factory and worked alongside the fire brigade.

There was also an internal siren in the manufacturing area; its sole purpose was to alert volunteer firemen they needed to attend the fire station. This existed and was in use well beyond the War years (1939-1945). It is believed the Company's fire station was built prior to the summer of 1939. It was single storey of brick construction with concrete base comprising of four vehicle bays, workshop, mess room and control room/office. It is understood the fire brigade was initially formed of volunteers. However after Britain's declaration of War (3 September 1939), the brigade became a full-time service with volunteers making up numbers as required. At about the same time a Works Police unit was formed and the two entities worked independently of each other, unless there were operational reasons to work jointly.

Little is known of firefighting equipment available to the brigade, however anecdotal evidence suggests a petrol engine trailer pump equipped with suction hose, canvas delivery hose and branch pipes was available. The Transport Department was located next to the fire station at the time and a vehicle was always likely to be available to tow the pump if needed. In addition, a hand cart with basic equipment was available for portable use. Its equipment consisted of canvas delivery hose, branch pipes, standpipe key and bar, plus a foam gun and container of protein foam. Whilst the hand cart may appear rudimentary it was practical in that it could go through buildings, rather than around them along narrow gangways/corridors and doorways.

Siebe Gorman Breathing Apparatus sets were available, which comprised of an airbag, oxygen bottle, mouthpiece and goggles. Several of these survived until the 1970s; possibly to remind new recruits how fortunate they were to have far better equipment at their disposal. Although the Siebe Gorman sets were cutting edge technology during the War years, they had been withdrawn from use many years earlier having been superseded by Draeger self contained compressed air Breathing Apparatus.

The Fire Station workshop held supplies of spare equipment and housed a fixed steam powered hose drying machine to enable the then standard canvas unlined fire hose to be dried for quick return to service. The hose was also repaired and fire extinguishers were maintained in the workshop.

During the War and for some considerable time afterwards much firefighting equipment was located along the factory streets and avenues to enable quick deployment in case of fire. The equipment would be held within wall mounted cabinets (red in colour) and generally consisted of a standpipe, key and bar, a branch pipe and two lengths of 2½ inch diameter canvas delivery hose. Fire extinguishers and hose reels were placed in all areas of the factory as required by both legislative and business needs.

Fire hydrants were also available on streets and avenues at approximately 25 yard intervals. The hydrants operated at normal town pressure of around 45psi, although pressure could be increased to 120psi on powering up the electric pump located near the base of the water tower. The pump would automatically cut in should a pressure switch indicate a drop in hydrant main pressure of 10psi. Three tanks of emergency water supplies (EWS) were located underground. These were referred to as dams by the old hands. In addition, the hydrant main could be supplemented with supplies from the elevated water tank (water tower) located close to the south east corner of the Factory.

After the War the site became home to the manufacture of Rolls-Royce and Bentley Motor Cars. Some areas of the site were leased to other businesses namely, Kelvinator Refrigerators, who manufactured for domestic and commercial markets and Chester Barrie (generally known as County Clothes) clothing manufacturers. These separate businesses, whilst occupying parts of the site, were independent entities and outside the scope of Rolls-Royce Fire Brigade other than receiving passing attention. Kelvinators suffered a serious fire on the site and moved to Bromborough in 1956. Chester Barrie moved to a new factory in 1961.

The Rolls-Royce Fire Brigade were known to have entered numerous 'Fire Brigade' competitions with other industrial brigades and had a number of successes. Unfortunately many of these events were not recorded and so the detail of whom, where and when is not known. It's a pity because history would have been kind to these men as they strove to be the best they could. They had great pride in their work and the business they represented.

1960s - The Factories Act 1961 gave fire authorities power to inspect factories with regard to fire safety. The act also made provision for means of firefighting and structural fire separation. Means of escape were included in previous legislation and were also added to this latest Act.

In the mid-1960s a van was converted to carry fire equipment. It consisted of a fixed hose reel that would be coupled to the nearest hydrant for a continuous water supply, 12 lengths of 2½ inch diameter layflat duraline hose, several branch pipes, standpipes keys and bars, foam gun and protein foam (approx 180 litres) and two portable self contained breathing apparatus sets. Prior to this vehicle, the Department would use small vans that had previously served the Transport Department. These were well maintained and roadworthy.

During the late 1960s the Works Fire Brigade and Works Police were amalgamated to form a single entity that became known as the Fire and Security Department. Rolls-Royce was not unique in doing this and many motor manufacturers and large industries went through or had already adopted the same generic 'Security' title. Needless to say the change was not welcomed by all the men but to their credit they came to accept, albeit grudgingly in some quarters, that change was inevitable. It would be fair to conclude that Rolls-Royce Fire Brigade, Crewe, ceased to exist from 1968 and a description more appropriate would be Rolls-Royce Fire and Security Department.

The Company's Medical Centre was opposite the fire station with an electronic link operated by Nurses to call the ambulance. The ambulance was a converted van equipped with stretcher, loading rails and portable first aid equipment including a Minuteman Resuscitator.

The rank structure changed following the amalgamation of Police and Fire Departments. In simple terms 'gate' control became the responsibility of the duty Sergeant based at the main gatehouse (accountable to the duty Sub Officer), whilst a

Sub Officer was responsible for fire operations, safety and administration including maintenance and patrols. The Sub Officer was based at the fire station and accountable to the Chief Fire and Security Officer. A three shift (watch) system was in operation to provide cover of 24 hours per day, 365 days a year. Officers worked a 19 day shift cycle followed by two days off. Average working week was 56 contractual hours. This would eventually change to four shifts with the average working week 42 contractual hours. More men were recruited to make up the additional shift.

At this time many areas of the site benefited from improved fire safety following installation of dedicated sprinkler systems. Sprinklers were a blessing because, not only did they warn of fire, they did something about it. The principle behind sprinklers is to contain fire, and on most occasions, extinguish them as well. All sprinkler alarms were linked to the Company fire station control room as were other systems, including automatic smoke/heat detection and manually operated break glass call points. Local fixed application systems were employed where appropriate. These being CO2, BTM (Halon 1301) and high pressure foam spray - consisting of water and Aqueous Film Forming Foam (AFFF) mix.

Dedicated emergency phones were supplied at the fire station for fire and medical emergencies and phones were duplicated at the main gatehouse to ensure a fast response. Emergency numbers were available to call from all site phones of which there were several hundred.

1970s -The Fire Precautions Act 1971 brought about major changes with regard to fire safety. This legislation gave power to the Fire Service to inspect premises in a far more prescriptive way, than it had in the past. The Fire Brigade was required to issue fire certificates to premises to ensure compliance with fire safety standards. This was followed with ongoing inspections to ensure standards were met.

In the late 1970s, the Company replaced the van, used to carry fire equipment and invested in a Dennis F8 (TLG 328) fire appliance that had previously seen service with Cheshire Fire Brigade. This served the business well. The value of the appliance far exceeded its cost. Carrying its own water supply (400 gallons) meant 'water on' happened much more quickly without the need to couple up to a hydrant. The whole ethos of Rolls-Royce Security was to provide the best service to employees and the business that it could. With this in mind Officers were required to have extensive knowledge of the site and processes. In short they were expected to know the whole site in fine detail. With regard to understanding processes, which were many and varied, they were not expected to fully understand detailed processes that took place just sufficient, albeit limited, knowledge to identify potential hazards and associated risks should an incident occur. They were also trained in first aid firefighting. The team with its limited resources never declared themselves, nor were they expected to be, in the same league as regular firefighters. There was clear recognition that a fire, even a small one, could render vital plant inoperable until it could be repaired or replaced. From receiving a fire alarm the team aimed to be anywhere on site with water on in two minutes or less and this was their great strength. They were well aware that expert capability in the form of Cheshire Fire Brigade would be on site within eight minutes (Home Office requirement) of an initial call out. Automatic total flood extinguishing systems (C02, Halon 1301) were installed in areas that needed a quick knockdown in case of fire without the need for intervention by employees or others. The automatic systems could be operated manually if required. There were also a number of fixed CO2 installations with manual operation only. Advances in two-way radio communications gave the security department a dedicated network and ensured a rapid response to incidents.

Over several years the Fire Station became a hub for on-site staff training. Fire teams, which were created by voluntary means, received block training in groups not exceeding 20 persons. Fire prevention and training was a key element. It was seen as the way forward and it was based around the legislative requirement to meet the following criteria: *What to do in an Emergency - 1. Raise the alarm 2. Communicate 3. Evacuate 4. Tackle the fire (if safe to do so).*

The Health and Safety at Work etc Act 1974 was the primary piece of legislation covering occupational health and safety in Great Britain. It's sometimes referred to as HSWA, the HSW Act, the 1974 Act or HASAWA. It sets out the general duties which: employers have towards employees and members of the public: employees have to themselves and to each other: certain self-employed have towards themselves and others.

The Health and Safety Act 1974 benefited the business and employees enormously and the Fire and Security department in particular by providing a transparent route to all aspects of safety, fire and otherwise. The forming of a joint Health and Safety Committee along with Departmental Safety Representatives allowed every employee to have a spokesperson that would listen to and act upon concerns where necessary. Safety Representatives received extensive training and their knowledge of fire safety improved, as did the message to all. Every employee within the business had a responsibility to ensure safe working. Safety Representatives became a key element in promulgating this.

1980s - The Security Department continued with additional employee training in *What to do in an Emergency.* Employees from all Departments were asked to undertake training, and to the credit of Management, Supervisors, Unions and Safety Representatives it worked remarkably well. It was no easy task for a Manager to allow a number of people to be off the job for between 60 and 90 minutes. Of course it had to be done to comply with legislation. There was rarely a need to remind Managers of this. Indeed some requesting the training, as members of staff moved on and were replaced by new employees.

The Department had the opportunity to upgrade the Dennis F8 fire appliance, which had given superb service, with an updated Dennis F38 (MTU 317H) that once formed part of the Cheshire Fire Brigade fleet of appliances. The company ambulance was replaced with an ex-county ambulance, which was far superior to the converted van previously used.

1990s - The Company invested in fire alarm upgrades in many areas with automatic detection installed where deemed necessary. In addition, a computerised monitoring system came on stream to compliment all alarm panels and activity including critical processes.

The introduction of the Fire Precautions (Workplace) Regulations 1997 changed many aspects of fire safety. One of the most important changes was that of risk based assessments that placed the onus on fire safety matters very much on the businesses involved, although policing would still be carried out by Fire Service Safety Departments. Risk Assessments needed to be carried out meticulously and the challenge was there to find a suitable and robust assessment method. West Midlands Fire Service provided an in-house course and training for a senior member of the Security Department to attend. The outcome was a method of assessment that was quickly introduced and modified on an ongoing basis. The end result was a Fire Safety Risk Assessment that satisfied all aspects of Fire Safety legislation as required under the Act, and in addition, considered building structures outside the scope of the Act, thus giving a comprehensive report on the Company's business fire risk status whilst being fully compliant with the Act. It was intended that every fire risk assessment would be reviewed every 12 months or earlier should any material change occur within the building or its surroundings. Sub Officers were trained to carry out fire risk assessments and were issued with a guidance manual to ensure a consistent approach.

Training of employees in *What to do in an Emergency* was ramped up and a former office within the fire station was converted into a classroom. It was rather basic but functional and met the needs for fire safety theory in relative comfort for attendees. In addition there was a fire ground outside the fire station that provided a suitable area for the use of extinguishers. During the demonstrations employees were shown how to use extinguishers and then given the opportunity to use them on live fires involving combustible materials and flammable liquids, while under strictly controlled supervision. In addition the opportunity was taken to give employees information on home fire safety, supplemented with excellent literature, booklets, leaflets etc. supplied by Cheshire Fire Brigade and the Home Office.

The Security Department was responsible for organising evacuation drills in all areas. Exercises were always planned with Department Manager's involvement and co-operation. The purchase of a smoke generator in the 1990s added realism to these exercises. All exercises were subject to proper scrutiny with a stopwatch used to accurately record evacuation times. Safety Representatives were asked to remain in the area under evacuation to witness proceedings and share their thoughts and observations with a member of the Security Department following the event. A formal written short report was a requirement following each exercise. New employees went through a more formal induction process with fire safety a key subject. Sub Officers or the Fire and Security Manager would carry out this training whilst formal there was an awareness that overload shouldn't occur and so appropriate paperwork was made available to cover the entire topic of fire safety and was considered a useful reference work.

Plans were made to replace the Dennis F38 fire appliance, which had given excellent service. A Dennis SS model was under consideration, amongst others. However changing circumstances within the business put the plans on hold.

In common with many businesses, the Company was forced to restructure to meet the demands of many changes in the world of commerce and manufacturing due to what many believed to be a worldwide recession. This was certainly challenging to our business as a whole.

As regards the effect on the Fire and Security Department, it was required to reduce employee numbers to a point where it was no longer viable to have a Company Fire Station. As a result, the Fire Station and appliance were mothballed and all alarms/ monitoring equipment were relocated at the main gate security control office. This was a significant change and very challenging. The Factory was no smaller as a result of the enforced changes, and indeed it could be argued, that the risks were higher. The business had to now rely on fire prevention more than ever. As expected the business survived the short term implications of the downturn in world markets. There wasn't much choice. As markets started to strengthen resources and investment were directed toward new product models and manufacturing plant, which gave little hope of reopening the Company fire station, and while this was regrettable, it was also understandable and was in fact the only way forward. The team could see that.

The Fire and Security Department played its part to the best of its ability to meet new challenges, which inevitably meant the Security Officers had to do more with less. As expected they rose to the challenge. Whether or not the decision to mothball the Fire Station was the right one is a matter of opinion, although there was always the possibility of it reopening if Management and insurers believed it to be advantageous to the business. The Factory was modernising for new models and improved production techniques and considerable investment was made in manufacturing and its support services. New owners in the form of Volkswagen AG took over the business in 1999. Investment in the Crewe Factory was considerable and the future was looking bright.

Millennium - Investment continued in the Crewe Factory and there was a good feeling about the business. The workforce appeared fully committed. Put simply 'The future looked very promising'. The then Fire and Security Manager took the decision to retire at the end of 2001. Thus ends this chapter in the history of Crewe's Rolls-Royce Fire Brigade and the Fire and Security Department.

Security Officers Training

1970s - Training was carried out in-house and on-the-job learning was the norm. The EWS tanks were used to carry out pumping drills with the trailer pump and the Dennis fire appliances in later years. A small library was created within the fire station consisting of Manuals of Firemanship. It was established with the aim of allowing Officers to study during downtime and silent hours.

1980s - It was recognised that more formal training was required to certificate level in First Aid. Initially this took place at the Cheshire Police Training Centre in Crewe and later it was provided on-site. The library grew and included a number of practical books that listed many chemicals used on-site, along with the means of extinguishing them in case of fire, and the dangers of chemical fires in general. Officers were encouraged to take advantage of the learning opportunities afforded by the small but ever increasing library. A publication widely regarded in industry as a fire safety 'bible' became available. A publication titled, Practical Fire Safety Precautions *(G.W. Underdown)* became available. This book became an excellent reference, due to its common sense approach to all aspects of fire safety and problem solving.

1990s - Instruction was given to certificate level in the use of Oxygen Therapy and Defibrillator and the need for more formal training in the use of breathing apparatus for quick rescue was identified. Sub Officers were sent to Teesside Airport Fire Training Centre for specialist training, and as a way of understanding fire operations, safety and chemistry, they were encouraged to attain the Institution of Fire Engineers (IFE) Preliminary Certificate. The Fire Protection Association (FPA) publication 'Fire Prevention' became a useful addition to the library as it helped to understand and interpret fire safety legislation and fire prevention. The FPA was formed by the Association of British Insurers (ABI) joining forces with the Fire Officers Committee (FOC). This joint enterprise created a platform for small and large businesses to learn and understand the fire risks at their respective companies. Rolls-Royce Motor Cars were members of the FPA.

Duties of Security Officers

The Security Officer's general duties were diverse and some of their tasks are listed below. It does not include security matters, only those related to fire safety and ambulance.

Ensure emergency vehicles were fully equipped and ready for emergencies.

Routine checking and testing of firefighting vehicles and ancillary equipment.

Inspect and maintain fire extinguishers. Officers were trained to achieve a 'competence' level in accordance with BS 5423 EN3. Pressure testing and re-filling of CO2 extinguishers was undertaken by an external company.

Inspect wall-mounted ¾ inch bore fire hose reels. Up to 50 were located on the site. They were maintained by the Maintenance team.

Visual checks on emergency exits (day and night). Formal checks were carried out during weekends when every door would be opened and closed. Doors that were permanently secure, push-bar, pad or ceramic bolt, automatic and semi automatic (balance weighted) would be tested for functionality to ensure smooth and complete closing. Safety Representatives also ensured their areas were compliant.

Weekly testing of fire alarms consisting of manual break glass call points, automatic smoke detection and automatic heat detection. Their servicing and maintenance was carried out by external companies in line with British Standards.

Fire sprinkler installations, including their pumps and water supply were checked and tested on a weekly basis. Their annual inspection was carried out by the insurer's representative, in the presence of a Security Officer and a member of the Maintenance team.

Hydrants were simply opened and closed in sequence to check they worked properly and had decent water pressure. In the early years, they were tested with a pressure flow meter by Security Officers. However, this work became the responsibility of the on-site Maintenance team as they included a programme of replacing stop-valves. Hydrants were on the ring main, with spurs off to more remote areas. Closing the entire ring main was not permitted under any circumstances without the written authority from the insurers and risk advisors. The hydrants were available on streets and avenues at approximately 25 yard intervals, and operated at normal town pressure, although pressure could be increased to 120psi on powering up the electric pump located near the base of the water tower. The pump would automatically cut in if the towns' main pressure dropped to 10psi.

Visual checks on emergency water supplies (EWS). Treating the static water in the tanks against waterborne diseases, such as legionella, was tasked to the Maintenance team. The three static tanks were located underground and older hands referred to these as dams. As the Factory expanded a surface EWS tank was built at the junction of Fifth Avenue and Fourth Street. A combined total of 80,000 gallons of water were held in the tanks. However, by the early 1980s, the surface tank had been removed and one of the underground tanks filled in.

Stand-by duties were undertaken during 'hot work' activities on the Factory site. Hot work was the term used to describe any form of maintenance or plant work that involved the use of a naked flame or heat. This work necessitated watching over contractors while they carried out their planned hot work, which included oxy-acetylene cutting, oxy-acetylene and electric welding, use of propane torches and blowlamps, and in some cases grinding and disc cutting, as well as soldering. This type of work was strictly controlled with formal hot work permits issued. There was also a requirement to stand-by during fuel tanker and LPG tanker (until the 1990s) deliveries prior to and during discharging.

Assist with medical emergencies by driving the ambulance as directed by members of the medical team (nurses), including transferring patients to the Company's Medical Centre or local hospital. In addition, Security Officers were required to provide first aid cover on occasions, when nurses were not on duty.

Each shift was allocated a section of the Factory to carry out inspections and maintain firefighting equipment and recorded all findings. Security Officers had to be dependable and adaptable and act as part of a team or alone. Although much of their work was routine, they were at times, caught up in dynamic situations where they had to act quickly and safely. They could be faced with one-off events that others had not witnessed in their entire working life. Working with experienced Officers brought the best out of new recruits and the value of on-the-job training cannot be understated.

Fire Extinguishers

All extinguishers had to meet the requirements of BS 5423 (British Standard). This would be superseded by BS EN 3 (European Standard). Fire extinguishers were located as required to comply with legislation and there was generally a tendency to provide more than the minimum requirement at the Factory. There were in excess of 800 extinguishers on site, which included the following types:

Water - Soda acid extinguishers were phased out in favour of CO2 cartridge propellant extinguishers to comply with British Standard 5423. These in turn would be supplemented by and eventually replaced with stored pressure (nitrogen) types of 9 litre capacity.

CO2 - A combination of 10lb and 12lb capacity with the majority being 10lb. The 12lb type was phased out due to their considerable weight, making them impractical for many potential users.

Foam - The 9 litre chemical foam was the norm until advances in technology made AFFF (aqueous film forming foam) far more suitable as an operational need. Stored pressure (nitrogen) types of 9 litre and 6 litre capacity were introduced in some office areas.

Dry Powder - The 9 litre cartridge internal and external CO2 cartridge types were the norm and were gradually replaced by stored pressure (nitrogen) types.

Bromochlorodifluoromethane 'BCF' (Halon 1211) - These small portable units were extensively used within the transport fleet until they were phased out in the 1990s as a requirement of The Montreal Protocol (1986), which came into force in 1989, and was revised in the UK in 1990. Whilst there was no doubting the many benefits of BCF extinguishers, a direct replacement was not available, and so the most suitable solution for most purposes became a 1 litre AFFF type.

The Water Tower

Standing at 90 feet above ground level, the imposing and enigmatic water tower certainly provided a mixture of myth and mystery as well as being a functional entity. There are plenty of anecdotal tales around this landmark. The most enduring were:

'A building worker was killed during its construction, not by a fall from height as some would suggest, but allegedly crushed by metal used in construction. There is no evidence to support this.'

'There was an anti aircraft gun mounted on top of the tower during wartime. There is no evidence to support this although there is anecdotal evidence of a gun being mounted on the flat roof on the third floor of the main office block in Pyms Lane. This part of the building was known for many years as the turret.'

'The tower was haunted. Clearly this was a myth, although during a still and foggy night, it was not a place for the faint hearted as looking upward from below it was a daunting sight as the tower disappeared into the mist.'

'Sirens were mounted on the tower. This is true. Just below the water tank a protected platform housed a siren. It was accessed by a vertical ladder from the

first stage platform. The siren was in place during the War to warn the locality of a potential air raid and also sound the all clear when it was deemed safe. After the War the siren's purpose changed and it became part of the UK national four minute warning network. The status of the sirens operating capability was inspected daily by the Security Department. It was simply a case of monitoring the warning device in the fire main pump house, located near the base of the tower. County Police were also required to check the siren status at regular intervals. A WB400 early warning voice receiver was located in the Company Fire Station. The later version WB1400 would be installed as an upgrade. The national four minute siren warning was disconnected during the 1990s when the government deemed it not fit for purpose in the changing political world.'

Many believed the water tower existed purely for firefighting purposes. This was not the case. The primary purpose of the tower was to supply water for the boiler house in case of a mains supply failure to the factory. Boilers at the time were coal fired and couldn't simply be turned off. They were required to be shut down safely and that took time, hence the supply from the tower. It is true the tower supply of water could be linked to the fire main and high pressure pump as a secondary supply if needed, in reality this was hardly ever the case and the bypass valves were rarely used. The tower height was calculated to ensure a head of water (height of water level) in the tank was approximately 86 feet. This allowed water from the pressurised town main to fill the tank by overcoming gravity and without the need for secondary pumping. An 86 foot head of water would ensure the boiler house supply was close enough to town pressure. The water tower was drained and withdrawn from use several years before it was dismantled in 2002.

Rolls-Royce Recollections

I remember my first day as though it was yesterday. I arrived at 05.45 hours and reported to the Company's fire station for my first shift. After introductions to my colleagues, the Sub Officer took me to his office and explained that as far as he was concerned, I had joined the Department as a Fireman. This was at odds to the job description of Security Officer that I'd applied for! He was quick to point out his tongue in cheek remark was due to his lack of knowledge on policing matters that even he was learning as the days went by. I fully understood his point.

An interesting day followed as I accompanied a fellow Officer as he inspected and tested every sprinkler installation on site. The factory was a mass of buildings and a complete mystery to me. I was fascinated and impressed at the workings of the sprinklers, pump engines and water storage tanks. Saturday afternoon was three hours of practical training, but prior to that the Sub Officer taught me how to run out a length of delivery hose. No water involved, just connect the hose to a standpipe that was fixed into a hydrant and run the length of hose out and attach a branch pipe to it. The hose was then made-up and the process was repeated until the Sub Officer was satisfied. I was enjoying myself and didn't notice the skin disappearing from the sides of my hands until I felt the pain, all due apparently to my holding the lugs incorrectly as I ran out the hose. My new colleagues referred to this as hose rash and I would soon learn how to avoid it. I needed to; otherwise a skin graft was on the cards. The Sub Officer pointed out that this was an occupational hazard. A term I would become familiar with over the years because the answer to all my 'accidents' would be as a result of occupational hazards.

It was then time for a training exercise which took the form of the Sub Officer disappearing and making an emergency call from one of the many phones on site or perhaps initiating an alarm from a call point. We didn't know when the call would be made or from where. When the call came we jumped onto our fire engine. This wasn't a fire engine at all. It was a converted van although; it looked and sounded the part. Having arrived at the scene we were tasked to deal with a fire related scenario as if it were the real thing. What an introduction to my first 12 hour shift. The next three weeks were spent shadowing colleagues as they undertook numerous tasks. I was now on a six month probationary period.

During my time with the Company there were numerous changes, and while many of our duties were routine, they were never boring. Life in the Department had plenty of amusing moments as well. I recall one such incident when an Officer was out on a routine fire risk patrol during silent hours (the term used to describe the times when there is no day or nightshift working on production). Officers were required to telephone from checkpoints, usually every 15 minutes (no two-way radio in those days), while patrolling their designated route. When it was realised that the Officer had failed to report on two occasions, it was decided to check his patrol area from his last point of contact. Just as we were turning out our missing Officer phoned in to let us know he'd had a 'bit of an accident' but didn't elaborate or need assistance and stated that he would be back at the fire station in a matter of minutes. When he returned he was an incredible sight. Uniform covered in some sort of yellow brown substance and he was soaked. We were initially concerned, thinking he had somehow fallen into a process tank and was in need of decontamination. However our concern soon evaporated, then erupted into laughter (very serious laughter), as he explained he was covered in wet clay/mud. The circumstances were: a deep hole had been excavated for new plant equipment to be fitted. The hole was about 12 feet deep with sloping sides and approximately two feet of water at the base. Our colleague knew it was there, it was mentioned in daily orders. It was also fenced off. Our man decided to take a close look at this hole in the ground, went a little too close and simply slid into it. Getting out proved difficult with the sloping sides and so he had to kick footholds into the clay and eventually climb out. The man whose name can't be mentioned was given the nickname Cassius from that day on. A clear reminder of his encounter with clay!

Another patrol of the Factory had the potential of turning into a serious incident. It also led to an important and beneficial change in equipment. The patrol took me to a remote part of the factory. Eerie silence as usual, which was quite normal. I walked past the window opening (frame not yet fitted) of a new extension on an existing building when a flicker of light suddenly caught my eye. I turned back to have another look and convinced myself it was a flame. It wasn't very big, but it was big enough to get my attention and treat it as a serious incident. I couldn't tackle it as it was too high above the ground. So off I ran to find the nearest telephone. It seemed an age, but was only a matter of seconds before I called our fire station. I reported my observations and requested an immediate turn out and suggested the attendance of Cheshire Fire Brigade.

I returned to the scene, and by now, the flame was giving off some serious light. It was issuing from the vertical wall of the building adjoining the extension. Moments later the team arrived and a hose reel was got to work, knocking the flame out fairly quickly. The seat of fire proved something of a challenge because it was between the building skin and involved the insulation. After what seemed an eternity, but was in fact a relatively short time, the fire was declared to be out. Lessons were learned from that incident and it was clear to all concerned that we had been fortunate to avoid a major fire. Cheshire Fire Brigade was not called due to a breakdown in our communications. An inquiry followed and the outcome was that all officers were equipped with two-way radios and our procedures were tightened to ensure no repetitions occurred. Luck was with us that night. The value afforded by purchase of two-way radios by far exceeded their cost many times over in later years

On becoming Manager I reflected on my interview prior to joining the Department. Mr. Jim Farmer was the Fire and Security Manager and I recall being quite nervous as I explained why I wanted to join the Security Department. Jim was a strict disciplinarian, yet always approachable and fair. As I began my new role as Manager I vowed to be as good as he was. No easy task I can assure you. He fought for and supported his team without fail. No wonder we all respected him. It was Jim who wanted a Rolls-Royce Security and Fire cap badge that was not only unique, but represented the best. The badge was designed and manufactured in-house at Crewe by the Aero Division of the Company. A limited number were cast in traditional eight point star design. The badges were issued to existing officers and new recruits on joining the Department. Tradition deemed it appropriate to present the cap badge to the holder on retirement, if they so wished. Some retiring members asked for their badge to be presented to the new recruit that would be replacing them. It was a matter of individual choice. Eventually the limited number produced ran out and were replaced with a rectangular badge featuring the Rolls-Royce trademark. The cap badges were produced using the lost wax method with the same technique and metal used in the manufacture of the Flying Lady (Spirit of Ecstasy) mascot. The Spirit of Ecstasy was always seen as a symbol of quality and excellence. Jim wanted his men to offer a service of quality and excellence to the business, and at the same time, have pride in the badge that he presented to them as part of their uniform. It worked.

Changes in fire safety legislation were particularly challenging and sometimes the rocky path to progress was smoothed by the many Fire Safety Officers I came to know. Always professional, their role of policing legislation was blended with good advice, mostly delivered on a goodwill basis and based on mutual respect. A particular County Fire Officer whom I had worked with in his fire safety role suggested it might well be beneficial to join the Cheshire Group of the IFE, of which I had previously obtained a very modest fire engineering qualification. Joining the Cheshire Group proved a route to meeting all ranks of fire officers and sharing information with more professionals in a role similar to my own. I was also pleased that several of my own staff was successful in obtaining the IFE Preliminary Fire Engineering Certificate. The Cheshire Fire Safety Panel, of which I became a member, was driven by the Fire Service and included members of industry and commerce. Therefore it was a good platform on which to learn, share experiences and sometimes help others in roles similar to mine.

On the occasion of a visit to Volkswagen Head Office in Wolfsburg Germany, I was given a tour of the fire station. Impressive to say the least and I happened to admire their newly acquired Bronto hydraulic aerial platform fire appliance. Next day on arrival at the Factory I was surprised to see the Bronto parked in front of the main office block extended to its full height. I discovered this was for my benefit so that I could view it working and witness its capability. On meeting the crew I was invited to board the platform, which I did with some trepidation as I had noted something of a breeze getting up. However I had to get on with it because my interpreter, a young German lady whom, I might add spoke better English than I did, had already jumped on. I remember the platform elevating in fairly quick time and as it stopped its ascent I was told this was half its operating height. At this stage I was asked if I wanted to go higher to which my interpreter said "Yes." I didn't get the chance to say no. Next minute or so we were at full working height, gently swaying in the ever increasing breeze. It was a moment to remember for sure.

2001 - 2015

Christopher Hannan, who worked in the Rolls-Royce Security Department from 1999 until 2015, gives a brief update of the work of Security Officers' work since 2001.

> *"Gradual changes were made to the Security Department after the Crewe operation became known as Bentley Motors Limited in 2002. The competencies of Security Officers were kept up-to-date with on-site specialist training, which included 'Confined Space' and 'Working at Height' training. The Sub Officers' advanced firefighting courses (three days) were held at Washington Hall in Chorley, Lancashire. As further re-structuring was introduced at the Factory, the Security Department became more involved in protecting the Volkswagen brand, as well as its own on-site work. This involved security work and the necessary risk assessments at promotional events, car clinics and motor shows, both in the UK and across the globe. The Rapid Response team was formed in the spring of 2015 to deal with emergencies and some of their day-to-day work included checking fire exits, testing the fire alarm system and the sprinkler pumps, which were carried out by the duty shift during weekends. The maintenance of fire equipment and firefighting training was delivered by outside organisations."*

Malcolm wishes to thank the Fire and Security team for their support, patience, tolerance and comradeship, while working alongside them, and members of the Maintenance Engineering team, in particular the late Dennis Walton, for contributing and sharing information regarding water supplies to and around the Factory.

Information for this chapter sourced from Malcolm Smith and Christopher Hannan. Malcolm and Christopher's comments/views, which are based on their memories in the Department, are considered to be anecdotal. They should not be taken out of context or to represent Company's policy or views.

*(**Above**) Rolls-Royce Fire and Security, winners of the Oldham Trophy, 1955. (**Below**) Aerial photograph of the Rolls-Royce factory and the fire station.*

*(**Above left**) Water tower at Rolls-Royce. (**Above right**) Rolls-Royce Security and Fire cap badge. (**Below**) Members of the Rolls-Royce Fire & Security Team in the mid-1970s, with their trailer pump, utility vehicle (Morris), fire appliance (Dennis F8) and ambulance (Austin). Back L to R: Mike Allen, Colin Boon, Bernard Bailey, Maurice Kirkham, Dave Bennett, Walter Moulton, Kevin Baker, Malcolm Smith, Mike Lunt and John Peake. Front L to R: Eddy Shephard, Jim Armstrong, George Lockett, Fred Robinson, Jim Farmer, Bert Steele and Terry Whittaker.*

Rolls-Royce's Dennis F8 fire appliance (TLG 328).

Rolls-Royce's Dennis F38 fire appliance (MTU 317H) outside the factory's fire station.

*(**Above**) Malcolm Smith promoting National Fire Safety Week at the Rolls-Royce Brooklands Restaurant, 1987. (**Below**) Malcolm Smith presented with a plaque by Geoff Shephard (Senior Divisional Officer at Cheshire Fire Service) towards the end of his career, for his outstanding fire safety work at Rolls-Royce. They are alongside the Silver Ghost (Reg: AX 201).*

CONCLUSION

Preparing for emergencies was the main focus of my work during the first ten years of my career (1980s). The daily routine of training on the drill yard paid off as high standards were met and fire brigade tradition of keeping fire stations and firefighting equipment in immaculate condition was upheld.

By the mid-1980s the number of call-outs averaged about 1,000 per annum, which included fires, special service calls, false alarms and standby duties. These calls gradually increased as we approached the 1990s and in the 12 months from April 1995 to March 1996, the total number of calls had reached 1,944.

Many changes took place during the 1990s. Firefighter safety continued to progress with further developments in uniforms and equipment and a fleet of specialised fire appliances became part of the establishment at Crewe Fire Station, although their use at incidents was very limited. Towards the end of the 1990s a shift towards community safety work emerged with the aim making people safer in their own homes.

During the Millennium, government policies forced fire and rescue services to make changes with a view to improve public sector performance in areas such as financial accountability and business planning. This course of action brought a commitment and investment in community work and plans were put in place to decrease the number of call-outs. As we approach the end of the decade the average number of calls at Crewe was in the region of 1,500 per annum.

This was also a time when firefighters were expected to have new skills as tactical firefighting became a 'hot' subject following studies in fire behaviour and ventilation. On-line learning was introduced and practical training in subjects such as, height safety, water safety and casualty safety at road traffic collisions were developed.

The roles of firefighters changed in many ways with community work seemingly at the forefront. Comparisons are highlighted in articles by *Chronicle* reporters, who spent time at Crewe Fire Station during 1968, and 40 years later in 2008.

June 1968 - *'Its 9am and the change of watch parade at the station at Crewe of Cheshire County Fire Service is complete. For White Watch, of which Ken Gardner is a member, another day's duty has begun. In common with his 30 colleagues at Crewe, Ken works a 56-hour tour of duty each week at his invaluable and, sometimes, highly dangerous job of protecting the public from fire and flood - and any other catastrophe, major or minor, which can strike anywhere, anytime, day or night. After the parade, during which he is instructed by his Sub Officer that he is No. 3 for the day, Ken begins the inevitable checking of the equipment that can mean life or death - the eight sets of breathing apparatus that are carried on three of the Station's appliances. This checking and testing of every item of equipment on a fire station is essential in Ken's work, for nothing can be left to chance. At 9.30am on this particular day the duty watch carries out what is termed in fire brigade language as a risk visit. Today it was to Morning Foods Ltd, at Crewe. Fireman Gardner, wearing undress uniform for the visit, leaves the station in one of the two appliances to spend an hour or so learning about the water supplies, the means of access, and any special risks which* *may be inherent in the premises. The information gathered during these inspections of all types of buildings is collated and carried on all appliances required to make an initial first attendance. Immediately on return to the station, Ken changes into full fire-fighting uniform and together with his colleagues prepare to spend a rather strenuous period on the yard. He is very ready for his tea break, for which he is allowed exactly 15 minutes. At 11.15am, the routine work of the station begins. There are no cleaners or char ladies on a fire station and the immaculate condition of the premises and appliances is a tribute to Ken and his friends. When the work is detailed by the Sub Officer, Ken finds he has landed a 'plum' job down the pit, cleaning the accumulated dirt and salt of the recent bad weather from underneath the district's petrol carrier. He disappears into the pit until 1pm, when he cleans himself for lunch. Precisely at two he is back in overalls and ready to press on with the job until 5pm, when he is allowed to clean up, have a cup of tea and prepare to hand over the watch to his colleagues coming on duty at 6pm. The whole of his working life is geared up to the fact that any second the bells may go down. If they do he will be aboard one of the appliances and out of the station in under 30 seconds. Promotion prospects are good with the brigade, from fireman to leading fireman to Sub Officer and then to Station Officer or the Officer-in-Command.'*

September 2008 - *'Fire prevention is as much a part of a firefighter's job as tackling blazes. Chronicle's Chief Reporter Belinda Ryan spent an afternoon with Crewe's firefighters to find out more about their work in the community. "An important part of our job involves working in the community and advising people about fire prevention," said Firefighter Gareth Roberts."We're even involved in a scheme to help the elderly now." The Crew Manager was speaking as we made our way in the fire engine from the Macon Way station to Waverley Court to give advice on fire prevention and install smoke alarms if necessary. As we went into a flat Gareth began a full home safety assessment with the owners. He ensured they had an escape plan should there be a fire and checked the smoke detector. Other checks included kitchen and cooking facilities, making sure the couple were aware doors should be closed at night and ensuring they tested their smoke alarm regularly. As Gareth went through the list of fire safety points his colleague, Firefighter Iain Dunne, explained that if the residents were over 65 the fire service also offered other assessments. This is part of a unique partnership with Age Concern, the NHS and Cheshire County Council and is aimed at gauging the needs of the older population. It involves the occupants completing a questionnaire and, if areas of need are identified, then the details are forwarded to Age Concern - if they agree. "It's to see if people may need other help, like getting out to pay bills, meeting people, making hot meals for example," said Iain. "We can find out what help people need, if any, because we go into their houses. We then pass on the information to the people who can best help." At that moment, Gareth gets a call to say there's been a shout. There's no time to waste - the call is to the Springfield*

School. With blue lights flashing and siren wailing, driver Mark Latham expertly weaves his way at speed through the Crewe traffic. The rest of the crew are, by this time, fully kitted out and ready for action. When we arrive it is obvious it has been a false alarm. Headteacher Mark Swaine apologises as he explains a staff member has set off the smoke sensors by accident. Gareth completes the necessary paperwork, which goes down as false alarm with good intent, and we head back to the station. "We get a certain amount of false alarms, but in cases like that there's obviously no bad intent," he said.'

Although the emphasis was now on preventing property fires, it would be true to say that most firefighters relished getting 'stuck in' at incidents. The excitement of attending emergencies was the appeal of becoming a firefighter in the first instance.

Firefighting has evolved in many ways since the days of Captain Sir Eyre Massey Shaw (1830 - 1908), the first Chief Officer of the Metropolitan Fire Brigade (London Fire Brigade). The attributes of a successful firefighter in the 19th Century as described by Massey Shaw were:

'A fireman to be successful, must enter buildings; He must get in below, above, on every side, from opposite houses, over brick walls, over side walls, through panels of doors, through windows, through loopholes cut by himself in the gates, the walls, the roof; he must know how to reach the attic from the basement by ladders placed on half burned stairs, and the basement from the attic by rope made fast on a chimney; His whole success depends on his getting in and remaining there, and he must always carry his appliances with him, as without them he is of no use.'

In the 20th Century a government inquiry into the British Fire Service, led by Sir Charles Cunningham in 1971, concluded that:

'A fireman must have some special qualities. He must have physical courage. On occasions he must voluntary face extremities of danger which confront few other people in time of peace. It is the element of risk and the demand for courage which set the fireman's job apart from others. But bravery is not the only personal quality needed. A fireman must be able to work as part of a closely integrated team, the watch to which he belongs. He must be prepared to obey orders without question, especially at an emergency incident. At the same time he must be able to show initiative when working on his own. All of these qualities may be needed in other occupations; but we know of none in which, together with courage in the face of danger, they are needed in combination to such a degree as in the Fire Service.'

On applying to join the fire brigade in 1979, I had to show average intelligence and strength by taking basic academic tests and carrying a standard sized person over a distance of 25 metres (fireman's lift). For the next two years I had to show the required qualities of a fireman as part of a team during my probationary period.

Firefighter training continued throughout my career until I called time on my full-time firefighting days in 2009, at the age of 54. However, a few months later, I felt there was still ‘life left in the old dog’ so I responded to an appeal from Cheshire Fire and Rescue Service (CFRS), who were looking to recruit part-time firefighters. I was still connected to the fire service as a Cheshire representative of the National Association of Retired Firefighters (NARF) and a board member of the Flamesavers Credit Union. With no known health issues and with 30 years firefighting experience at the sharp end, I expected to be welcomed with open arms. Not so. I had to prove (on paper) that I was confident, resilient, communicated effectively and could solve problems. I also had to have a commitment to diversity and integrity, was open to change and that I had a commitment to excellence. Despite ending my career as a Crew Manager (Leading Firefighter), CFRS’ Human Resource Department gave my application the ‘thumbs down’ as in their words, there were too many areas of development.

Although this rejection felt like a slap in the face as no judgement had been made on my firefighting skills, the reality was that I wasn’t prepared for life after the fire service. CFRS had offered no vocational qualifications, so I was given the same treatment as anyone else applying to become a part-time firefighter.

Firefighters of all generations look back on the good old days when reflecting on their careers, and whatever decades they served, they usually claim that their days in the service were the best. But one thing is for sure. Despite changes in the fire service throughout time - some for the better and some for the worse - firefighters will always put the public’s safety first, and when called to duty, the words of Sir Eyre Massey Shaw and Sir Charles Cunningham will always echo in their ears.

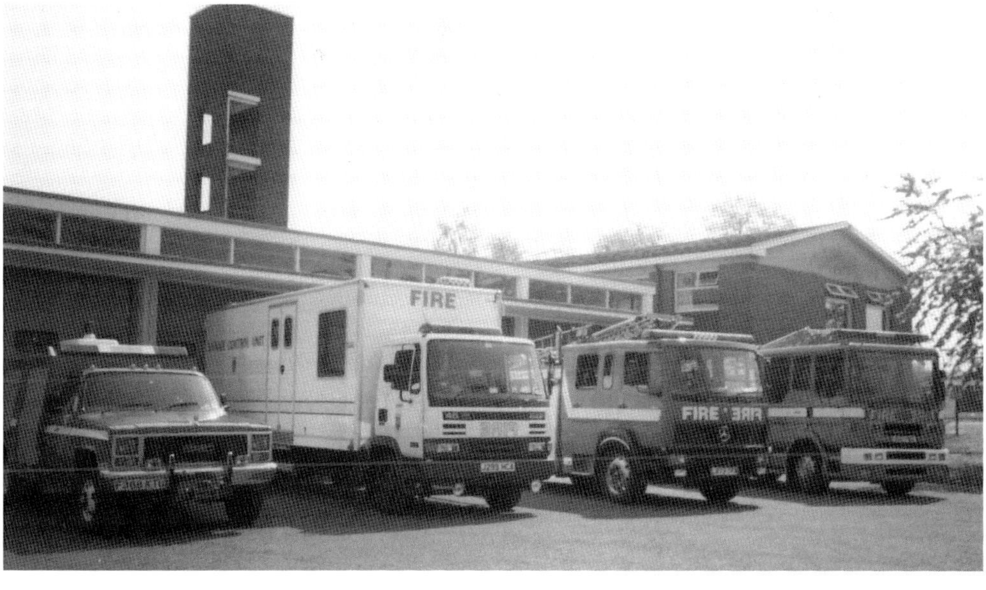

Crewe fire appliances in 2000 - L to R: GMC, Leyland DAF, Mercedes 1124 and Dennis Sabre.

BOOK SPONSORS

FLAMESAVERS CREDIT UNION

A Credit Union was launched in 1992 for members of Staffordshire Fire Brigade. In 2001 it expanded to include members of Cheshire Fire Brigade and a few years later it was re-named Flamesavers. In 2010 membership was opened up to members of Greater Manchester Fire and Rescue Service and in 2014 members of all fire and rescue services throughout the country were allowed to join. Former Crewe Firemen Dave Williams and myself, who became directors of Flamesavers in 2001, continue to serve on the board. Jenny Steele and Gary Williams, who both worked at Crewe Fire Station, also served as directors.

*(**Above**) The Flamesavers Credit Union Team - Board of Directors and Staff, 2022. Back L to R: Dave Williams, Steve Rhead, Gordon Allen and myself. Front L to R: Ann Fisher, Andy Bell and Lisa Downs. Absent: Alan Anderson and John Berrisford.*

GAVIN PALIN FUNERAL SERVICES
Independent Family Funeral Services

Funeral Directing had always been an ambition for Gavin Palin and his wife Paula, so in 2009 they ventured into opening Gavin Palin Funeral Services in Nantwich. Max Kelly, who had been a casual employee since 2011, became a full-time member of staff in 2015, and three years later Jordan Palin joined the team. With their caring, professional and personal approach, they will help organise your loved one's funeral to be individually tailored to your requirements. As well as the traditional hearse, funerals with alternate means of transport can also be provided by horse and carriage, motor bike, 4 x 4 vehicles, lorry, tractor and trailer and a fire engine.

Gavin Palin's 'Dodge' Fire Appliance used as an alternate means of transport at funerals.

CHESHIRE FIRE AND RESCUE SERVICE

Crewe's new fire station is due to be operational by 2024. It will be located on the same site as the existing fire station, which was opened in 1966. In 2021 Crewe Fire Station's area covered approx 99 square kilometres of Cheshire. It had 123 premises with site specific risk information, one Control of Major Accident Hazard (COMAH) site and had five listed buildings in the area (2 x Grade one and 3 x Grade two). The total number of incidents (fires, special services and false alarms) in the Crewe area in recent years were: 626 (2017/18), 674 (2018/19) and 547 (2019/20).

Artist's impression of the new fire station at Crewe.

(**Above**) *Dennis F12 (1951) and* (**below**) *Bedford TK (1968).*

*(**Above**) Dennis F61 (1978). (**Below**) Dennis SS135 (1988).*

*(**Above**) GMC (1990). (**Below**) Mercedes 1124 (1990).*

Leyland DAF (1994).

Dennis RS133 (1994).

*(**Above**) Dennis Sabre (2000). (**Below**) Mercedes Atego (2003).*

*(**Above**) Mercedes Sprinter (2004). (**Below**) Leyland DAF (2016).*

*(**Above**) Crewe Firemen at Beech Street in 1961. Back L to R: Jack Harding and Bill Taylor. Front L to R: Sam Caruth, John Norman, Marsh Cartwright and Colin Tirrell. (**Below**) Sub Officer Ellis Moss and Fireman Don Meredith in the Control Room at Beech Street in the mid-1960s.*

*(**Above**) Christmas Party at Beech Street in the mid-1960s with Station Officer H. Whalley. (**Left**) Youngsters in the fire engine cab. Chris Norman (bottom left), followed in his father's footsteps and became a fireman in 1978.*

Fire engine crash near Basford Sidings in 1965.

CHESHIRE COUNTY COUNCIL

FIRE BRIGADE COMMITTEE

OPENING

OF THE

New Fire Station
Macon Way, Crewe Road, Crewe

BY

THE RT. HON. ALICE BACON, C.B.E., M.P.

(Minister of State, Home Office)

at 2-45 p.m.

on Monday, 18th July 1966

Opening ceremony brochure cover.

Guests and dignitaries at the fire station opening ceremony on 18 July 1966.

Alice Bacon MP inspecting the firemen.

Displays by firemen at the opening ceremony.

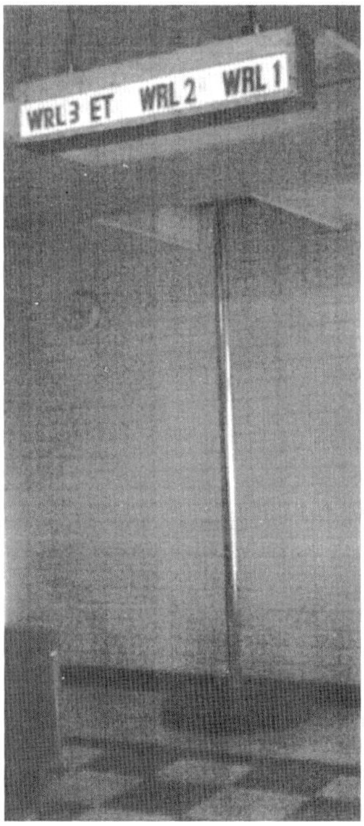

(Top) *Children alongside the Fireman's Pole with Fireman Colin Tirrell at a Christmas Party at Macon Way Fire Station in the late 1960s.* ***(Left)*** *Fireman's Pole and the fire appliance display panel at Crewe.* ***(Above)*** *Crewe Fire Station in the late 1960s.*

*(**Above**) Sub Officer Harold Howard, 1968. (**Below**) Training with the new breathing apparatus in 1969. Standing L to R: Len McIntosh, Richard Green, Peter Larcombe and Ellis Moss. Sitting L to R: Jack Rowley, Derek Mellor, Ken Gardner, Colin Tirrell and Don Meredith.*

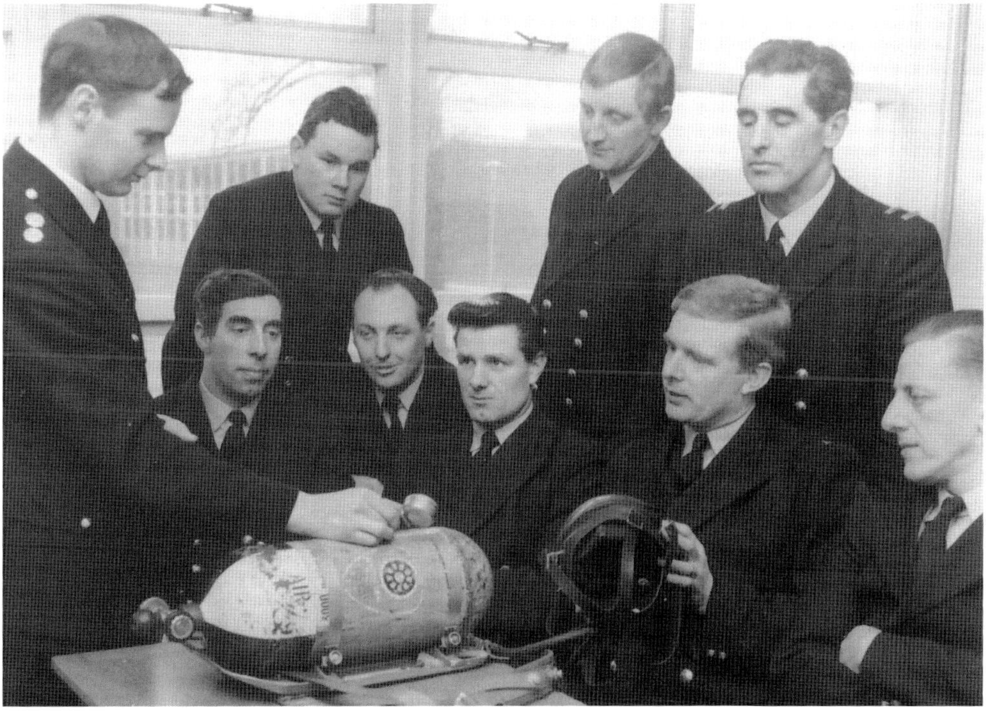

(**Above**) *Off-duty firemen socialising during the mid-1970s. L to R: Ron Hill (Fire Officer at the Crewe Teacher Training College), Marsh Cartwright, Len McIntosh, Dave Colclough (Brigade Mechanic), Barrie Lunt, Dennis Cotton (Fire Officer at the Crewe Railway Works), Ken Gardner, Jack Rowley and Richard Green.* (**Below**) *Sub Officer Ellis Moss and Fireman Geoff Shaw in the Control Room at the Macon Way Fire Station during the mid-1970s.*

*(**Above**) Sub Officer Ellis Moss receiving his Queen's Silver Jubilee Medal in 1976 from Cheshire County Fire Officer Brannon. (**Below**) Crewe Firemen (part-time) in 1976. Back L to R: Alan Taylor, Ray Stafford, Ronnie Whitehead and Ray Burrows. Front L to R: Roy Wood, John Peever and Dave Langer.*

(**Above**) *Blue Watch with their aerial appliance in 1978. L to R: Dave Rouse, Dave Greatorex, Maurice Higginson, Keith Roberts, Gerry McCabe, Alan Ollier, Dave Hanley, Colin Tomkinson, Barrie Lunt and Mick Clays.* (**Below**) *Training in the Breathing Apparatus chamber in the late-1970s.*

*(**Above**) Fireman Geoff Shephard is joined by Cath Dodman (fire station cleaner) in Crewe town centre in 1981. One of the youngsters looking on is Craig Welch who later became a fireman. (**Below**) Red Watch Firemen. L to R: Brendan Grant, Ken Gardner, Neil Harrison and Chris Mannix with the new Hurst Rescue equipment in the mid-1980s.*

(Above) *Training exercise at Basford Hall Sidings. A staged incident involving a petrol tank wagon and a railway-carried flask wagon in the mid-1980s.* ***(Opposite page top)*** *Crewe Firemen. L to R: Bob Longworth, Chris Spencer and Ian Swan with Sarah Thoplis in her new electric wheelchair in 1988. Funds towards the cost of the wheelchair were raised from a sponsored fire engine pull.* ***(Opposite page bottom)*** *Green Watch Firemen. L to R: Andy Wainwright, Peter Turner, Pete Shields, Chris Spencer and Bob Longworth in the mid-1980s.*

*(**Above**) Fireman John Roberts (left) and Fire Prevention Officer Dave Holman (right) receiving their long service and good conduct medals from the Duke of Westminster, 1988. (**Below**) Fire Engine (Dennis F8) Pull in aid of Children in Need in 1989.*

*(**Above**) White Watch dressed up for the Remembrance Sunday Parade in 1990. Back L to R: John Roberts, Paul Bickerton, John Griffiths, Paul Buckley and Brian Tuohy. Front L to R: myself, Kevin Birtles and Chris Norman. (**Below**) Green Watch at a fire in the early-1990s. L to R: Graham Atkinson, Paul Rowlands, Peter Turner, Dave Langer and Bob Longworth.*

*(**Above left**) Leading Fireman Bob Longworth with his long service and good conduct medal in 1992. (**Above right**) Station Commander Roy Howarth in the early-1990s. (**Below**) Fire Prevention Officer Dave Wilbraham in the early-1990s.*

*(**Above**) Gwyneth Dunwoody (MP for Crewe and Nantwich) with Station Commander John Lloyd and members of Green Watch in 1994. L to R: Keith Stubbs, Geoff Carter, Steve Hughes, Colin Tomkinson, Andy Wainwright, Bob Hughes, John Speed, Alistair Mackie, Peter Turner and Bob Longworth. (**Below**) Firefighters Chris Norman, Lindsay Johns, Dave Hanley (Crewe) and Bob Partner (Chester) training on the safety boat at Winsford Flashes in the mid-1990s.*

*(**Above**) Red Watch in the mid-1990s. Back L to R: Dave Williams, Jerry Whiteman, Paul Rowlands, Martin Poole, Steve Burrows, Tony Kitchen and Nigel Pordes. Front L to R: Stuart Saunders, Gary Williams, Bob Longworth, Alan Corbin and Terry Kelly. (**Below**) Green Watch in the late-1990s. Back L to R: Geoff Carter, Philip Dean, Bob Hughes, Steve Hughes, Alec Thomasson, Keith Stubbs, Pete Shields, Peter Turner and Colin Tomkinson. Front L to R: Mike Jones, Andy Wainwright, Steve Davies, Lindsay Johns and John Speed.*

*(**Above**) Millennium Open Day guest Bruce Jones alias Les Battersby (Coronation Street) with Station Commander Peter Wilding and Mrs. Jill Wilding. (**Below**) Con-Op Rod Broome, a former Crewe Fireman, receiving his long service and good conduct medal from Cheshire Lieutenant W.A. Bromley-Davenport in the early 2000s.*

Red Watch (2000). *Back L to R: A. Dunning, C. Holmes, G. Williams, S. Burrows, N. Pordes, M. Poole and D. Williams. Front L to R: D. Wade, P. Kilgour, P. Wilding, J. Haag, J. Dunne and A. Corbin. Absent: M. Sopp and A. Kitchen.* ***Green Watch (2000).*** *Back L to R: C. Tomkinson, J. Speed, P. Leigh, P. Smith, J. Bostock, B. Hughes, P. Shields and D. Hanley. Front L to R: M. Higginson, I. Seel, S. Hughes, A. Wainwright and P. Hanby. Absent: A. Thomasson.*

White Watch (2000). *Back L to R: P. Rowlands D. Keelan, K. Birtles, A. Mills, S. Benbow, T. Kelly and J. Caulfield. Front L to R: B. Grant, R. Benson, L. Cliffe, P. Moorcroft, G. Goodwin and A. Wainwright.* ***Blue Watch (2000).*** *Back L to R: A. Williams, A. Ollier, T. Lewis, L. Bowen, R. Harden, F. Bratley and M. Clays. Front L to R: C. Welch, myself, P. Edwards, S. Herbert, L. Johns, M. Clarke and P. Gresty.*

*(**Above**) Crewe Firefighters with local musician Paul Spencer (Dario G) and his wife Kath, and Deputy Mayor Mick Roberts and Mrs. Ann Roberts at the Open Day in 2002. (**Below**) Fundraising Car Wash for the Fire Services Benevolent Fund and for Underwood West Nursery and Infant School in 2003 with Fire Cadets washing the Mayor's (Councillor Stan Davies) Bentley.*

*(**Top**) Firefighters Pete Shields and Mitchell Clarke with the Mayor and Mayoress (Councillor Steven Roberts and Mrs. June Roberts) during the VE Day Celebrations in 2005 and (**above**) Firefighters Allan Williams and Glen Whelams with a vintage fire appliance at the same event.*

Watch Manager Steve Barnes with Megan Birkett (fire safety competition winner) and former Station Commander Norman Turner at the 2006 Open Day.

***(Above)** Crewe Fire Cadets at the Nantwich Family Fun Day, Barony Park, Nantwich in 2007. **(Below)** Group Manager Richard Gorst and Admin. Manager Bev Dyer presenting Crewe schoolgirls Gemma Thorley and Sophia Faddes with their prizes after winning a fire safety competition in 2008.*

Blue Watch 2022. Back L to R: Ryan Younger, Aiden Fiske, Dom Page, Joe Webster and Matty Lyon. Front L to R: Mark Huxley, Kev Simpkins and Iain Dunne. Absent: Jon Woolley, Richard Douglas and Neil White.

*(**Above**) Red Watch 2022. Back L to R: Dan Mistreanu, Leigh Bowen, Dan Hough and Tom French. Front L to R: Louie Burton, Barry Earnden and Paul Gresty. Absent: Dave Jackson, Kerry Blease and Joel Olszewski. (**Below**) White Watch 2022. L to R: Phil Moorcroft, Daniel Cope, Matt Hole, Phil Cornes, James Silver, Rob Carney, Alex Flude and Gary Walker.*

*(**Above**) Green Watch 2022. L to R: Ken Wong, Ashley Andrews, Ashley Brown, Sam Woodcock, Sam Welland, David Brightwell, Paul Leigh, Michael Hubbard, Ben Burgoyne and Nick Regan. (**Below**) Crewe Fire Safety Advocate Phil Carter fitting a smoke alarm.*

(**Above**) *White Watch practising their RTC skills at a scrap yard: L to R: Mark Latham. Phil Moorcroft, Gary Walker, Phil Cornes, Liam Davenport, Daniel Cope and Matt Hole.*
(**Below**) *Firefighter Matt Hole cutting a car during RTC training.*

Firefighters Leigh, Woodcock and Regan training with the ladder during the Covid 19 pandemic.

*(**Above**) Water installations in the grounds at Crewe Hall. (**Below**) Crewe Firefighters Andy Wainwright (left) and Ian West (right) on a rescue mission with the UK Search and Rescue Team following the Indian Earthquake in 2001.*

Drill tower with the siren on top.

*(**Above**) Siren at the fire station, used to alert part-time firemen to fires in the past.*
*(**Below**) Firefighters in Macon - Crewe's twin town in France.*

*(**Above**) Crewe Firefighters Janssen Bostock, Paul Dunn, Brendan Grant, Rikki Harden and Mitchell Clarke with dignitaries from Macon and Cheshire during a visit to Macon in 1996. Also in the photo is John Lloyd (Crewe's Station Commander) and Simon Snape (Cheshire's Deputy Chief Fire Officer). (**Below**) Firefighters in Bischofsheim - Crewe's twin town in Germany and their fire station in 2004. Back L to R: Dietmar Zaia, Olaf Zerjeski and Robert Latin. Front L to R: Gregor Gaudron, Reiner Zerjeski and Harald Engert.*

Crewe Firemen - winners of a Cheshire fire brigade fishing tournament in the mid-1970s. L to R: Ellis Moss, Dave Holman, Peter Neary and Fred Pickering.

Crewe Firemen - finalists in Cheshire Fire Brigade's annual snooker knockout at Chester Fire Station in 1976. L to R: Ellis Moss, Dave Greatorex, Barrie Lunt and John Roberts.

*(**Above**) Crewe Firemen - winners of Cheshire Fire Brigade's snooker knock-out tournament in 1991. L to R: Chris Norman, Kevin Birtles, John Roberts and Alec Thomasson. (**Below**) Crewe Firemen - finalists in the Commander Bayley Football Tournament (Willaston) in 1992. Back L to R: Alec Thomasson (Manager), Nick Gough, Paul Holmes, Dave Williams, Ian West, Bob Hughes, Rich Wainwright and Richard Gorst (Assistant Manager). Front L to R: John Speed, Rob Benson, Andy Wainwright, myself, Chris Hughes and Paul Dunn.*

Crewe Firefighters who represented the England Fire Service football team during the 1980s and 1990s. L to R: Paul Bickerton, Russ Brown and David Brightwell.

*(**Above left**) Former part-time Fireman Ray Stafford MBE, one of the Fire Station Sports Days organisers. (**Above right**) Members of Red Watch with their guests at the 2009 Sports Day. Back L to R: John Dunne, Edward Timpson (MP for Crewe and Nantwich), Dan Hough, Jay Haag, Nigel Pordes, Martin Poole, Matt Hole and Joel Olszewski. Front: Councillor Margaret Simon (Mayor of Crewe and Nantwich Council). (**Below**) The snooker table before it was removed in 2004.*

Crewe Fire Station's Sports Days at Macon Meadows and at the Cumberland Sports Centre.